Die Heimat des Abenteuers ist die Fremde.

("The home of adventure is the unknown.")

— Emil Gött

Mein Feld ist die Welt

("My field is the world.")

— motto painted above doorway to ships in Hamburg

waiting to take emigrants to the New World

To travel hopefully is a better thing than to arrive.

— Robert Louis Stevenson

For my restless "nation,"
wherever that mythical place may be…

…and whoever my true "compatriots" might include…

… for after all, we each come from one place,
regardless where we might find ourselves today.

Chasing Restless Roots: The Dreams that Lured Us Across America
volume 2 of the pentalogy *Oceans of Darkness, Oceans of Light:
Our Family's Trials and Treasures in the New World*

Volumes 1, 2 and 3 are available as E-books and
available on-line via Amazon.com, etc.

author: Michael Luick-Thrams
with Anthony J. Luick and Gary Luick
copyright: © 2015 Michael Luick-Thrams
published on behalf of the TRACES
Center for History and Culture
Printed by Sigler Companies. Ames, IA USA
ISBN 978-0-9857697-6-5

Contents

Parts I – III a, with the first of three conclusions ("from the *persona*: my disrupted granny") are in Volume I: *Roots of Darkness: Our Dreams and Nightmares in America*

Part V and VI, with the final conclusion ("for the *polis*: my derailed country"), plus:
Supplements
Sources and Commentary, including footnotes and image registry
Disclaimer and Acknowledgments
are in Volume III: *Tap Roots Betrayed: How Our Dreams Got Derailed in America*

both by the same author; further information at www.roots.TRACES.org

Jeandelle, Gramma, Dad, Lorraine and Sheranne; circa 1990

By the time my father's family posed for this casual snapshot in the yard of Gramma Luick's simple frame cottage in Thornton one hot mid-summer day on the Iowa prairies, his—well, our—family had been roaming across the North American continent already for over 350 years. For a third of a millennia, the Luicks (or the lineages into which they married after arriving in the New World) had been wildly chasing American dreams—voracious longings that led us from coast to coast and to myriad adventures.

All through my childhood, Gramma served as the hobby historian for the paternal side of my extended clan. (With a dozen aunts and uncles, twenty cousins, scores of great-aunts and -uncles who we knew personally, and over a hundred second cousins we knew of, the Luick-Thrams tribe constituted a sizeable village in itself!) Whenever she had even a remote reason to do so, Charlotte took no small pride in rattling off her oft-sung chorus of "We're Scotch-Irish, English, Welsh, German, Dutch and Dane!" I admired her seemingly infallible authority on the subject and—like a kid pulling the string of a talking doll—goaded her relentlessly with insistent pleas of "Come on, Gramma—say it again, will ya?"

Now a well-therapized, middle-age adult and a Ph.D.-toting historian, I would have been so grateful if traumatized "Little Lottie" had gone beyond merely singing her rote chant. If only her endless inner seas of unresolved pain, the bottomless oceans of darkness that she carried inside her, had allowed her to go beyond the cutesy or flip, into the real and essential! Had she found the fortitude to wade into the truth of who she was and from where she, where *we* had come, Gramma could have helped those of us who followed to better understand whatever it was that led at least two of us grandkids to have recurring nightmares for years about the secret-swallowing stairs in the center of the Luicks' spooky farmhouse.

Instead, by reducing our family chronical to hollow jingles but otherwise deleting from her account all differentiated-if-difficult facts, she neatly guarded ugly secrets and sustained dark lies. She deprived us of a legacy that is rare and inspiring, not to mention potentially edifying about how to be better people. Our grandmother, in effect, stole from us a rich birthright, far more valuable than any sham appearances of decency. By not being honest or forthcoming about who we'd been, she limited who we could become—as individuals, as a family, as a nation: She hid our road map to an improved world.

As it was, except for generalities superficially sketched in oral accounts that forever shifted depending on our grandmother's mood at any given time, we learned little of detail. It seemed that as great as her need to talk about her and her husband's families was, her need to *not* talk about them in "too much" depth was much greater. Pity, though, for by the time she married into it in 1934, the Luick clan had accumulated a genuine wealth of experiences. On-hand from the founding of Boston and Dutch Nieu Amsterdam (today's "New York"), to the opening of the Northwest Territory and Gold-Rush-drunk frontier California, my family both changed the North American landscape and was forever changed by it. As a whole, my lineage has fought too many wars (the Pequot, Revolutionary, 1812 and Civil, two World Wars, Vietnam and Afghanistan); weathered repeated economic cycles of what once were known as "panics;" and persevered in the face of storms, plagues, locust infestations and attacks by "Injuns" or wild animals. Ever restless and always pursuing elusive happiness, my family searched a spectacular continent for a worthy home before settling down for over a century and a half in one unspectacular North Central Iowa county—Cerro Gordo, "Fat Hill" in Spanish. In that unassuming heartland of America, the people who literally made, then shaped me, dabbled in darkness even as they sought Light.

Though trained as a historian and not a psychologist, I believe deep in my bones that history also can inform us about the people we are as individuals, based in part on the people we have been as families. It has been my quest to understand myself that has led me all my conscious life (already as a boy, later as a geeky teen during the U.S.' Bicentennial) to gather, then dissect the stories of my people. I did so instinctively, as I intuited at some point that the damaged and damaging man who I had inherited as a father did not begin his unhappy life raging and violent. Even as a youth, I sensed that a similarly sensitive, alert, hurt little boy laid hidden deep in Dad's core, beneath the ceaseless ranting and raving that left me so hurt, confused and sad.

In now recording the wanderings of my people—of my father's, his mother's… of *all* our people—I no longer do such rigorous digging and dissecting solely for my own edification: These, "our" stories, are also *yours*—just with different names, dates, locations, etc. Perhaps, in reflecting on our disasters and achievements, our acts of folly as well as wisdom or kindness, our bravery and cowardice, our despair and hope—our

Shelley with baby Greg, Gramma and Sheranne, 1990; the weather house on the wall adorned the farmhouse living room and dated back decades, as did her ol' desk

darkness and Light—you'll reflect on your own. I hope so, for if we are to survive as a nation, let alone as a species, it will be only if each of us takes a long, hard look at ourselves and, through honest reflection, evolve into human beings more fully able to live peaceably with each other and with a planet now in slow-motion freefall.

———

Imagine for a moment:

You live in a cold, damp, crowded land. Crop failures, disease and hunger stalk you and your family more years than not. Wars, religious strife, extortionate taxes and church tithes reign virtually unopposed by those who shoulder most of their burden. You essentially belong—per the German label for such servitude, *Leibeigene*: literally your body—to a local lord whose written permission you need to walk away from such misery. If you stay, you know that a stifling social hierarchy will grind your dreams and vitality to nothingness—a shadow of your erstwhile hopes and ambitions. To stay means spiritual death; to leave everything you've ever known seems your only chance of building a life you truly want.

democracy "at the stump" in the America of the mid-19th century

If you and your family amass the means needed to leave Europe's late-feudalistic, pre-urban and -industrial conditions, you can only dream of a land touted as bursting with unlimited opportunities, of overnight fortunes and success. With few exceptions, its wealth grows yearly exponentially, its average standard of living achieves levels the highest human beings have ever known in the history of the world, and your children are almost certain to be taller, healthier, materially better provided for and happier than they'd ever be in the land of your birth. And, as a country sans landed gentry or inherited titles, it offers you the chance to be the master of your own fate. Rare in an era of tyrants, the young republic's governance is more hands-on democratic than that of any other country at the time.

So, what's not to like about any of that? If, however, such socio-economic-political enticements are not enough, there's also gently rolling, treeless rich soil to be had for the taking. Vast forests, lakes and coastal waters choked with immense schools of fish, mineral deposits in size and number matched by few places on the planet abound. The rich flora and fauna—in large patches, virginal—only hint at a natural diversity and abundance still common in much of the New World, but long-vanished in the Old.

With only 46 million inhabitants a century after the country's founding as a sovereign state, America in 1876 was a largely unspoiled, endless array of teeming shores, churning waterfalls, soaring mountains and grass-carpeted plains. Such magnificent landscapes only stoked the nation's superlative narratives, its can-do spirit which both charmed and appalled staid European visitors and new immigrants alike. For most of the century and a half from the War for Independence from Britain till the end of World War I, America's vast natural resources fed rates of growth that would have made today's Chinese envious.

All that extraction, however, exacted a price—and a steep one. Reducing an estimated 60-90 million bison in the country at the time of its founding to less than a thousand by 1900 is only one example of the shameless pillage we Americans inflicted on the Eden we claimed as ours. The passenger pigeon fell prey to our ladies' hat crazes, just as the heath hen—once "the poor man's food"—was foolishly harvested to extinction by the hungry of the Northeast. Other examples existed in droves already decades ago, but have failed to move us to find ecological equilibrium soon enough.

Saint Anthony Falls, mid-19th century—today the heart of Minneapolis

Still, in the early days of our New World history, North America's wilds provided riches and an abundant life for millions of newcomers who supplanted the natives who once had lived here so harmoniously. As agrarians, my people (as did the majority of most Americans' ancestors who were in the country before 1930) lived inseparably close to the land. Toiling with the soil for 355 years, my family tore it from its natural state, then wrestled from it wealth unlike anything our Old World forebears could have dreamt of obtaining.

In the process, the land itself provided the core, the basis of a United States society now so adrift. To understand where we are, we must know how we got to this place. To find a way forward, we must look back. To cast a new vision to guide our country into a new century, we must understand the visions that have directed our people up to now, then recalibrate the Dream to fit the faulty world they have left us.

We have always pushed forward… despite all perils, self-made or external.

———

PART III b

Children of Pioneers

Section 5:
Louis & Mary (Hunt) Luick family

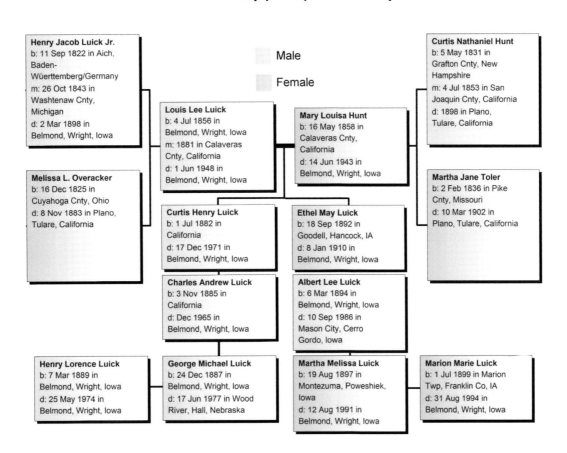

Henry Jacob Luick Jr.
b: 11 Sep 1822 in Aich,
Baden-
Wüerttemberg/Germany
m: 26 Oct 1843 in
Washtenaw Cnty,
Michigan
d: 2 Mar 1898 in
Belmond, Wright, Iowa

Melissa L. Overacker
b: 16 Dec 1825 in
Cuyahoga Cnty, Ohio
d: 8 Nov 1883 in Plano,
Tulare, California

Louis Lee Luick
b: 4 Jul 1856 in
Belmond, Wright, Iowa
m: 1881 in Calaveras
Cnty, California
d: 1 Jun 1948 in
Belmond, Wright, Iowa

Male

Female

Mary Louisa Hunt
b: 16 May 1858 in
Calaveras Cnty,
California
d: 14 Jun 1943 in
Belmond, Wright, Iowa

Curtis Nathaniel Hunt
b: 5 May 1831 in
Grafton Cnty, New
Hampshire
m: 4 Jul 1853 in San
Joaquin Cnty, California
d: 1898 in Plano,
Tulare, California

Martha Jane Toler
b: 2 Feb 1836 in Pike
Cnty, Missouri
d: 10 Mar 1902 in
Plano, Tulare, California

Curtis Henry Luick
b: 1 Jul 1882 in
California
d: 17 Dec 1971 in
Belmond, Wright, Iowa

Ethel May Luick
b: 18 Sep 1892 in
Goodell, Hancock, IA
d: 8 Jan 1910 in
Belmond, Wright, Iowa

Charles Andrew Luick
b: 3 Nov 1885 in
California
d: Dec 1965 in
Belmond, Wright, Iowa

Albert Lee Luick
b: 6 Mar 1894 in
Belmond, Wright, Iowa
d: 10 Sep 1986 in
Mason City, Cerro
Gordo, Iowa

Henry Lorence Luick
b: 7 Mar 1889 in
Belmond, Wright, Iowa
d: 25 May 1974 in
Belmond, Wright, Iowa

George Michael Luick
b: 24 Dec 1887 in
Belmond, Wright, Iowa
d: 17 Jun 1977 in Wood
River, Hall, Nebraska

Martha Melissa Luick
b: 19 Aug 1897 in
Montezuma, Poweshiek,
Iowa
d: 12 Aug 1991 in
Belmond, Wright, Iowa

Marion Marie Luick
b: 1 Jul 1899 in Marion
Twp, Franklin Co, IA
d: 31 Aug 1994 in
Belmond, Wright, Iowa

Curtis Nathaniel Hunt's extended ancestors

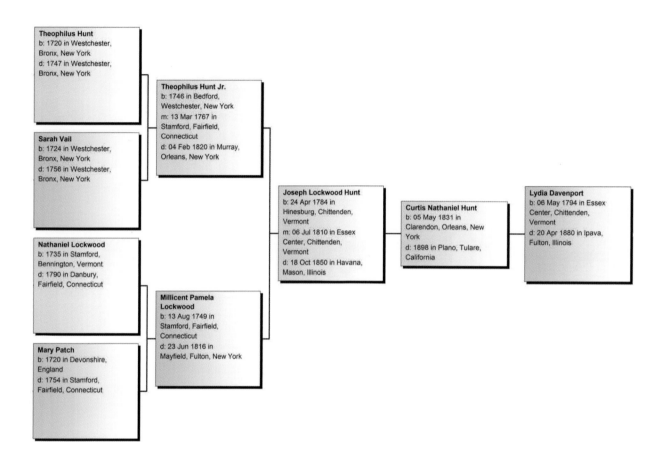

Theophilus Hunt
b: 1720 in Westchester, Bronx, New York
d: 1747 in Westchester, Bronx, New York

Sarah Vail
b: 1724 in Westchester, Bronx, New York
d: 1756 in Westchester, Bronx, New York

Nathaniel Lockwood
b: 1735 in Stamford, Bennington, Vermont
d: 1790 in Danbury, Fairfield, Connecticut

Mary Patch
b: 1720 in Devonshire, England
d: 1754 in Stamford, Fairfield, Connecticut

Theophilus Hunt Jr.
b: 1746 in Bedford, Westchester, New York
m: 13 Mar 1767 in Stamford, Fairfield, Connecticut
d: 04 Feb 1820 in Murray, Orleans, New York

Millicent Pamela Lockwood
b: 13 Aug 1749 in Stamford, Fairfield, Connecticut
d: 23 Jun 1816 in Mayfield, Fulton, New York

Joseph Lockwood Hunt
b: 24 Apr 1784 in Hinesburg, Chittenden, Vermont
m: 06 Jul 1810 in Essex Center, Chittenden, Vermont
d: 18 Oct 1850 in Havana, Mason, Illinois

Curtis Nathaniel Hunt
b: 05 May 1831 in Clarendon, Orleans, New York
d: 1898 in Plano, Tulare, California

Lydia Davenport
b: 06 May 1794 in Essex Center, Chittenden, Vermont
d: 20 Apr 1880 in Ipava, Fulton, Illinois

Martha Jane Toler's parents

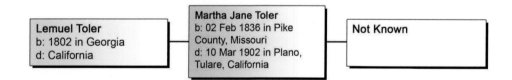

Lemuel Toler
b: 1802 in Georgia
d: California

Martha Jane Toler
b: 02 Feb 1836 in Pike County, Missouri
d: 10 Mar 1902 in Plano, Tulare, California

Not Known

Louis Lee and Mary Louisa (Hunt) Luick

born:	4 July 1856	16 May 1858
where:	Franklin Grove, Iowa/USA	Calaveras County, California/USA
married:	fall 1881	**where:** California/USA
died:	1 June 1948	14 June 1943
where:	Belmond, Iowa/USA	Belmond, Iowa/USA

Happily, not only taut group-think, layers of cultivated lies or webs of sick secrets hold families together. There is also love—tenderness, affection and empathy—that connect family members to others, too. Were it not so, the phenomenon of family would neither function nor be worth all the work.

If there is one at all in my father's lineage, the poster family of a contented and truly happy recent generation could be that of Louis Lee and Mary Louisa (Hunt) Luick. It seems that more than most other nuclear-familiar sets of humans wearing the name "Luick" they embodied The Good Life as celebrated already by the earliest Western philosophers. Improbably and utterly coincidentally, this one photographic image of their closely-situated family during a musical moment not only contains likenesses of three generations of the Luick family, but at least four ancestors of mine.

Louis, Curtis, Henry, Ethel, George, Mary (Hunt), Albert & Charles Luick; circa 1896

Maybe Great-Great-Grampa Louis loved heading such a large immediate family, given that as a child he had to survive the chaos of drifting among a revolving cast of kin and new step-family. Perhaps, the familiar environs of Belmond seemed an agreeable, cozy place to sink roots after the many serial moves that followed his suddenly finding himself in an early patchwork family. After Louis' father ran away with a neighbor's wife and took refuge in Missouri, the boy's life would never be the same. (No, your needle isn't stuck: it *is* the same timeworn tune Grampa George and Olga sang—just an older rendition crooned eighty years earlier!) By the time he finally returned to Iowa—more than twenty years after his frantic, jolted mother, Melissa, dragged him with her to find refuge among relatives in Michigan, then moved her family on to California with a new husband—he'd seen enough. For the rest of Louis' long life he rarely left northern Iowa—or the company of his and Mary's nine children and their myriad offspring.

———

chapter 39: patchwork pioneer families

When Louis Luick entered the world on the Fourth of July 1856, "Belmond" did not yet exist. His family had just sailed per prairie schooner into the heart of the sea of grass that then covered the Upper Midwest. There, baby Louis' family's crude cabin stood near one of the rare stands of trees that shadowed the streams then still dissecting the prairie. Having set up shelter in the shade of "Franklin Grove," the German-Yankee Luick-Overacker family began the very-American tasks of building a town where there had been none, after first forming farms out of the rich loam soil that had lain undisturbed for more than ten thousand years. Along with wheat and oats, the preoccupied pioneers also seeded future conflicts that would ripen and take head, too—yielding, in part, unhappy unions that eventually would give way to adulterous temptations.

When nine-year-old Louis' father, Henry Luick, Jr., stole off one morning (as an ironic bard one day would lampoon publicly, "just as the sun was shedding his first beams over the mountain tops") with his neighbor Charles Johnson's alluring wife, Lydia, to hide out with her for two years in the Show-Me-State, Louis' mother took him, still-nursing baby Charles Grant, four-year-old Frank Eugene and 13-year-old Barbara with her as she sought solace among her people back in Michigan. (The Overacker clan dated back to Nieuw Amsterdam.) Despite having been abandoned by a scheming husband she dubbed "Mad Bobcat," Melissa also took along with her swelling band of transients Henry's half-brother, Gottlieb, 16.

Barbara Luick, mid-1860s; typical late-19th-century American stage coach like the Luicks would have used

Young Louis' step-uncle, Gottlieb Luick—whose name means "love of god" in German—would stay in the Wolverine State. Later, he would take over his mother's farm, from where he could watch the rising fortunes of his cousin, Gottlob Luick—whose name in German means "praise of god." In 1873, with his brother Emmanuel, Gottlob co-founded a millwork company, Luick Brothers Lumber. Gottlob served as Ann Arbor's mayor from 1899-1901, and in the teens first as the vice-president of the Huron River Manufacturing, then as an officer of the Star Motor Car Companies as they attempted to build early automobiles in Washtenaw County. When he retired in 1931, Gottlob donated his lumberyard as the site of what is still today Ann Arbor's farmers' market.

original caption: "Gottlob Luick in a white shirt in Fifth Avenue doorway of his building in 1895. Emmanuel sits on the right, young Albert Luick sits on the ground, and Oscar Luick stands on far left. The Luicks worked in the shop alongside a changing ethnic mix of hired laborers. Germans, Irish and African Americans established their presence in the neighborhood before the Civil War and built churches nearby. Italians and Greeks joined them after 1900."

Unlike his father's cousin, Louis didn't see a future in Michigan, so drifted back to Iowa. The 1870 census records him resting his head in his father's new home of Oskaloosa, a town founded thirty-five years earlier by Daniel Boone's youngest son, Nathan. (It's being a center of Quakerism on the prairie may reflect that Daniel had been raised and his mother had remained a practicing Quaker.) Louis' older brother, Sylvester David, worked in that booming center of bituminous mining as a butcher. Their father, Henry Jacob—48 years old in 1870—farmed near Oskaloosa but was about to open a restaurant and, in nearby Eddyville, the Luick House Hotel.

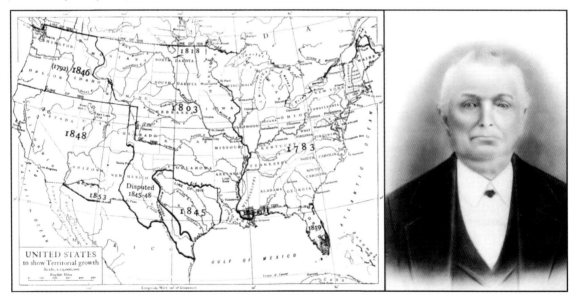

When Henry Jacob Luick, Jr., arrived in America in 1833, it included neither Texas nor the West Coast.

Although it likely took place after Louis left the Luicks in South Central Iowa to rejoin those in the north, Henry would fund Luick House Hotel in part with a windfall from distant Germany—as announced miles away in the *Jackson Sentinel* on 14 November 1872 in Maquoketa, Iowa:

> Mr Luick, an active and intelligent German of Eddyville, has fallen heir to $55,000 and has gone to Germany to reap his reward.

More than thirteen months later, on 19 December 1873, Cedar Fall's *Gazette* confirmed:

> H J Luick, who was one of the heirs to a large estate in Germany, has just received his portion which amounts to $92,000 in gold. His name ought to be spelled without the "i".

While Mahaska County's seat had an air of Quaker plainness about it and later would host a Friends-run college, relationships between the adults with whom adolescent Louis lived there were anything but "simple." In 1865 Louis' oldest brother, Michael Henry Luick, had married the widowed Sarah Jane (Lathrop) Baker—the same year that one-time-judge Henry committed the criminal offense of running away with a married woman: Sarah's older sister by eleven years, Lydia Marie (Lathrop) Johnson. If the webs between those of consenting age in the Luick domicile weren't tangled enough, 20-year-old Sylvester married Lydia's daughter, Irene Marie Johnson, on 25 September 1868—a week and a day after Irene turned eighteen, a month before Irene's mother and Henry legalized their until-then illegitimate relationship.

The U.S.' 1840s annexation of half of Mexico changed the course of Melissa (Overacker) Luick Arnold's life.

Louis' convoluted homelife in Southern Iowa's coal country may have proven to be too dense or the clear call of Western adventure had grown too great—or both—for as of 1872 he had joined his mother and his step-father back in Belmond. Melissa had married the one-time Brethren then, later, Congregational pastor, John Arnold, on 12 November 1868—less than two weeks after Henry had wedded Lydia in Oskaloosa. Had Louis attended both of his parents' weddings, plus that of his older brother Sylvester, he would have had to have spent most of fall 1868 bouncing back and forth, hundreds of miles across much of the north-south height of the then dirt-road-gridded Hawkeye State.

Louis' new stepfather knew all about perpetual motion and constant change. Born in New York state in 1816, by the time of the 1850 census John Arnold and a 30-year-old wife "Harriet" farmed in Lorain County, Ohio, the parents of three small children. Only one of them, their son Francis, appeared ten years later on the 1860 census, by which point the Arnold household resided in Austin Township, in South Central Minnesota's fertile Mower County. By then, just a year before the start of the American Civil War, the national head count found John married to a 26-year-old "Susan" and the father of three additional young children.

The forename of the middle one, Kansas, age 4, mirrored the fraught times, for by the year of the child's birth the territory of the same name had witnessed three-dozen slayings attributed to slavery politics. A fellow Congregationalist pastor, the New England abolitionist John Brown, had gone to Kansas ostensibly to protect his pioneering sons, but the bloodbath that he instigated either inspired or appalled an already-tense young nation—its people's responses to the murderous events determined by their personal political inclinations. That Congregational pastor Arnold chose to christen his son as a namesake of such an impassioned, inflamed cause suggests his allegiances.

period image of Lawrence Massacre, led by abolitionists like John Brown

At that time, slavery as an institution in itself, unpaid (agrarian) versus paid (industrial) labor, and the admission of territories as new "slave" or "free" states reflected a diversity issues at the core of the American identity—private as well as public. They had gone unresolved since the founding of one of the world's first constitution-based republics in 1787. Those volatile issues reached deep into the young nation's delicate psyche; at even the seemingly most innocuous provocation they would explode with a visceral force, sending shock waves across the entire continent. In such a highly politicized atmosphere individuals associated their various group memberships with personal character and their very worth as a person. The ensuing conflicts—seen in national contexts but lived out on a local level—played out even on the isolated, half-empty frontier. Specific skirmishes between vying groups were often the least restrained and the most deadly where the fewest people lived or established bodies reined.

It was likely personal rather than political passions, however, that led John and his third wife, Melissa (Overacker) Luick Arnold, to set off cross-country for California. Louis later recounted that he was sixteen, so this move likely took place in 1872 rather than 1876, as reported in some family chronicles. Besides the exact year of the cobbled-together family's trek into the Great American West, a second remaining mystery consists of means to get there. In 1869 Union Pacific had used a silver hammer to sink a golden spike into the last rail joint in America's first transcontinental railroad connection—with its statutory eastern terminus conveniently being in Council Bluffs, Iowa.

According to the 1870 Wright County census John and Melissa's newly-fused families comprised a household of eight souls—with Louis, that'd make nine. Why such a long-distance journey—supposedly by covered wagon, pulled by oxen—wasn't undertaken instead per rail poses yet another puzzle. Melissa's 1870 wealth of $2,500 in real estate and $300 in "personal property" (more than $50,000 in 2013 dollars)

scenery Arnold-Luick family saw as it trekked to California; Louis, age 16

reportedly equaled more than eleven times that of her new, twelve-year-older spouse.

With that kind of capital, couldn't Mr. and Mrs. Arnold and entourage have traveled first class, with porters to tuck in their trunks for the days-long ride? For if they really did endure a several-month land trip to California's Central Valley, the Luick-Arnold assemblage would have walked most of the way, as roads were sparse and, when extant, typically poor. Plus, given the increasing scarcity of livestock fodder along the way across the plains, deserts and then mountains, pioneers often walked alongside their wagons rather than further tax already-burdened beasts. Besides sparing the animals having to drag even more weight across the country, the migrants spared themselves the agony of bouncing about hard-wood wagon seats the whole way, atop jarring roads or rutted trails, for too many months.

Whenever or however Melissa, John and their combined offspring reached the Golden State, they found family waiting for them in the bountiful San Joaquin Valley. Two of Melissa's eleven brothers, Adam and Howard, owned ranches near Porterville, in Tulare County. According to one family historian, Howard Overacker

> left Michigan for San Francisco in 1851 to mine for gold but was not successful and returned home. In 1856 Howard and his wife, Deborah, returned to California and purchased 300 acres south of Niles, where they ranched. Adam, one of the original settlers of [Jones County, Iowa], traded his Iowa farm for 500 head of sheep in northern California in 1854 and purchased 320 acres near Livermore [...] in 1866, where he engaged in ranching.

At some point after arriving in the Plano district of Porterville, Louis and his kid brothers, Frank and Charles, struck out on their own. Family lore has it that they tried their hands at various endeavors in their struggle for financial self-sufficiency. After they found that fist-sized nuggets of gold weren't lying around in the much-advertised land of milk and honey, waiting to be gathered up like so many eggs into an already-groaning basket, the Luick boys took turns being career creative. Between them, they "punched" cattle and sheared sheep, picked citrus fruit and harvested wheat. For a while, Louis also drove a stage coach and worked as a teamster.

Dell, Frank, Michael and Louis Luick shearing sheep, circa 1900

Work as hard as they might to sink deeper roots in the Central Valley, 1880 proved to be a turning point for the Luick-Overacker-Arnold clan in California—with irreversible consequences. For one, Louis and Charles withdrew from endless rounds of odd jobs for a spell and took a live-in position at the New River J Ranch in Lerdo District, Kern County. There, their cousin Rosetta (Overacker) Robinson's husband, George, hired the pair—now respectively 22 and 16 years old—to work with him and three other hands: Wisconsin-born brothers Thomas and Albert Coyle (21 and 13), and Alexander St. Marys, a 30-year-old Illinois native. Rosetta's father, Melissa's Civil-War-veteran brother Anthony, lived next door with his daughter, Lucy—yet another of Louis and Charlie's infinite army of cousins. Between the nine of them buzzing about it, the New River J ranch constantly stayed a busy place.

In the adjacent county, however, the Luick boys' mother and step-father weren't faring so well. At the moment that some short-hire census taker trapped Melissa at home in what she or (more likely) he noted as "Plano Village," "M. Arnold" cited "self" both as head of her home and as "keeping house." Melissa's son from her almost twenty-five years of marriage with Henry, Frank Luick, had turned 19 by

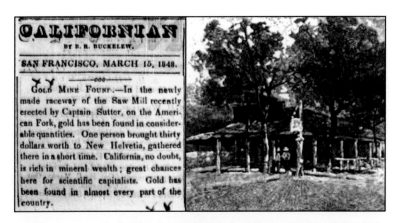

gold's discovery in California, 1848; first building in Visalia, built 1852

the 1880 census, which listed him as a "farmer," and Melissa and John's ten-year-old daughter, Eva Dora, as living "at home." (Melissa had been 44 when she gave birth to Dora, her tenth child.) Their husband and (step-)father, John, however, for unknown reasons warranted his own census entry, with a separate address.

Both homes of the Luick-Arnold line, however, were about to vanish, as later that year John died suddenly—and three years later Melissa also passed from this life. The two, though, did not leave much of a worldly legacy for their heirs, as attested by the probate estate case filed in Tulare County Superior Court in Visalia on 11 December 1883. As one of Louis' grandsons noted:

> [Melissa] owned 9 acres with one acre usable and it had a $160 mortgage on it with an interest rate of 1% per month. She had owned [it] about one year [or so, following John Arnold's death.] It sold on the courthouse steps for $180 to the guy that had […] originally sold it to her and was carrying the mortgage. She had personal property that the court valued at $50 but that wasn't included in the probate.

With the loss of their strong-willed matriarch, the three Luick brothers, who'd followed Melissa and her second husband to the West Coast some decade and a half earlier, no longer felt drawn to remain mountained-in on a valley floor, vast as it might have been. As they considered various futures for themselves as individuals and as a family, the call of the wide open Iowa prairie stirred something deep inside—likely a hunger for a place and for people to whom they felt they belonged. So, in 1885 or 1886 they packed up their lives in "paradise" and moved back to Iowa—this time, documentably, by train. And, at least in Louis' case, no longer single.

―――――

chapter 40: a Golden State

Mary Louisa Hunt had a lot of life behind her already before she added "Luick" to her moniker. Unlike her Midwestern future husband, she'd been born 315 years after the first recorded European presence in today's "California." It was the fantastic natural wealth of that occidental Eden that drew Mary's people to risk losing the lives they knew back East, for dreamy ones they imagined enjoying one day out West. The mortal risk, however, was real: Mary's grandmother had died on the wagon-train trek from Missouri to Calaveras County—a destination ominously bearing the Spanish word for "bones." An early explorer for the Viceroyalty of New Spain, Gabriel Moraga, had assigned the name to the area after he found Native-American skulls and bones he falsely believed to be the remnants of famine or tribal warring over hunting and fishing grounds.

Per one of the few detailed documented sources on-hand, Mary's maternal grandfather, Lemuel Toler—whose surname came from the Old-English term "*tollere*," a "tax gatherer"—had gone

enslaved Native Americans being marched to the Presidio in Spanish-colonial-era California's bay area, November 1817

west to the Mother Lode area (California). He arrived with three little girls in a covered wagon (his wife died on the trip). [Mary's mother] Martha Jane Toler was born 1836 and died in 1902. She had two sisters, Sarah Toler and Safronia [sic] Toler. They married very young. Martha Jane married Curtis Hunt. Sarah married Joseph Hunt, his brother, and Safronia married Daniel Hunt, a cousin of Curtis and Joseph Hunt.

The Tolers had set off from Missouri, but they weren't alone: They were joined by tens of thousands, across the entire Midwest—including the recently opened northwest frontier, a sparsely populated crescent arching from Southeast Wisconsin through Southeast Minnesota to Southeast Iowa. As one of the Hawkeye State's first comprehensive chroniclers, Benjamin Gue reported half a century later that:

> In February, 1848, an event occurred in California which largely affected the settlement of Iowa for several years. A laborer employed by Colonel Sutter (a Swiss immigrant, who had built a mill on the Sacramento River), while digging a race for the mill, discovered gold dust in the excavation. It was soon found that gold in large quantities existed in the alluvial deposits of many of the streams of the Territory which had recently been acquired from Mexico. The discoveries soon became known to the public, causing great excitement. The contagion reached the Mississippi Valley, as glowing accounts came of rich deposits and sudden fortunes made by the gold diggers. Then began an exodus from Iowa and other western States. The tide of immigration which had been flowing into the prairie States was suddenly diverted toward the newly discovered gold-fields of California.

> Early in 1849 thousands of citizens of Iowa, allured by the prospect of acquiring sudden wealth, formed companies in various localities for the purpose of making the journey over the plains. Wagons were fitted up with camp equipments, provisions, tools and arms for defense against the Indians. They were generally drawn by oxen, for cattle could subsist on grass along the route, while horses would require grain to be transported the entire distance. It was necessary for the emigrants to carry with them enough supplies to last for the entire journey, which took from four to six months. Large, strong wagons were made for these trips, as rough roads were encountered through the mountain regions. These wagons were also used as the night camps for defense against Indian attacks. Almost the entire journey was through an unsettled country, portions of which were in regions infested by roving bands of hostile Indians. The wagons were covered with canvas and drawn by from three to six pair of oxen. At night the encampment was made secure by forming a corral with the wagons, while the oxen were left to graze on the plains. Progress was slow, as the cattle could only travel from fifteen to twenty-five miles a day.

> During the years 1849, '50, '51, '52, long lines of California teams traversed the main roads leading westward through Iowa, from the Mississippi to the Missouri. They furnished a good home market to Iowa farmers for their surplus hay and corn, early in the spring before the grass had grown to supply feed for the slowly moving teams. Thousands of gold seekers from Illinois, Indiana, Michigan

mid- to late-nineteen-century wagon train, pulled by oxen

> and Wisconsin made their journey thus over the Iowa prairies in those years. It is doubtful, on the whole, whether as much wealth was brought back by the thousands of Iowa men who swelled the army of gold seekers as was expended by them in outfits, subsistence, loss of time and the various unavoidable expenses attending the venture.

> Whether Iowa gained or lost in population from the great hegira is not easy to determine. Thousands of Iowa men remained in California, but other thousands from eastern States, who traversed its fertile prairies on their journey in search of gold, remembered the beautiful country they had passed through and, after a few years, returned to make it their home.

In the early years of this removal from the Heartland to the Promised Land, the vast majority of arrivées consisted of young males. With three daughters on the female-scarce frontline of the California Gold Rush, Lemuel Toler—by then approaching fifty years of age—simply had to wait for suitable suitors to come round who might improve his family's fortunes. Having arrived on the West Coast about 1850, according to one of Saphronia's great-grandsons, the motherless Toler girls were living with their father at Halfway House (probably between Valley Springs and San Andreas) in Oct of 1852. The diarys [sic] of [legendary miner-cum-journalist-turned-hell-raiser] Alfred Doton [sic] tell a story of meeting and trying to court Martha Jane Toler.

Alfred Doten, circa 1860s

Maybe young Martha Jane—fittingly, from the Aramaic *Marta* for "lady" or "mistress," and the Medieval English form of *Jehanne*, an Old French-feminine form of *Iohannes*, from "god is gracious" in Hebrew—possessed excellent intuition. Perhaps my Great-Grampa George's future grandmother foresaw would-be-lover Doten spending his last days soaked in begged-for whisky and dying alone in a had-been-boomtown boarding house, for as the empty-handed author left the Tolers' wayside home for the last time, the attractive lass smote him, yet he ever again only wrote of her. In any case, his diary entries that refer to his frustrated attempts to "come in contact" with Martha Jane are vague. And, their meeting took place unexpectedly, by a coincidence driven by hunger:

> <u>Woods Creek, Stockton, San Francisco: Sunday, June 22 1851</u>
>
> —Clear, warm & pleasant—Today Messrs Spicer, Everbeck, Caswell, Snodgrass, Fenton and myself took a pasear up to the quartz vein. Our horses were fresh and in good condition and the 14 miles we had to go were made extremely short—We raced "some" going up—After cruising about for a spell we saddled up and started back—We took a turn further up the road and took supper at Toler's house about a mile or so above the Double Springs—Here we saw some pretty girls and ate supper there with much satisfaction and after passing quite an agreeable time we started on again and after racing a little on the road we arrived at Chinn's ranch at 10 in the evening and soon arrived home—We took a drink of the river—very cold water—snow melting—

That the "*pasear*"—Spanish for "stroll" or "ride"—Doten took with colleagues consisted largely of a pleasure spree and an equestrienne sprint fit well the carefree lifestyle the once-pious New England native had taken up on the West Coast, far from watchful parental eyes. Doten had left Plymouth, Massachusetts in March 1849, within mere weeks of hearing about the discovery of "fist-sized rocks of gold lying on the ground, waiting to be picked." With his father's blessing in mind and the elder Doten's money in his pocket, 19-year-old Alfred had then set off for California. He sailed aboard the *Yeoman* around Cape Horn, at the tip of South America, in order to reach the northern half of Mexico that the U.S. had just wrestled from its nearest Latin neighbor and annexed as its own.

Typically, such hemispheric sailing-ship voyages took five to eight months. Some sea-born souls willing to brush with death in order to rush to the gold opted to sail to the Isthmus of Panama, ride in canoes and on mules for a week through malarial jungles, then board a ship bound for California. While others suffered the overland route across the North American continent, each option offered its potential hazards, ranging from sudden death at sea to slow disaster on land.

Catering to the material needs as well as immaterial whims of the rich and the hopeful alike,

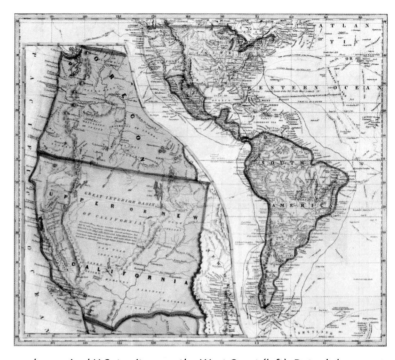

ships bearing goods from around the world came to San Francisco as well. Ships' captains found that their crews deserted to go to the gold fields. The wharves and docks of [the city] became a forest of masts, as hundreds of ships were abandoned. Enterprising San Franciscans turned the abandoned ships into warehouses, stores, taverns, hotels, and one into a jail. Many of these ships were later destroyed and used for land fill to create more buildable land in the boomtown.

newly acquired U.S. territory on the West Coast (left); Doten's long route

boomtown San Francisco, 1851 and (right) harbor with abandoned ships from around the world

Doten's voyage around the Americas was most exotic but not in the least unique. Between 1848 and 1855 the discovery of gold lured a third of a million of not only Anglo but also Latin Americans, Europeans, Asians, and even Australians to a previously sparsely populated paradise. About half came on ships, the other half via the California or Gila River Trails, respectively from the mountainous northeast or desert south. Called "Forty-niners" in reference to the initial surge of gold-seekers who really did find nuggets lying around, in total tens of billions of today's dollars of the stuff enriched a select few with unimaginable wealth. The majority, however, eventually left the increasingly depleted goldfields with little more than they had started with.

In the process, however, those seeking overnight fortunes transformed the West Coast of North America, as well as virtually assured the fate of a young republic poised to soon break into two yet seemingly destined to ultimately form a vast, united powerhouse. San Francisco, for example, claimed less than a thousand inhabitants in 1846 but by the time my great-x3-grandmother wed a few years later it had reached almost 50,000 souls.

two views of San Francisco Bay from the same perspective, November 1848 (left) and November 1849

Already in 1849, as new ranches and farms, roads and towns spread across California, the early Anglo residents wrote a constitution and chose a governor and legislature. With a population of only 92,597 at the time (and as a part) of the last "Great Compromise" of the pre-Civil-War United States, California became a state in 1850. The push to codify the grabbing arose out of the lack of property laws or a system of staking claims in the gold fields—but lacked provisions for countering the devastating damage such intensive mining caused rivers, bays and lakes, not to mention the very land itself.

When he set off from the staid site of the Pilgrims' landing for the latest Promised Land, the young Alfred Doten could not have foreseen the his colorful life ahead. His trip there from New England took seven months—plenty of time to dream about the imagined life that led him to board that ship back in Plymouth in the first place. Like so many other gold-fever victims, though, he quickly abandoned the city lights of the boomtown he found beyond the Golden Gate and set off for the bustling gold fields, in land.

There, according to one chronicler,

> Alfred Doten would discover a lifestyle that included fighting, whiskey and women. The upright young man would metamorphose into a destitute drinker always fixated on the next strike[....] Upon arrival in San Francisco, he wrote a wide-eyed letter to his father, describing the free flowing liquor, the gambling and the prevalence of "the dust." Doten was eager to find his own gold [and] fell in with a crowd of rough miners. In the Calaveras diggings, they worked hard by day, washing hundreds of buckets of pay dirt to sift out the flecks of gold. By night, they drank.

ad for new clipper-ship lines from Boston to the West Coast of North America

(standing, from the left) Rebecca, Laura Ann, Alfred, Samuel & Charles;
(seated) Euphalia, Cornelia, mother Rebecca (Bradford), father Samuel,
Eunice & Lizzie Doten, taken in Plymouth, Massachusetts; circa 1848

Doten's father, Samuel, a sea captain and descendent of Plymouth's first families, had joined other men back on Cape Cod to form the Pilgrim Mining Company. Per the company's charter, members got free passage to California. In return, they were to return two-thirds of their gold finds to their investors. Within only a few months after the gold-seeking Yankees disembarked, however, they found no fortunes and voted to disband—despite young Alfred's pleas to the contrary, in defense of his father's investment which, by then, was forever lost.

Suddenly on his own, Doten had to find a viable way to support himself. Soon after gold had been discovered, San Francisco had briefly become a ghost town as most residents swarmed in the direction of the Mother Lode. In the pop-up mining settlements like the ones Doten frequented, "Argonauts" as the forty-niners were then also called

> lived in tents, wood shanties, or deck cabins removed from abandoned ships. Wherever gold was discovered, hundreds of miners would collaborate to put up a camp and stake their claims. With names like Rough and Ready, and Hangtown [earlier named "Dry Diggings," today "Placerville;" Happy Camp, Whiskytown, etc.], each camp often had its own saloon and gambling house [much like "Halfway House" inn run by my great-x4-grandfather, single-parent widower Lemuel Toler.]

For his part, foreseeing a flourishing, high-markup market, enterprising Alfred Doten opened a small store that doubled as a local watering hole. Filled with mostly young, ambitious-but-frustrated men, it served as a stage for violent confrontations between cultures and personalities—as he recorded in his journal one mid-summer Sunday:

camp post office, 1850s; gold nuggets; 1925 gold-panning half-dollar

> Lower Bar, Calaveras County: June 13 1852
>
> All day the store was full of drunken Chilenos, French, etc., and the day passed off finely with plenty of jabbering and quarreling and several fights in which some eyes were blackened and noses bled——but no one was hurt very bad.

Blacked eyes or bloody noses, however, were the mildest forms of violence that became daily fare in Doten's new life in the Golden West: After some Mexicans shot an American in a bar fight, the 22-year-old adventure seeker joined a vigilante mob in rounding up the Mexicans and hanging them from a tree.

a hanging at old Mexican customs house, 1851; vigilante medal, 1856

That Alfred Doten could join a self-appointed pack, not once but repeatedly, and hang untried accused of grave crimes suggested something about his character. So did his peers' assessments of him—which were not always complimentary. One, published supposedly as "a joke" by Doten's later journalist colleague at the *Virginia Daily Union* in Nevada, Samuel Clemens (the future, celebrated writer "Mark Twain") suggested that hard-drinking Doten didn't always win the hearts of those who knew him best. Certainly, the Missouri-born Clemens knew Doten's dark side: He once attended the hanging of a prostitute's killer with the five-year-elder reporter.

Under the headline "Convicts," Clemens wrote in Virginia City's *Territorial Enterprise*:

> Some one (I do not know who) left me a card photograph, yesterday, which I do not know just what to do with. It has [several names, including A.M. Doten] on it, and appears to be a pictured group of notorious convicts, or something of that kind. I only judge by the countenance, for I am not acquainted with these people, and do not usually associate with such characters. This is the worst lot of human faces I have ever seen. That of the murderer Doten (murderer, isn't he?) is sufficient to chill the strongest heart[.] I am very glad to have this picture to keep in my room, as a hermit keeps a skull, to remind me what I may some day become myself. I have permitted the Chief of Police to take a copy of it, for obvious reasons.

Possessing a complex, contradictory character, Doten clearly made enemies as well as friends. According to one source, while the owner of the *Gold Hill News* in Nevada, he

> kept a loaded six-shooter in an open desk drawer to discourage dissatisfied readers. "Can you shoot?" was the first question he asked a job-seeking reporter.

In any event, as the most easily accessible gold disappeared and gold-mining became both more costly and difficult, Americans

began to drive out foreigners to get at the most accessible gold

Samuel Clemens, age 15, 1850; Comstock Lode miners, 1880s: the right photo's original caption extolled "To Labor is to Pray"

that remained. The new California State Legislature passed a foreign miners tax of twenty dollars per month [$570 in 2014 values], and American prospectors began organized attacks on foreign miners, particularly Latin Americans and Chinese.

Even more destructive to the welfare of minorities than Anglo discrimination against non-American "whites" or Asians, ecological catastrophe plagued old-resident Native Americans as

the huge numbers of newcomers [drove them] out of their traditional hunting, fishing and food-gathering areas. To protect their homes and livelihood, some Native Americans responded by attacking the miners. This provoked counter-attacks on native villages. The Native Americans, out-gunned, were often slaughtered. Those who escaped massacres were many times unable to survive without access to their food-gathering areas, and they starved to death.... Native Americans, dependent on traditional hunting, gathering and agriculture, [also] became the victims of starvation as gravel, silt and toxic chemicals from prospecting operations killed fish and destroyed habitats. The surge in the mining population resulted in the disappearance of game and food gathering locales as gold camps and other settlements were built amidst them. Later, farming spread to supply the camps, taking more land from the use of Native Americans.

drawing of natives; original caption: "River Operations at Murderer's Bar"

Those who had peopled the "New World" for at least ten thousand years swiftly fell victim to inadvertent exposure to diseases earlier unknown to them, as well as to deliberate attacks. They succumbed in large numbers to introduced diseases such as smallpox, influenza and measles. Some estimates indicate case fatality rates of 80–90% in Native American populations during smallpox epidemics. By far the most destructive element of the Gold Rush on California Indians was the violence practiced on them and their environment by miners and settlers. Miners often saw Native Americans as impediments to their mining activities. Retribution attacks on solitary miners could result in larger scale attacks against Native populations, for example, [with] reprisals often targeted tribes or villages unconnected with the original act.

Were their decimation by raging new viruses or at newcomers' grasping hands not enough, targeted discrimination and intentional extermination claimed further fatalities.

The Act for the Government and Protection of Indians, passed on April 22, 1850 by the California Legislature, allowed settlers to continue the Californio practice of capturing and using native people as bonded workers. It also provided the basis for the enslavement and trafficking in Native American labor, particularly that of young women and children, which was carried on as a legal business enterprise. Native American villages were regularly raided to supply the demand, and young women and children were carried off to be sold, the men and remaining people often being killed in genocidal attacks [...] against tribespeople in or near mining districts occurred. Despite resistance in various conflicts, the Native population in California, estimated at 150,000 in 1845, dropped to less than 30,000 by 1870. [Their] pre-European population [...] estimated at 300,000, had already been decimated, almost exclusively due to diseases carried by the Spanish settlers. Factors of disease, however, do not minimize the tone of racial violence directed towards California Indians. Peter Burnett, California's first governor, declared that California was a battleground between the races and that there were only two options towards Indians, extinction or removal. California, apart from legalizing slavery for Native Americans, also directly paid out $25,000 in bounties for Indian scalps with varying prices for adult male, adult female and child sizes. California with a consortium of other new Western states stood in opposition of ratifying the eighteen treaties signed between tribal leaders and federal agents in 1851.

Upon arriving in California the White, Anglo-Saxon Protestant Alfred Doten found himself in a multi-ethnic population of newcomers and drifters, with only one close confidant, "old Morris." Stranded as he was in an almost all-male world, Doten craved mitigating female contact. In his daily log, he recorded

> his binges, noting he had a "spree," or "bender," or that he got "infernally drunk" with the other men[.] Back in Plymouth, Doten had a sweetheart, but in California he pursued sexual relationships, primarily with women of color. One day, Doten lured a young Native American woman into his tent. He was about to "lay her altogether," he wrote, when a "damned old bitch of a squaw came in as mad as a hatter[.] I told her she might go to the devil for her pains and spent some few minutes cussing her in good round English."

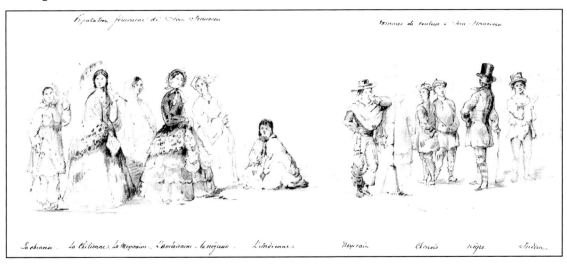

Gold-Rush era inhabitants: Chinese, Chilean, Mexican, American, "Negro" and "Indian" women; Mexican, Chinese, "Negro" and "Indian" men, drawn by Swiss merchant-consular Gottlieb Rudolf von Rütte, 1850

Still, Alfred Doten seemed to differentiate between the women of color from whom he sought short-term sexual satisfaction and the "white" women he desired as romantic objects—including my then-sixteen-year-old great-great-great grandmother, Martha Jane Toler.

> Lower Bar, Calaveras County: July 3 1852
>
> I went down as far as the Halfway house which is kept by Mr Toler—I saw his three daughters looking as blooming as ever and wanted much to kiss one of them but didn't...

His fascination with the girl he at times referred to as "the adorable one," "dear one," "girl from Missouri" or simply "M" would stretch over two years. And while his ambiguous diary entries hinted at stolen moments of physical intimacy and what he perceived to be mutual interest, "Miss Martha" consistently remained out of reach. Her father's deep and persistent distrust of Doten frustrated the restless Yankee's recurrent advances. The less able he was to satisfy his desires, the more he fixated on Martha Jane and her family.

> July 4th 1852
>
> We did not have much of a time here today. Morning myself and others fired our guns to make some noise—Some Chilenos were a little tight and the Chinese were somewhat noisy... Spicer said that Morris was [about a mile from the Tolers' inn] at the Double Springs cooking for 120 dollars a month—

original caption: "California Gold Diggers, Mining Operations on Western Shore of the Sacramento River"

Devious Doten used every opportunity to chase contact with Martha Jane—and to try to woo her.

> **On the Calaveras River: October 14 1852**
>
> At sunset I arrived at the Halfway House where I stopped for the night—Saw old Morris and the Toler gals as a matter of course—After supper Silas Stuart played the violin and after he had done, I took it and just astonished the crowd with my playing and singing—The Toler girls were much pleased—

Apparently, at least one of "the Toler girls" felt so "much pleased" by the inn's dashing guest, that an exceptionally excited Doten had occasion to write the following entry:

> **October 23rd**
>
> —About sunset a special messenger arrived from the Halfway House from Morris, telling me to come down there immediately. I got my horse and started off. Had quite a moon to light my way, got there about 8 o'clock. Took supper, Morris then had a private confab with me. He wanted me to write a letter for him to his wife as he cannot write very well. But the most he had to say was that a young lady [Martha Jane Toler] had fallen in love with me and desired to see me. He introduced me and in a room with two of her sisters we did up some of the tallest kind of courting. She was bashful in the extreme and I felt as awkward as she did. I took the fiddle and fiddled up quite a conversation, in fact I broke the ice which was about 2 feet thick with an old fiddle. Staid all night.

A day later, Doten followed up his cliff-hanging previous entry:

October 24th, Sunday

—Forenoon I wrote a letter for Morris to his wife asking her to come out here &c. The rest of the day I was maneuvering about the enemy, trying to bring my guns to bear. About 4PM I got her in a corner by herself. Declared my passion—loved in return—all right on both sides—wait till next spring—happy hearts—fluttering gizzards—honey and so on. Left for home again at sunset filled with love and joy and thought I was being wafted through the air astraddle of a cobweb towards regions of bliss. Dreamed of heaven all night.

miners working a wooden sluice and panning on the Mokelumne River

Doten avoided naming explicitly in his journal what had happened to forever alienate innkeeper Lemuel Toler and thus complicate courting Martha Jane. Whatever it was, it wouldn't go away, no matter what love-sick Alfred did to distract himself, and no matter what vices he might employ to take his searing focus off the very thing he could not have but longed for more than anything else.

October 30 1852

—Forenoon I took a bath in the river—very cold—[...]—Afternoon about four o'clock I rigged up in my best bib and tucker and saddled up my horse and started for the Halfway house in fine spirits and feeling very happy in the thought of who I was to meet there—I rode up to the door in fine style, dismounted, saw the old man Toler—Said how de do, Mr Toler—He said nothing, but merely nodded—Just as I was about unsaddling, the old cuss stepped up to me and said, "look here, I don't want you to unsaddle your horse here, I want you to leave here, and that damned quick"—I said "very well"—saw Morris, but no chance to speak to him—Caught a glimpse of the adorable one—Cast a glance of withering scorn upon Old Toler, sprang into the saddle and was off in a most furious hurry—I sank the rowels deep into the flanks of my steed, never cast a glance behind—ground my teeth in despair—and while my steed flew like lightning over the road I breathed further curses, not loud, but very deep—Rode as far as the bridge—turned back and rode back as far as the Douglas and Rany's Ranch about a mile above Tolers, where I tied up for the night—Went supperless to bed and lay awake all night cursing old Toler, and revolving plans in my mind for running away with his daughter. Oh, Martha, you will raise the devil with me yet—

1882 cartoon depicting San Francisco landlords as vampires; a "typical ranch house" in book from the era

Some nemesis by the name of "Perry" played a role in my great-x4-grandfather Lemuel Toler's deep distrust of Alfred Doten, who referred to his fellow shopkeeper with burning contempt. He didn't need external enemies, though: he had an adequate internal one—and suffered for it.

October 31st, Sunday

Morning I turned out, feeling supremely miserable. Took three cocktails but they only made me feel more dummy... After breakfast I saddled up my horse and rode up and down the road for two hours, til I felt a little better. Road down to MacDonald's ranch, stopped there about an hour or so, and then went up to my camp, feeling like a fool. At night I rolled in my bed and dreamed all night that I was a jackass chasing a firefly through a briar swamp.

Yes, indeed: The Martha Jane Toler Love Bug had bitten poor Squire Doten—an' bit 'im bad!

On the Calaveras River: November 16 1852

—A little shower—Forenoon I rode down to the Halfway house—saw old man Toler—the girls were gone on a visit to Stockton but were expected today on the stage—The old man wouldn't have anything to say to me and wouldn't let me talk to him—He was in a terrible state of agitation—I went in to see Morris and he told me that all my hopes in that quarter were completely dished and Perry has been the means of the whole of it {God eternally damn him to the hottest of all the hot corners in hell}—I took dinner there—Had a long talk with Morris—Told him to talk to the old man Toler—told him to talk with her also—About 2 o'clock PM the stage came up and the Toler girls arrived, so I sent Morris into pay my bill, and I saddled up and started off as I did not wish to see the girls—I left the old man Toler pacing up and down in the bar room with tears in his eyes and in a terrible agitation—Poor Morris took it much to heart and when he shook hands at parting he cried as well as myself—I rode slowly away without looking behind and feeling sad and sorrowful—And all this is caused by the poisonous tongue of that snake in the grass, Perry—I rode up as far as the New York Ranch where I stopped for the night—

Alfred Doten and the Tolers lived in a place, at a time marked by both boundless striving and endless strife. In his thick diary Doten took turns recording the latest outbreaks of ethnically-charged crimes even while noting the fortunes of those closest to the target of his affection.

> Spanish Gulch: February 23 1853
>
> ...Heard that the Mexicans are robbing and killing the Chinamen at a great rate... Joe Hunt is also married [as of 16 February] to Miss Sara Jane Toler, the sister of Martha...

Questions of ethnic origin dominated both social discourse and personal reflection at the time Doten was tagging the Tolers. Only two years after statehood, about one of every sixth person hailed from China. Several hundred Chinese arrived in California in 1849-50. More than twenty-thousand additional Chinese landed in San Francisco in 1852. One observer held:

> Their distinctive dress and appearance was highly recognizable in the gold fields, and created a degree of animosity towards the Chinese.

Chinese ghetto, as illustrated in Mexico, California and Arizona; Being a New and Revised Edition of Old Mexico and Her Lost Provinces *(1900); Chinese miners cradling for gold*

Twenty-thousand mostly male Chinese immigrants skewed even more the local male-to-female ratio. Given the extreme scarcity of women and girls in California's goldfields, young men like Doten took note of each female among them—even married or minority ones. All seemed fair game:

> Spanish Gulch: May 4 1853
>
> —Clear, warm and pleasant—Morning I rode down to the Henrietta ranch, made inquiries but could not find the old Scotchman I was after to build our kiln—Heard he had gone up to the "Hill," so I turned about to go home again—stopped at the N.Y. ranch and got some watermelon seeds—Stopped also at Boyd's house and Mrs Boyd gave me a few more—very pretty, pleasant little woman—went on to McDonalds and the boys there would have me stay all night—The bright eyes of "Miss Martha" also inspired to make me stay, so I picketted [sic] out my horse on the ranch and staid [sic]—Evening I was introduced to McDonald's young wife—had a fiddle there and having plenty of dancers we contrived to pass a merry evening indeed and I went to bed extremely happy for I saw the bright eyes of the dear one that notwithstanding all that had been said and done she was mine yet, my case was by no means hopeless—

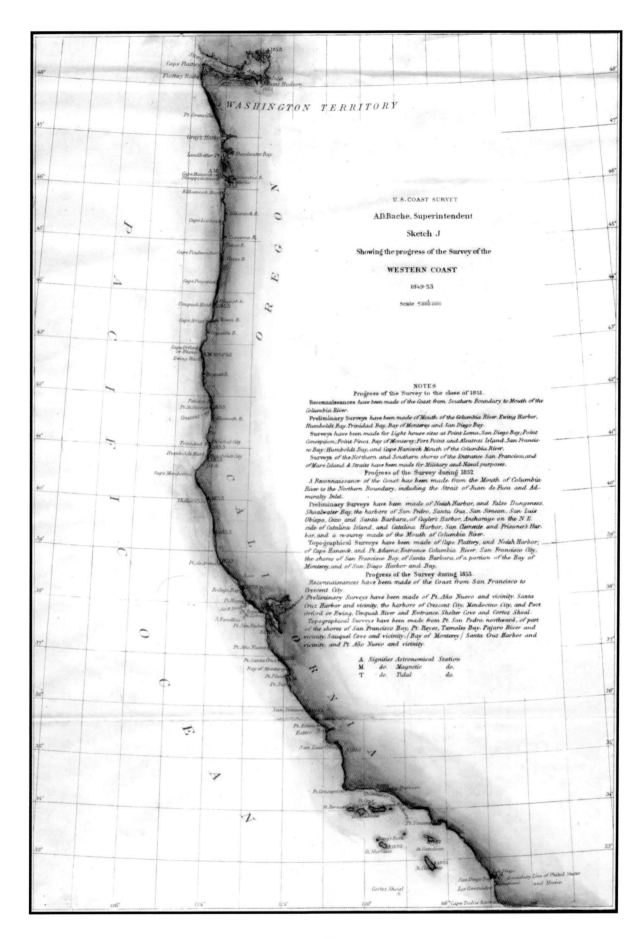

U.S.COAST SURVEY

A.D.Bache, Superintendent

Sketch J

Showing the progress of the Survey of the

WESTERN COAST

1849-53

Scale 5.000.000

NOTES

Progress of the Survey to the close of 1851.

Reconnaissances have been made of the Coast from Southern Boundary to Mouth of the Columbia River.

Preliminary Surveys have been made of Mouth of the Columbia River, Ewing Harbor, Humboldt Bay, Trinidad Bay, Bay of Monterey and San Diego Bay.

Surveys have been made for Light house sites at Point Loma, San Diego Bay; Point Conception; Point Pines, Bay of Monterey; Fort Point and Alcatras Island, San Francisco Bay; Humboldt Bay, and Cape Hancock Mouth of the Columbia River.

Surveys of the Northern and Southern shores of the Entrance San Francisco, and of Mare Island & Straits have been made for Military and Naval purposes.

Progress of the Survey during 1852

A Reconnaissance of the Coast has been made from the Mouth of Columbia River to the Northern Boundary, including the Strait of Juan de Fuca and Admiralty Inlet.

Preliminary Surveys have been made of Neah Harbor, and False Dungeness, Shoalwater Bay, the harbors of San Pedro, Santa Cruz, San Simeon, San Luis Obispo, Cozo and Santa Barbara, of Cuyler's Harbor, Anchorage on the N.E. side of Catalina Island, and Catalina Harbor, San Clemente and Prisoner's Harbor, and a re-survey made of the Mouth of Columbia River.

Topographical Surveys have been made of Cape Flattery, and Neah Harbor; of Cape Hancock, and Pt. Adams, Entrance Columbia River; San Francisco City, the shores of San Francisco Bay, of Santa Barbara, of a portion of the Bay of Monterey, and of San Diego Harbor and Bay.

Progress of the Survey during 1853

Reconnaissances have been made of the Coast from San Francisco to Crescent City.

Preliminary Surveys have been made of Pt. Año Nuevo and vicinity, Santa Cruz Harbor and vicinity, the harbors of Crescent City, Mendocino City, and Port Orford or Ewing, Umquah River and Entrance, Shelter Cove and Cortez Shoal.

Topographical Surveys have been made from Pt. San Pedro, northward, of part of the shores of San Francisco Bay, Pt. Reyes, Tamales Bay, Pajaro River and vicinity, Sauquel Cove and vicinity, Bay of Monterey, Santa Cruz Harbor and vicinity, and Pt. Año Nuevo and vicinity.

A   Signifies Astronomical Station
M   do.   Magnetic   do.
T   do.   Tidal   do.

30

quartz stamp mill, 1850s; miners excavating bluff with water jets, 1860s

The next day, the emotional rollercoaster Doten chose to remain on took yet other new turns.

Spanish Gulch: May 5 1853

...This forenoon I was busy in a room with M——courting and getting more hopelessly in love than ever——Oh me, poor fool——Found that she was all right yet, and still was the same——Had a long conference together——After dinner I took leave of them all...

A fortnight later, however, Doten detoured from his obsession with Martha Jane Toler long enough for a dalliance with a Chinese woman—suggesting double standards on several levels.

Spanish Gulch: May 21 1853

...Evening Bill and I went up to Kelso's on a pasear——"Maria" has fell in love with me and wants to have me for her lover as she is a yellow gal and it would hardly do for me to marry her legally——She is worth 15.00 dollars——She is a real good looking girl of fine shape and no doubt a fine bedfellow——

Assessing a dollar value to bedding "unmarriageable" Maria and buying a new mare both warranted apparently only casual references in Doten's journal:

Spanish Gulch: Sunday, May 29 1853

... Bought Rathbone's horse for 75 dollars——

31

"Horse Auction" from Mountains and Molehills: or, Recollections of a Burnt Journal *by Frank Marryat, 1855*

Taking his new equine acquisition for a ride, though, provided Doten an excuse to meet with the evasive daughter of the angry innkeeper—which he recorded in disappointed detail in his diary:

> Spanish Gulch: May 31 1853
>
> —Clear and pleasant—Morning I saddled up old Rathbone (our horse) and started for Brown's ranch on a pasear—Brown's ranch about three miles below the bridge across the river from the Halfway house—I had fondly expected to meet the adored one here according to appointment, but she sent word that she was otherwise engaged—The fact of it is that she has a large quantity of beaux besides myself and for reasons of her own refused to see me—So I suspect all is pretty near at an end between myself and her as I can't stand any such nonsense as that—

As Martha Jane proved evermore elusive, Doten's focus on her grew increasingly bittersweet—at times even bizarre. Still, he seemed to enjoy causing "more stir" at Halfway House.

> Spanish Gulch: June 1 1853
>
> —Clear, warm and pleasant—Forenoon I rode out with Mrs Brown, both of us on horses—first time I ever rode in company with a lady on horseback—We rode down past the Halfway house and I saw Miss Martha and the other girls cutting about the house like mad and peeking at me from every corner—I merely nodded to them and passed on—we rode down as far as the Oak Ranch, where Mrs Brown had some errands to do, and then came back home again in fine style—Took dinner, after which I gave Mrs Samuel Brown a few lessons in riding on horseback—Mrs Harold of the Oak Ranch came over on a visit—I had to take her home again—She rode Mrs Brown's horse and I rode old Rathbone—led her horse back—more stir among the girls at the ½ way house—altogether I managed to pass a very pleasant day of it—

Arranging even casual contact with Lemuel Toler's oldest of three daughters took on a game-like quality—and at times drove Doten mad with its intricate intrigue and communicating by proxy.

> Spanish Gulch: June 2 1853
>
> —Forenoon I rode over to the Halfway house, to see Morris—The old fellow was right glad to see me &c—Miss Martha was hovering about, but I had nothing to say to her—I learned much that I wish to know about matters and things &c—Went back to Brown's to dinner—Left word with Mrs Brown what to tell Martha from me when she should next see her—also left word with Morris—After dinner started for home—passed over and took leave of Morris and the girls—

Despite his romantic obsessions and sporadic romantic rendezvous with Miss Martha Jane, Alfred Doten still had to deal with daily life in the complicated world of gold-rush-era California.

> Spanish Gulch: June 22 through 24 1853
>
> Fencing, deepening the well, killing a big rattlesnake—Some Indians camp "within gunshot," gathering seeds and roots and hunting—AD gets a letter from Dr Quimby—Young has been away a week longer than expected on a money collecting trip, and the boys "begin to think strange of it."

"Winter of 1849" (left) and "High and Dry: Former Ships in San Francisco" by Frank Marryat, 1855

In gold-crazed California not only natives but also newly arrived Anglo-Saxon men went missing. Some estimates hold that one of every twelve Forty-niners perished in the process of stealing the region from the Mexicans, who had stolen it three centuries earlier from its aboriginal inhabitants. Once they had effectively exterminated the "native threat," those outsiders pouring into the West Coast in search of overnight riches faced endless work and danger every day. Still, at night they distracted themselves amply with whisky and women:

> **Spanish Gulch: June 25 1853**
>
> —Clear and pleasant—Afternoon we went down to James's bar—Helped Kelso get his boat across the river, got a rope stretched across and established his ferry—Yesterday Kelso and George, a man that was working for him, were rafting lumber down from Middle bar and just above here the raft George was on struck a rock and was dashed to pieces—the current was very swift and as cold as snow could make it so that George was immediately swept down the stream and has not been seen since—A reward is offered for his body—Kelso sprang in to assist him and came near losing his own life—George was about 25 years of age and a good steady man, and bore a good character—Evening Kelso opened his house—Everything in the liquor line was free for the evening—I played the violin, we also had two Italian musicians, one with a violin and the other a clarinet and together with Mrs Kelso's tambourine, we managed to get off some pretty good music—The house was crowded —dancing, singing, and kicking up was the order of the night—The ladies of the town were in and we had several waltzes and polkas—Steven and his wife were there, also Mrs Donelly and daughter &c—We had a fine time and a most glorious jollification and kept it up till daylight, when we broke up and Bill and I came home—The boys from the Spanish gulsh were there, except Spicer and Moody—

The times were both turbulent and exciting. On one hand met by revolving dangers, on the other the miners and those who lived from them witnessed superlatives up-close on a daily basis.

> **Spanish Gulch: Sunday, June 26 1853**
>
> —Clear and cool—Forenoon we slept off the glories of last night—Afternoon Young arrived, safe and sound . . . He made a raise of some money—On the road we passed teams bound for Stockton with the bark of the big tree at Murphy's—31 feet [about ten meters] in diameter—

"Logging, Back of Visalia;" details from a later regional postcard

While their days unfolded in the wilds of the West Coast, those fueling the Gold Rush periodically trekked to swelling settlements like Stockton or San Francisco for rest, supplies or simply a break. Oddly, "AD" Doten wrote an account of one such pilgrimage to the Bay in detached third-person. Still, the details he recorded provide a colorful glimpse of the material world in which he moved while driven by intangible impulses:

34

Spanish Gulch: June 27 through July 3 1853

AD rides old Rathbone to Stockton and takes the steamer American Eagle to San Francisco, spending part of the voyage with a Missouri girl, to whom he gives five dollars—In San Francisco he visits Seth, Eunice and Emerson, and buys an accordion and several pieces of sheet music, including "Ben Bolt," "The Girl I Left Behind Me" and "Camptown Races," a bow and string for his fiddle, clothing, a subscription to the Alta California, and some Chinese raffle tickets and a number of lesser items—He returns to Stockton on the HT Clay, visits with a number of Plymouth friends, finds his partner Bill, who has come down with the wagon, picks up his chest at Job Churchill's and with Bill purchases $137 worth of supplies, including flour, pork, sugar, coffee, tea, five gallons of brandy, chili, gunpowder, mackerel, spices, lard, chemical soap, ham, axes and a grindstone—Bill goes home by the short route with the wagon and supplies—Alf, having been much taken with Maj Stemmons's daughter Maria on the way down, takes the longer route on Rathbone and stays overnight at the Stemmons's house, where he plays the violin and sings and notes, "Miss Maria Stemmons looked on with all her big blue eyes and almost made me fall in love again"—The next day he stops at the Halfway House, where he learns that Martha Toler is to be married two days hence, and enters five Hurrahs! and goes home—Spicer and Moody come over from Spanish Gulch the evening of the third, and they have music and get "a little obscure."

cartoon (1850) titled "Independent Gold Hunter on His Way to California," with original caption: "I am sorry I did not follow the advice of Granny and go around the Horn, through the Straights, or by Chagres [Panama]." View of San Francisco in 1850, painted in 1878 by George Henry Burgess

Even drinking himself into obscurity, however, couldn't change what Doten couldn't control. On the day of his would-be lover's wedding to another, the displaced Yankee merely tersely noted:

> Spanish Gulch: July 4 1853
>
> Clear, warm and pleasant—Today we did all we could to celebrate our national birth-day by firing guns, drinking brandy—music and making a fuss generally—get passed off finally—Young was especially afflicted with a toothache, so did not join the festivities of the day as he might, but still we had a glorious time—oh my heart is breaking for the love of—that Toler—

Still, over the next few weeks Alfred Doten's smitten heart continued to sting—as evident here:

> Spanish Gulch: July 6 through 30 1853
>
> —A.D. rides to Campo Seco for some clothing, but can't get it, as the dry season has nearly emptied the camp—He makes a 30-mile ride to "Douglas's flat" near Murphy's to pay a debt for Young, finds his old friend and enemy [shop-owner] Perry keeping store there and ignores him, takes a look at the diggings there, returns by the way of Ballecito, where he visits his cousin, James Bradford, and finds everybody "doing very well indeed," at the mining—He writes a letter to Eunice, buys a pair of shoes at "the Hill," allows Mr Brown to condole with him on losing Martha Toler, reads Old London Bridge and Branch of Brandywine, celebrates his 24th birthday by firing "two guns in honor of I" and holding "a bit of a soiree and fandangle," finds [that his dog] Gumbosina delivered seven pups.

---

chapter 41: fountains of youth

Whatever the unnamed circumstances behind Lemuel Toler's adamant rejection of Doten's advances towards his oldest daughter, instead of a flashy, famous-but-penniless adventurer, Louis Luick's future

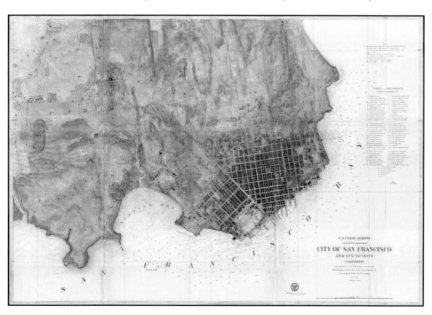

mother-in-law Martha Jane married a down-to-earth, land-owning stockman on the Fourth of July, 1853. Thoughtful Curtis (originally an English surname meaning "courteous" in Old French) Nathaniel (Hebrew for "god has given") Hunt had left his aging Vermont-born parents behind in Illinois when he decided to venture, alone, out west to seek what would prove a respectable living.

1858 map "City of San Francisco and Its Vicinity"

Currier & Ives lithograph of City of San Francisco. Birds eye view from the bay looking south-west*, 1878;*
a panoramic view, with San Francisco Bay in the foreground and the Pacific Ocean in the background

The 1880 census showed Curtis and Martha Jane residing next to Melissa (Overacker) Luick Arnold—but for some reason their second-oldest surviving daughter, Mary Louisa, was missing from the rolls of what would become a total of nine children. While she seems to have not been living at home at 22, her neighbor's son may have "known" her in the biblical sense, for she and some man conceived a child around the time of Mary's 19th birthday in May 1877. Although Mary gave birth to a daughter, Anna Leora, on 20 January 1878 in Plano, Tulare County, the 1880 census lists Louis as a "farm laborer" on the New River J ranch in Kern County. The two would not marry, however, until 1881—when Anna could not

only walk, but also talk. Were she here today, what might she say about why her presumed parents seemed to vacillate so long before finally marrying?

Did the girl, in fact, belong to another sire but, when they later married, Louis generously claimed Mary's fatherless child as his own? Family-history researchers often find that Victorian-era obituaries and even "official" marital records were habitually "corrected" by family members to hide embarrassing, inconvenient truths—such as Lydia (Lathrop) Johnson Luick's claiming that she and Henry married in "1865" when the puzzle's pieces suggest

Louis Lee and Mary Louisa (Hunt) Luick at the time of their marriage, 1881

that to be the year the two love-struck neighbors high-tailed it out of Belmond. (Records attest that the wedding only took place at the end of October 1868.) That Anna Leora (Luick) Forristal's obituary lists Louis and Mary as her parents does not explain why they only married three years after her birth—or why her age at death so widely varied from that of her ("half"?) siblings, who with one exception lived at least eleven, but as many as twenty-six years longer than she—as shown in a statistical analysis of Louis and Mary's "official" offspring who reached majority age.

Excluding their daughter Ethel May, who died at 18 from typhoid, Louis and Mary Luicks' eight offspring who survived to adulthood lived long lives—on average dying at the age of 86.75! Their parents, respectively, died about a month shy of 92 and at age 85. The lack of a single recorded case of child mortality in the Luick-Hunt family was rare for rural families of that era.

What was the "secret" of the extraordinary longevity of the Luick-Hunt lineage? Could it have been solely genetic? Was it, as Louis himself said, through hard work or gardening? Or was it something else—perhaps something physically immeasurable? Could it have been a pervasive, sustaining love of music—*and* of each other?

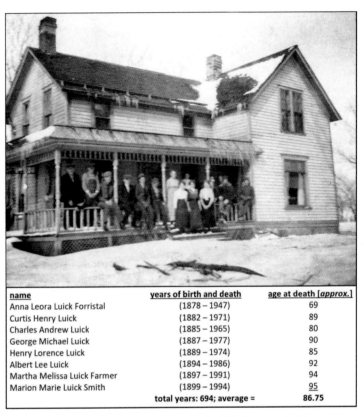

name	years of birth and death	age at death [approx.]
Anna Leora Luick Forristal	(1878 – 1947)	69
Curtis Henry Luick	(1882 – 1971)	89
Charles Andrew Luick	(1885 – 1965)	80
George Michael Luick	(1887 – 1977)	90
Henry Lorence Luick	(1889 – 1974)	85
Albert Lee Luick	(1894 – 1986)	92
Martha Melissa Luick Farmer	(1897 – 1991)	94
Marion Marie Luick Smith	(1899 – 1994)	95
	total years: 694; average =	86.75

Luick family with guests, circa 1910; Ethel likely one of girls on steps

the Luicks' was a "Man's World:" Leslie and Myrle with Louis on left; Henry in middle of men, 1912-13

———

After Louis returned to the land of his birth, one of the first things he did—as visible in the milky, self-snapped photo at this chapter's opening—was to outfit his little band of children into a... little band. Despite the family's recorded frequency of moving about—among rented farms as far-flung from each other in those horse-drawn days as Hickory Grove, Iowa Falls, Latimer and Belmond—Louis pulled together a rag-tag ensemble of other flatland musicians to create a lifting local sound. He named his amateur crew the "Felt Boot Orchestra" as

> the musicians wore felt boots to keep their feet warm. Sometimes this determined and dedicated band walked miles to dances and those felt boots were a necessity. The music was sweet and full of swing! Louis and the band made a bright interlude in the long Iowa winters.

Louis (center) with Felt Boot Orchestra members under a canvas roof

Those "long Iowa winters," however, could be "bright" only on an interlude basis: They also could be bleak and brutal—as Louis, Mary and their surviving children were to find out in January 1910, when

It was a sad and sudden ending that came to the life of Ethel May Luick when she died at her home last Saturday morning after only a week's sickness of typhoid fever contracted while working at the home of James Courtney at Meservey. Miss Luick is the daughter of Lewis [sic] and Mary Luick and was born at Goodell, September 18, 1891. She was a young lady of a bright sunny disposition, kind and obedient to her parents, ever thoughtful of her people and friends. Such a disposition made her many friends who ever felt that to know her was to love her. Funeral services were held at the home Monday afternoon conducted by the pastor of the Methodist Episcopal Church, J.A. Kettle, and interment made in the cemetery. She leaves besides her parents five brothers, three sisters to mourn her death, though they feel like saying,

Sleep on, beloved, sleep and take thy rest,
Lay down thy head upon the Savior's breast.
We loved thee well, but Jesus loves thee best.

In the land of the living, however, survivors must press on with the tasks of navigating daily life—and few farm families can eke out a living from only irregular playing gigs. When he wasn't making music, Louis scraped together the pennies to at least shelter and shod his big brood by running the township's road grader, hauling fill dirt, driving dray, cutting firewood or executing any number of other off-farm activities. Still, those were just turn-of-the-century day jobs; he dedicated all his remaining energy—and nights—to his true passions: his and Mary's family... and music.

If he were out mostly pretending to pursue a dud career by day, gifted Louis was fully into coaxing his beloved fiddle sing at night. His second-youngest grandson, Gary Luick, remembers

> my father telling us kids about his father would play the violin at the corner of 3rd and Main St. in Belmond, [which would have been in front of] the Ralph Jenison place. You would hear the music all over town. I still have the violin that my grandfather used.

Today home to about two-and-a-half thousand inhabitants, Belmond is still a cozy little Iowa prairie town—despite having been hit by two devastating tornadoes and a major flood since 1966. A century ago, though, strolling along its elm-lined avenues or sitting in a buggy parked on some darkened side lane with your sweetheart in your arms on a warm summer evening, listening to Louis Luick's lilting refrains waft through the streets from over in front of Ralph and Mabel's place... it would have been like watching a flickering moving-picture show right out of Victorian heaven.

violin once owned and played by Louis Lee Luick, now in Gary's care

Belmond's main street, preparing for a parade, circa 1910

While the image of Great-Great-Grampa Louis making his fiddle sing for Belmond's grateful townsfolk is expressly romantic, what sort of Earthly reality interrupted his bliss after he put his polished wooden baby to bed, closed its worn case and trundled home to dutiful Mary and a house full of lively Little Luicks? He and his long-suffering wife still had to pay at least the most basic bills. If nothing else, they had to *feed* all those mini-mouths they'd borne.

None but one of the documents related to Louis' work life suggest anything close to resembling worldly "success"—the exception being the 1920 census, which listed him as "sperintendant" of "Public Roads." Yet, what did that misspelled title really mean? Other sources cite him as "driving a road grader"—but specifically for 36-square-mile Pleasant Township. He wasn't makin' big bucks doin' that, and he wasn't settin' aside a cool mil for a rainy day in the process, either. But, did it matter? The entirety of all remaining physical traces of the man suggests that, at least to him, it did not!

photo (circa 1910) likely of Louis' road crew, as it came from his collection

Louis and Mary's shared married life of some sixty-two years was, above all, a modest yet contented one, filled with family, surrounded by simple pleasures. From the outside, looking back, they seem to have realized The Good Life—if *they* realized it or not.

———

chapter 42: the soul tenderers

Despite some ten thousand years of pursuing sedentary agriculture, followed most recently by two and a half centuries of industrialized production, it seems to me that there are still basically three kinds of human beings in the world. That'd be: hunters, gatherers and "soul tenders," the last being that select minority charged with the task of caring for—or at least blessing—those in the first two groups.

I see "hunters" as those women and men who are constantly seeking a super savings at the local discount store, an engaging conversation partner perched atop a barstool down at the corner pub, a compelling book to read at night until heavy eyes overpower light interest… or another dusting of cocaine to snort up an already-raw nose, a warm penis or vagina to fondle, an umpteenth shot of icy vodka to gulp down… a sense of "family" or belonging to some *ersatz* group… or any

Danny Jones, circa 1970; Bertha (Hadsall) Juhl, Helen (Juhl) Johnson, Bertha's great-granddaughter Anne Dahlby, Charlotte (Juhl) Luick & Anne's aunt, Donna (Gullickson) Tuttle, at Bertha's 85th birthday, April 1978

other number of distractions from that one ultimate, inescapable "find"—death.

"Gatherers" are those people obsessed less with collecting experiences than with amassing mountains of material goodies: backless closets full of long-forgotten clothes and shoes, garages full of unused junk, parking lots jammed with luxury cars…. hundreds of porcelain thimbles, or assorted dolls assigned fancy names… or tilting yachts, massive sparkling "rocks" posing as "rings," "friends" who when you really need 'em really aren't… groaning bank accounts, trophy partners or children, immense McMansions, endless compact discs or books or boyfriends or…

And the "soul tenders" who faithfully follow other two main sorts of humanity? Those are the high priests, the shamans, the monks or nuns and Sunday school teachers, the doctors and nurses or midwives… the (hi-)story scribes, the sociologists and therapists, the drug counselors or battered-shelter doorkeepers… the poets and the songwriters, the painters and sculptors.,. the Holocaust survivors or rape victims or "clean" addicts who quietly roam from school to school, warning half-comprehending kids of the deadly trap of (self-)hate. We are the Eternal Human Salvage Crew, searching for meaning among the ruins we all, collectively, leave behind.

We—and, yes, I include myself—are the under-loved, under-paid philosophers who each day, every hour ponder unanswerable questions that the "hunters" choose to ignore and the "gatherers" refuse to

me as late hippie; Darleen, Gordon and me at Omega House, fall 1986

entertain. We ring mostly unheard alarms about the perils of seductive-yet-vacuous trivialities, even as we agonize over the evils of soul-numbing materialism. We scorn the hunters and gatherers as "less evolved," yet wrestle with our own fascination with both. We are the ones, so hungry for "family," for a lasting, indelible sense of belonging that we shift through dried bones and paper fragments, grainy microfiche and faded maps, looking for clues to who "we" are and to which of the infinite sub-groupings of humanity we might "really" fit. We are the ones who, hard as we try, fail to find large, lively families to be "enough," who keep looking for meaning among the debris of the imagined and glorified Unknown. We are the ones who down-home folks like child-rich-but-dollar-poor Louis Lee and Mary Louisa likely would have warmly invited to join their loud and crowded table, then thrown questioning, strained looks at each other as they realized their guests were really unintelligible aliens.

John Baker (standing), Mingonette, Adelbert "Dell," Jessie, Sarah (Lathrop Baker, sitting) & Michael Luick;
Michael & Sarah (Lathrop Baker) Luick home in Belmond, circa 1890—note violin player on the porch roof

Even if we did not know them personally we stalk these sorry souls, our unsuspecting ancestors: We read their mail and supposed thoughts; we dissect their diets and design in our minds the interiors of frontier shanties they "must" have lived in. We search for deeper, lasting "truths" and, in the process, leave them no shred of privacy or spare them not one possibly condemning assumption or allegation. They are "ours"—they "belong" to us just as much we so ardently yearn to "belong" to them—so we demand that our forefathers and -mothers deliver what we didn't get from the parents or other blood-bound kin we knew but found, ultimately, lacking. As my wise cousin Barbara has promised that "the dead have no egos," we appeal to our ancestors' selfless, all-knowing ghosts and wait for wisdom to pour forth from cooked stories of their own myriad hopes and dreams, their various successes or failures. We hope for something better, for someone wiser or kinder, some moment that was fuller and more redeeming than the empty, damning moments of the eternal, insufferable, self-replacing "Now" we otherwise try to flee.

Ian, Gerry, Deb (Luick), Jared & Jamin Wass, 1991; Dena, David, Paige & Sherri (Mahaffey) Luick, 1992

All the while, we know that each of us enters this world possessing the same "capital:" a body, a mind and limited time on the planet. We all also exit the world with the exact same "return" as any other mortal ever had upon checking out: a biography which belonged completely and solely to him or her—to each one of us, whether or not we ever "own" it.

Clergy of various religions, under-appreciated hospice workers and "death-and-dying" helpers (an altruistic body that includes agnostics as well as atheists) maintain the process of finally letting go of whatever limited time we each will have had includes a "flash-by" review of the Life one has made, of everything we have ever experienced compressed into one impressive momentary "show" as we bow out, then move on. The difference is, some make more out of their allotted time than others—and some leave behind more obstacles for those yet to come to surmount than the rest of us do. Some of us learn to live life well; others, less so.

To which group do...?

———

Last night, unable to sleep for all the chatter and clatter being made by the ghosts I schlepp around with me at present like little, invisible monkey babies clinging to my tortured psyche, I finally threw my legs out of bed at 2:33 and stumbled to my cluttered desk. As I so often do when I can't fall back to sleep in Dresden, I fell back on comfort food for the soul, spiritual nourishment that I can find only on a faraway prairie. I picked up the phone and tried familiar numbers until I eventually found "connection" with some unwitting sap back in the Heartland—that mythical, only half-real "place" that I also carry around in my crammed, rattling noodle.

Hoping to still the ravenous, unrelenting mental hunger to confirm if the Luick-Hunt clan was really as happy as I hoped (and "need") them to be, I dialed Louis' grandson—who ironically lives near my recently widowed sister, but as so often in fraying America, the two cousins never meet to seek moments of shared solace.

"Hi, Gary!" I bid, "How are things in Iowa?"

"Oh, hi, Mike!" My Grampa Donald's much-younger cousin coughed, then affirmed, idly, "They're doin'."

"So, Gary, I'm callin' 'cause I'm strugglin' with Louis and Mary, as I'm just not finding enough to bring them 'alive' in my narrative, to get a sense of who they really were and why we should care."

"*Oka-a-ay*" Gary stalled to think, "how might I help?"

"Well, just like I had to turn to Gramma Luick's aunt, Della, for clues about from what sort of parental home Charlotte's mother hailed, I'm lookin' for hints about who Louis and Mary were, as suggested by what their children became."

"What ya mean?"

"Well" I bargained, "don't children mirror the adults around them?"

"Oh, I see what ya mean. Well, that's easy" I felt relieved to hear coming from the other end of the imperfect phone connection. "Where do ya wanna start?" Gary asked.

"How about with Anna Leora?"

"Whattaya wanna know?"

"Well," I took a breath, unsure how much intimated scandal my Midwestern cousin could stomach, or at what rate, "I'm still puzzled why her reported parents only married three years after she was born—"

"You know, I did hear somethin' 'bout that—like she wasn't Louis' or somethin' like that."

"That's what I suspected, Gary—to be honest."

"You know, I asked her husband, Harry Forristal, once, about it." The abrupt silence begged a concluding comment—but none came. I speculated if maybe the line had gone dead.

"Gary—you still there?"

"Children mirror the adults in their lives…"

All I got back was a blank "Yep," followed by more low-level humming typical of trans-Atlantic-phone calls. ("Maybe it's the NSA filters that make that buzzing sound" I often offer.)

The ensuing seconds of heavy silence made me prod "So, like—what did Harry say?"

"You still got the compiled materials I emailed ya, Mike?"

"Ya, I sure do, Gary."

"Anna's obit should be there"—his words sent my fingers flipping through the unnumbered pages—"and that will answer some of this."

"Here it is!" I almost shouted as I found it among hundreds of pages of data. "Here's Anna's obituary—" my voice trailed off as I began to softly mumble out-loud highlights of what the tiny print in front of my wrinkled nose had to reveal about a woman who'd likely been born an illegitimate girl "adopted" sans paperwork by my great-great-grandfather:

Anna Luick was born in Plano, California, on January 20, 1878 to… and passed away in the Lutheran hospital on May 24, 1947 at the age of… married in 1894 to… who passed away about ten years ago. To this union were born ten children: three sons and seven daughters, all but two of whom remain to mourn the passing of a loving mother… Besides the above, her father, age 91, the following brothers and sisters… Also nineteen grandchildren and three great-grandchildren…

I suddenly stopped reading out loud.

"What's the matter?" Gary wondered.

"*Hum-m-m*" I harrumphed, "the rest is sortta poopy."

"Really? What's it say, again?"

While not a great worker in her church life, she was baptized in the Belmond Methodist church a few years ago and her interests were found in the standards for which her chosen church stood. She was a typical pioneer mother and wife who faced the hardship of a life with courage and fortitude. Internment was…

Interior and exterior views of Belmond's Methodist Episcopal Church; "Rev. Chapler" in inset, early 1900s

"*Yeah-h-h*" Gary interrupted, "that sounds about right."

"But what about—" I began to grouse.

"Let's see" my small-town informant delayed, then deflected with "there was Curtis."

"Curtis Henry?" I checked, unhappily yielding to Gary's naked diversion.

"Ya—Curtis Henry. He built the house they lived in, and I think he might have been the one who was a truck driver."

Curtis Luick making a delivery in Belmond with his dray wagon, circa 1933

"Is that so?"

45

"Oh, yeah. He'd make deliveries all through town, of all kinds o' things—machinery parts an' fencin', ice during summers an' such. But his grandson, Steve, he lives out East somewhere—he runs a bed-and-breakfast in this big ol' Victorian place with columns… maybe in Upstate New York, maybe somewhere out by Buffalo. I think, though, he used ta work with drug addicts, or run a foundation for children…"

"I'll try to find him on the web" I pressed, absently, starting to finally feel faintly drowsy. "What about Charles Andrew?"

"His wife was Mable."

"Would that have been 'Mable Brooks'—Lorena Jenison's mother's half-sister?"

"Ya, that's right. Anyways, she and Uncle Charlie lived up in Clear Lake…" Gary's voice tapered off as I heard him shift his weight in a creaking desk chair, before resuming. "He had a small farm up there somewhere, I think south of the Lake—but that's all I can really say 'bout him and Mable." Pause. "Oh, other than that Mable, she run a beauty salon up there at The Lake—"

Mable (Brooks) Luick with assistant in Mable's beauty shop in Clear Lake, 1930s; note framed Civil War veterans monument lithograph behind Mable, likely honoring her veteran father, James Wesley Brooks

"Okay" I pushed, trying to outrun sleep, which was gaining on me fast, "George Michael came next—but I've basically got that chapter covered, so who's next?"

"Really? Uncle George was a great ol' guy—but if ya don't wanna know anything 'bout him…"

"No, it's not that" I stalled, "but—well, it's not so easy, Gary."

"What's not so easy?"

I looked around the darkened apartment, looking for something even though I had no idea what it might be. "Ya know, it seems he wasn't the loveable old man we all thought he was. At least, not only."

"He wasn't?" Gary said nothing for a hushed, awkward moment, then asked "What ya mean?"

"You know Velma's kids, my grampa Donald's two nieces and nephew, the Jacobsens, right?"

"*Ya-a-a*" Gary inhaled.

"Well, Jan said Velma told her that she once found a white KKK hood and pointed hat of Great-Grampa George's tucked away, out in the barn, and—"

"Geo-o-orge?" Gary balked, incredulously. "We talkin' 'bout the same person?"

"Yeah—that's what I asked, too. Look, Gary" I hurried on, "we can pick this up about Great-Grampa George being in the Ku Klux Klan another time" I lied, "but for tonight, who's next?"

Only too happy to leave controversy behind, my fellow Iowan waltzed right along with me as he offered "At the other end, there was the girls."

Instead of challenging Gary, drilling him on why he just leap-frogged over Henry Lorence and his father (also named "Albert Lee Luick," but not the banker who will appear later in this family saga) I asked "Have anything on Ethel May—the girl that died of typhoid in Meservey?"

"Nope—only what's in the materials I sent ya." He drew a deep, difficult, raspy breath. "I meant Mattie and—"

"That'd be 'Martha Melissa' if I'm not mistaken."

"That's the one."

George (right) and brother Curtis Luick, circa 1905

"Hey, I remember Aunt Mattie so well! I got this great, really clear color picture of her and Marion that I took as a teen in the late Seventies, when Ethel Luick Tuttle and I visited them, at the time they were livin' in the same retirement center in Belmond. I'll send it to you." A delicious sense of lightness came over me as I remembered the lovely hours I spent with those sweet little ol' Luick ladies, two souls indelibly connected already as wee lasses, who remained inseparable their entire lives.

Ethel May Luick's undated gravestone in Belmond

damaged photo of a religious pageant at Belmond's Reformed Church, late 1920s: Ethel's death came suddenly and too young. Did religious beliefs comfort her surviving family?

Great-Aunts Mattie and Marion seemed like Siamese twins surgically separated, despite being born two years apart and non-identical. Of the two, Mattie (above, on the right; to the right, on the left) was the talker.

caption on photo back reads "Old Town School, May 13 1915" and mailed to "Mr & Mrs Lewis Luick;"
Mattie likely tall girl in white dress in front of window, Marion the girl dressed in white in center front

"They were great" Gary concurred. "Mattie loved ta dance. She'd go up every Saturday night to the Surf, at The Lake, and dance."

"Really? But what'd she do when she wasn't on the dance floor?"

"For a while she had the café down on Main Street—that's where she was that time when Lawrence Welk and his band was passin' through Belmond and stopped to order a pile o' burgers. Oh, ya—Mattie talked 'bout that for years!"

Lawrence Welk and Norma Zimmer (left), 1961; Mattie's café on Belmond's Main Street, December 1941

"How neat!" I feigned. As my eye lids grew unignorably heavy, I asked "And, after runnin' the café? Then what'd she do after that?"

The Wright County Dairy Interests Association President, Floyd Templeton, announces the June Dairy Banquet to be held at the Belmond High School on June 27. The banquet, catered by Mrs. Mattie Farmer, will be served at 6:00 p. m.

Don Warren, WHO Radio & TV announcer, will be the guest speaker for this annual event, which has traditionally attracted about 700 Wright County residents.

One of the highlights of the June Dairy Banquet will be the selection of a Wright County Dairy Princess. Selection will be made from a list of five candidates. There will be a panel of three judges who will select the young lady who will represent Wright County in the state contest later in the fall. The candidates for the 1967 Wright County Dairy Princess crown are: Mary Ann Ramaeker, Eagle Grove; Nancy Dannen, Alexander; Audrene Obrecht, Ames, and Darlene Malaise, Woolstock.

Miss Dianna Marts, 1966-67 State Dairy Princess, from Franklin County, will be a guest of the Wright County dairymen. Miss Marts has been the Dairy Interests' ambassador in promoting dairy products for 1966 and 1967.

The Wright County Dairy Interests Association is a promotional association, doing everything they can to promote milk and milk products. The nutrition and taste appeal of quality dairy products is never questioned. It is just a matter of good salesmanship. Wright County processors and producers have joined hands to get this job done.

notice in Wright County Monitor, *22 June 1967; WPA poster promoting milk consumption, 1941*

"Yeah, when things at the café just weren't workin' out any more, she tried her hand at catering—but later on the side, you know, for special events and such. Her food was the glue."

"I can imagine, that ya can't live from catering in a town of less than two thou—"

"So Aunt Mattie worked as the head cook at the school for years—and she made the best damned chicken-and-gravy over biscuits! I'd go in and get seconds and thirds. Not everybody got to do that" he boasted, paused, then added reflectively "*Yea-a-ah*, she took good care of me. She an' Ross—"

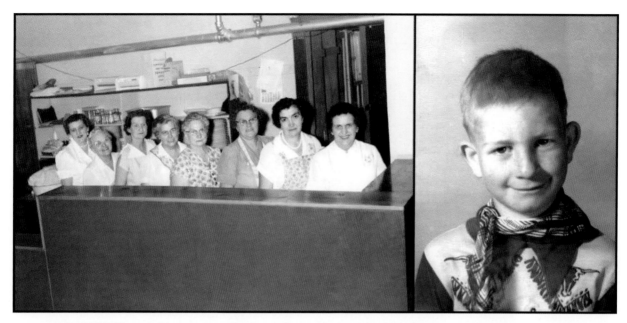

Marion (third from left) and Mattie (at head of crew) behind school cafeteria counter; Gary Luick, 1953

"That'd be 'Ross Farmer,' wouldn't it?"

"Ya, Ross 'Farmer'—though, they didn't have any kids. He was the love of her life—but it didn't last."

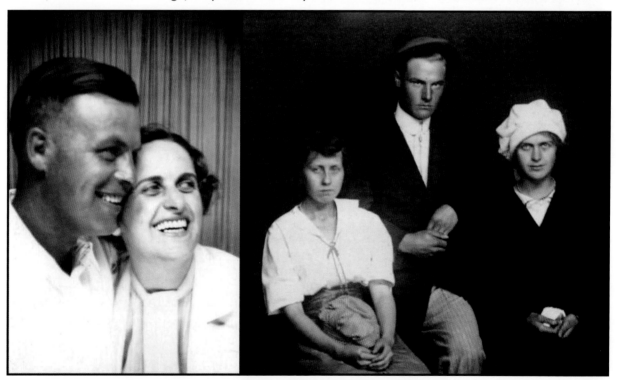

Ross & Mattie (Luick) Farmer (left), likely 1930s; with unidentified friend (white blouse), likely mid-1910s

"Why's that?" I wanted to know—but instead got:

"I thought Ross was always dyin' my hair red! I had the reddest hair you could ever imagine, growin' up as a kid—but it was only hair gel he was puttin' in it that whole time!"

"But you thought it was red hair dye?"

"Yes, sir—I sure did!" my cousin clucked, then conceded "but, they was all only playin' with me! I believed that was why I had red hair, all through school—"

"But, Gary, back to Ross Farmer: Did he die or leave her? Why did you say it didn't—"

Ronald, Marion (Luick), Charles "Laverne" and Richard Smith, mid-1940s

"But we've not said anything about Mattie's kid sister, Marion Marie" Gary interrupted.

"But" I protested in vain.

"She was Ronny's and Richard's mom. Their dad was a salesman."

"The 1940 census says Luverne was 48 then" I interjected, conceding defeat, "an' sold candy."

"'Candy?' Could be—but he later worked at the General Mills plant, with soybeans, millin' 'em inta mash fer breakfast food."

"But you were sayin' 'bout Marion—"

"Ya, she worked with Mattie, in the school kitchen, for a while—but they lived with Henry..."

————

chapter 43: a forbidden love

"*Huh-h-h*" I sat up, confused but at least fully awake again. Cousin Gary, far away across the Atlantic, said nothing. "I thought Henry lived with Louis and Mary" I objected into the silent phone. "Several censuses in a row show him—"

"That was earlier, before Grampa and Gramma died. Later, Marion's family lived with Henry."

"You're talkin' 'bout 'Henry Lorence Luick,' right?"

Henry Lorence Luick (center), circa 1910: homo-erotic images from (top left) Greece (480 BCE), Persia, (1627), Sappho in Homer's Greece; (lower left) the Sac & Fox tribe (1830s), & from Qing-Dynasty China

"The one and only."

"But I thought—"

"He lived in the basement and—"

"In the *basement*?" I howled.

"Yep—like I said: in the basement."

"But state and Federal censuses from 1895 through 1930 list a 'Henry' each time, save for one, living with a 'Louis' and a 'Mary' so—"

"Look down further on that same page—to the 1940 census. By that point, Grampa and Gramma were really old. It was the Depression; they couldn't work. So, Marion and Luverne married and was moved in with her parents and older brother."

"Oh, here it is!" I called out. "And, it seems little Ronald was just two at the time—so wasn't it pretty crowded in that little Arts-and-Crafts, one-story bungalow?"

"Well, that's why Henry lived in the basement."

Henry Luick and his youngest sister, Marion (Luick) Smith, in yard of Henry's bungalow in Belmond, 1930s

"You said that, Gary—but most houses in the rural Midwest in that period didn't have finished basements as we know them. They didn't have the treated building materials or the durable liquid sealants: You *couldn't* have lived in a basement in those days—it'd have been too cold and damp to be healthy." I thought for a moment, then asked "And besides, where'd Henry have cooked? That little house hardly could've have had two kitchens—and certainly not a full one in the basement because—"

"He had the run o' the house."

"What! What do you mean, 'Henry had the run of the house'?"

"It was *his* house."

"*His* house?"

"Ya" Gary confirmed, nonchalantly, "*his* house."

"Did Marion's family pay rent to occupy the upstairs? I mean, how'd that work? If it was Henry's house, why'd he live in the basement other than—"

"'Cause he was diff'rent?"

"He was 'diff'rent'?"

"Ya."

"What do you mean by 'different,' Gary?"

"Well, you know." I swore I could hear disembodied Gary mincing words. "In the summer, we boys'd be down at the crick, fishin' an' stuff, an' they'd say things…" his voice and charged words evaporated as the pressure to tell old truths built.

"What kind of 'things'?"

"Like—like, he liked boys" Gary blurted out, as if forced to reveal something he ought never to let pass his lips.

"Henry liked boys?"

"Ya."

"Sorry, Gary—I didn't hear that: What'd you say?"

"I said 'yes,' Henry liked boys."

My eye lids were anything but heavy now. My heart began to beat faster, stronger, as it began to soak in: *So, I'm not the first or only Luick man who longed to be close to other men* I thought to myself.

Gary coughed, faintly, then asked "So, anything else ya wanna know?"

"What do you mean—what are you trying not to say here, Gary?" I pressed him into an invisible corner, asking pointedly "Are you saying that Uncle Henry was a pedophile, or that he longed to be intimate with members of his own gender? There's a *big* difference there, ya know."

Henry (on right of train-prop railing) and with an army buddy (on left), likely as recruits for World War I

Gary again fell silent on the other end. So, I waited. In the churning void that now hung in the air between us like black, battered boulders tumbling round in a lightless cosmic drum, pieces began to fall into place for me. As images of Klan-member Great-Grampa George's "soft" kid brother—dressed in a smart cardigan sweater, accessorized with a fabulous striped tie—flashed through my dizzy head, I thought to myself *It all makes so much more sense now* before I finally bid Gary "You know, Mom said that she and Dad would pay 'Old Uncle Henry' to come and watch their place west of Thornton when they were first married." I looked around, uncovered and then recounted the related notes from a phone interview I'd conducted a short time before with Phyllis, who said

> I liked Henry. He was a good-looking, gentle man—big-framed, neat and tidy, and well-dressed. He liked to cook and bake pies. He was so pleased one time when he came up and discovered that we had ripe elderberries growing on Doc and Norma's place. He promised he was goin' to bake elderberry pie while we were gone and save us some for when we got back from the trip. Boy, was *that* good!

———

chapter 44: The Good Life

Henry Lorence Luick seemed to have been what in English is called a "jack of all trades"—someone with an amateur ability in many different types of activities but who is not necessarily expertly competent in any special one, as a vocation. Henry's military-service record shows he enlisted at "29 yrs 4mos" in the Wright County seat of Clarion on 23 July 1918. After he returned on 29 May 1919 from a tour of the bloodied battlefields of the First World War, Henry showed up in the 1920 census as a "shearer of sheep," then, a decade later, as a "laborer—odd jobs." By the 1940 census his cited professional status had graduated to "laborer—sugar beet factory"—likely the one on the western edge of Belmond, in part built due to the efforts of our shaker-mover cousin, banker Albert Lee Luick. Perhaps, by need, Henry also substituted at Crystal Sugar's massive brick building outside Mason City, above the tree-lined banks of the winding Winnebago River, across from the dust-spewing Northwestern States Portland Cement pits. If he did, he frequented the same sugar-beet plant where my young father and, earlier, my maternal grandfather, Elmer Thrams, worked winters—when our fields were frozen shut and lay fast asleep under knee-deep snow—to earn extra dough.

cover pages of two of Henry Luick's insurance policies, both of which were offered by locally-based firms

Apparently, Henry also earned extra grocery money by holing up down under Marion's family's constant footfalls, in the basement of the small house he owned. He netted additional pennies as a seasonal farmhand or doing bits o' this an' that—that is, whatever paid, out-of-home dabblings his parental-care duties allowed: His aging mother and father lived with their bachelor son until their respective deaths in 1943 and '48. Thereafter, Uncle Henry was his own master.

Henry with a close friend and solo in a U.S. Army portrait, both taken while a soldier in World War I

It also seems Henry Lorence (like his father, Louis Lee) was what in German is called a *Lebenskünstler*, literally an "artist of life" who can live by her or his wits, especially in the pursuit of leaving time otherwise "wasted" in a dreary world of work to follow other, unpaid endeavors such as art, leisure… or simply savoring physical pleasure. Most of us Late Victorians shirk back when we hear the socially-slanderous term "hedonist" (derived from the Greek for "delight"), but that is the closest, one-word English translation for the German concept of a *Lebenskünstler*. As a matter of historical fact, however, as the world's free encyclopedia tells us, "Hedonism is a school of thought that argues that pleasure is the only intrinsic good. In very simple terms, a hedonist strives to maximize net pleasure (pleasure minus pain)." Taking this ideal one codified step further,

> Ethical hedonism is the idea that all people have the right to do everything in their power to achieve the greatest amount of pleasure possible to them. It is also the idea that every person's pleasure should far surpass their amount of pain. Ethical hedonism is said to have been started by a student of Socrates, Aristippus of Cyrene. He held the idea that pleasure is the highest good.

But, the classical philosophical concept behind today's hyped, commercialized call to "live ta the max" predates the pleasure-drunk Greeks. In the Sumerian *Epic of Gilgamesh*—one of the first written accounts of such allegorical mythology—the alewife Siduri advises a wandering king

> Life, which you look for, you will never find. For when the gods created man, they let death be his share, and life withheld in their own hands. [Fill] your belly. Day and night make merry. Let days be full of joy, dance and make music day and night. And wear fresh clothes. And wash your head and bathe. Look at the child that is holding your hand, and let your wife delight in your embrace. These things alone are the concern of men.

Henry and a young friend on a trip "out West," likely late 1920s or early 1930s

Music prettified The Good Life already in early Egypt, where tombs showed harpists pleasing feasting guests. According to Professor Pedia, the wall decorations adorning burial sites of the noble dead also "sometimes contained hedonistic elements, calling guests to submit to pleasure because they [could not] be sure that they [would] be rewarded for good with a blissful afterlife"—a premise illustrated by a royal song attributed to the 12th or an earlier dynasty:

> *Let thy desire flourish,*
> *In order to let thy heart forget the beautifications for thee.*
> *Follow thy desire, as long as thou shalt live.*
> *Put myrrh upon thy head and clothing of fine linen upon thee,*
> *Being anointed with genuine marvels of the gods' property.*
> *Set an increase to thy good things;*
> *Let not thy heart flag.*
> *Follow thy desire and thy good.*
> *Fulfill thy needs upon earth, after the command of thy heart,*
> *Until there comes for thee that day of mourning.*

Ancient Greece's "laughing philosopher" Democritus—also known as the "father of modern science"—promoted a hedonistic philosophy he held supported the idea that the supreme goal of life consists of "contented cheerfulness," and claimed "joy and sorrow are the distinguishing mark of things beneficial and harmful." Democritus' compatriots, the Cyrenaics, taught that

> the only intrinsic good is pleasure [...] not just the absence of pain, but positively enjoyable sensations. Of these, momentary pleasures, especially physical ones, are stronger than those of anticipation or memory. They did, however, recognize the value of social obligation, and that pleasure could be gained from altruism[.] Cyrenaicism deduces a single, universal aim for all people [as] it follows that past and future pleasure have no real existence for us, and that among present pleasures there is no distinction of kind[.]

However, some actions which give immediate pleasure can create more than their equivalent of pain. The wise person should be in control of pleasures rather than be enslaved to them, otherwise pain will result, and this requires judgment to evaluate the different pleasures of life. Regard should be paid to law and custom, because even though these things have no intrinsic value on their own, violating them will lead to unpleasant penalties being imposed by others. Likewise, friendship and justice are useful because of the pleasure they provide. [The] Cyrenaics believed in the hedonistic value of social obligation and altruistic behavior.

The later Greek philosopher Epicurus dismissed superstition or notions of divine intervention. He qualified the teachings of his predecessors, the Cyrenaics, in as far as he believed that

the greatest good [is] to seek modest, sustainable "pleasure" in the form of a state of tranquility and freedom from fear and absence of bodily pain through knowledge of the workings of the world and the limits of our desires. The combination of these two states [constitutes] happiness in its highest form.

Though Epicureanism is a form of hedonism, in that it holds pleasure to be a sole, intrinsic good, it differs from "hedonism" as a school of thought or even an unconscious way of life. Consider:

its conception of absence of pain as the greatest pleasure and its advocacy of a simple life…. In the Epicurean view, the highest pleasure (tranquility and freedom from fear) [is] obtained by knowledge, friendship and living a virtuous and temperate life. [Epicurus] lauded the enjoyment of simple pleasures [and] had a unique version of the Golden Rule: It is impossible to live a pleasant life without living wisely and well and justly (agreeing "neither to harm nor be harmed"), and it is impossible to live wisely and well and justly without living a pleasant life.

back row: Ralph Forristall, Charlie Luick, Howard, Gladys & Mary Frstl. flanking barely-visible Mable (Brooks) Luick; Myrtle (Jenison) Luick with sons Leslie & Myrle, Curtis Luick; baby Velma, George & Lorena (Jenison) Luick; Mary (Hunt) Luick, Harry Clyvender & Leora (Luick) Forristall, Louis & Henry Luick; on hammock: Albert Luick, Edith & Esther Forristall, Marion & Mattie Luick; on ground: cousins Donald, Lee & Voral Luick, Leola Forristall; circa 1920

To what degree did Louis and Mary Luick's brood live "wisely and well and justly" in the small-town world to which they clung so tightly? As their distant ancestor, the Sumerian alewife Siduri, called them to do, they literally made "music day and night"—standing there, at the corner of 3rd and Main, letting their hearts pour forth over obliging catgut strings. From the Surf dances they swung at to the sagging hammocks they swung in, the family's days were marked by pleasure and raw sensuality. As they filled their bellies on Mattie's "damned good" chipped-chicken gravy and Henry's prized elderberry pie, they shared food and drink with lusty gusto. Their slow, prairie summers were punctuated by Curtis' eternal hammering on the snug home it took so long to build for his two offspring and by Luverne's hawking sweet, candied wares. Charlie's wife—Lorena Jenison Luick's aunt, Mable Brooks Luick—up at The Lake, sold beauty. And, as indicated by the many photos of the man reveling in the presence of his siblings, later children and especially (great-)grandchildren, George clearly valued family above most else.

Pleasure laced the entire fabric of the late-Victorian life that generation of Luicks sustained, long after the plump monarch who lent a noble name to the optimistic era they enjoyed had died on distant, never-visited shores. Unlike me, it didn't seem important to my paternal great-grandfather, his many brothers and sisters, and their parents what lay beyond the prairie's soft, verdant edge. For them, their flat-but-full world was enough.

The Cyrenaics beckoned the Luicks with the assurance that "momentary pleasures [are] stronger than those of anticipation or memory" but they failed to provide detailed instructions about what to do when giddy anticipation drives one mad or memories make one inconsolably sad. Did Louis play more happy or melancholic tunes? Whichever, he had to stay in the moment, to remain present, at least while playing, in order to unify the various notes and harmonies together into one pleasing sound. Unlike his future historian great-great-grandson's normal mode of approaching the world, Louis and those who played with him had to reside in the rolling moment rather than linger in what was a bar before or try to play what was still a page ahead. It seems the Luick-Hunt clan embodied "yes" to pleasure, "no" to lasting lamentations or to great goals set in a shimmering mirage of a fancied tomorrow.

Marion (Luick) Smith's husband, Laverne, 1940s. The two bottom photos on this spread show domestic and commercial life in the Belmond of the late 1910s.

Louis and Mary (Hunt) Luick's sons: George (left), Charlie, Curtis, Albert and Henry; circa 1910

And Louis and Mary's children—how well did they adhere to the advice of the ancients; how closely did they follow time-tested recipes for success in the pursuit of happiness? In terms of fulfilling social obligation and gaining pleasure from altruism, at least the oldest, Anna, proved to be "not a great worker" in the choosey eyes of her chosen church family. And, while George's flickering, ill-considered involvement with a resurgent Klan likely didn't include any lynchings and hopefully didn't result in the wonton beatings of "degenerates" like his own kid brother, the larger movement meant immeasurable pain for thousands of its mostly dark-skinned victims. Happily, unlike Nick or Della up the road, none of Louis and Mary's many children are recorded as to having become enslaved to Demon Drink.

A notice in the *Globe-Gazette* on 7 July 1962, however, suggests Henry didn't always remember that "some actions which give immediate pleasure can create more than their equivalent of pain:"

Reported Beaten by Hitch-hiker

An elderly Belmond man is in Mercy Hospital at Mason City recovering from a beating by a hitch-hiker, who also robbed him and took his car Friday evening.

Henry L. Luick, 73, was treated for a broken jaw by a Clear Lake physician and later admitted to the hospital.

Luick told deputy sheriffs he had picked up two hitch-hikers at Garner and let one out in Clear Lake. The other stayed in the car and was coming to Mason City. Luick said he could not remember what happened until he woke up in a ditch by a gravel road south of Clear Lake.

The beaten man wandered into the farm home of Raymond Rooks, who called the authorities.

Luick's car was found later in Clear Lake. The hitch hiker was described as being in early 20's.

Henry Luick, above, 1950s; ad for his favorite Belmond Main Street hangout, below

It's a warm summer evening—a Friday in early July 1962, the year of my birth: I've been riding around in my mother's belly for some four months by now. The weekend—the first since the Fourth—is starting and my dandily-dressed great-granduncle Henry is in his fat sedan, headed from Belmond to Mason City in those pre-freeway days via Garner, where Highways 69 and 18 intersect. He picks up two young men out looking for excitement—at least one of whom is in his "early 20's." One gets out in Clear Lake—the home of a cooling swim and the hot Surf, a tasty treat at the A & W drive-in or the Corner Drug's packed soda fountain, a flick at the Lake Theater or a round at the well-attended skating rink. But, the other young buck? He chooses to stay in the car and ride on with the well-attired old man—for a lift? Or, for a few bills in exchange for a forbidden thrill? The two converse as Henry's sedan rolls towards Mason City—but then, on a whim, in search of intoxicating pleasure the driver (presumably still the older man) departs from the shortest route and heads down a quiet "gravel road south of [the] Lake…" but what happened next? What made Henry turn down that country lane? What was he looking for—a sympathetic ear, a reassuring smile… a warm body part? Whatever it was he wanted, his young passenger suddenly wanted none of it—and felt justified to slug an old man in the face so hard, from up close, that he shattered Henry's jaw, then left the helpless man unconscious, lying in a grave-like ditch.

Yes, indeed:

> some actions which give immediate pleasure can create more than their equivalent of pain. The wise person should be in control of pleasures rather than be enslaved to them, otherwise pain will result, and this requires judgment to evaluate the different pleasures of life.

More than just the physical risks of pursuing Earthly pleasures, a practicing hedonist should consider social costs. As Anna's obituary cites, Louis and Mary never had their oldest child baptized: Did they have any of the rest? Either social pressure or personal conviction led Anna to be baptized just a few years before her death at the age of almost 70. And the rest? For each member of the Louis and Mary Luick family the 1895 State of Iowa census marks their "religious belief [as] none." Having been a census enumerator myself for the 1990 census to earn rent while writing a master's thesis, I know that

Henry with one of the first autos owned by a member of his family

census takers vary greatly in the degree of both the skills they bring to their assignment and the accuracy or thoroughness with which they leave it.

Riding what is the sinking side of the crest of the long wave left by the nation's fading Third Great Awakening, many Americans overestimate the religiosity of our ancestors. And, we also too often confuse "church-ism" for "religiosity." Having no "religious belief" in the late 19th century did not necessarily mean that Louis and Mary's family did not possess some sort of spiritual faith; that designation could just as easily have meant "no denominational affiliation," for in the rural North Central Iowa of the late-Victorian era, openly declaring one's self an agnostic or atheist would have been akin to public treason. Still, like many urban Americans today, some brave souls alive then practiced their faith quietly, outside the sanctuaries of church congregations they found lacking. To accept our ancestors' religious non-affiliation is one thing, but in the hyper-religious American Heartland—then as well as today—to openly endorse even "ethical" hedonism would mean virtually total social ostracization. If Louis and Mary's family had "too freely" pursued worldly pleasures, with no visible church involvement to balance such behavior's certain disapproval, they would have been scorned by the churches of the communities between which they floated. Unabashed non-conformity would have called the entire local moral fabric into question—an unsettling process that, per records and accounts on hand, did not happen.

———

chapter 45: the last pioneers

Instead of contempt, surviving records suggest that Louis and Mary Luick family's unbridled pursuit of The Good Life attracted their neighbors' respect or even endearment. Quite simply, theirs was a generation of modest people making their lives as enjoyable as possible despite hard work and losses like that of their young daughter or sister, Ethel. Not driven by philosophies they most likely would not have known, they lived the best, most pleasurable lives they could.

Mary and Louis in Belmond garden during a visit from George, Donald and "Buddy" Luick; summer 1938

And, it seems no 20th-century community celebration would have been complete without having at least one Luick on hand—as documented by a *Globe-Gazette* article from 24 October 1931, detailing the festivities observing Belmond's founding 75 years earlier:

young Belmond-area violin player

PROGRAM GIVEN AT ANNIVERSARY

Belmond Celebrates 75 Years of Existence With Old Time Features.

BELMOND, Oct., 24.—Entertainment including old time songs, accordion selections by R. H. Rierson and Ernest Haupt, violin selections by Lewis Luick and H. J. Brooks; vocal solos by William Nelson and Ralph Baker, harmonica selections by J. T. Heim, harmonica and guitar duets by William and Harry Genlow, selection on the hones by Dell Luick, music by Cooper's orchestra, songs by the M. E. male quartet, H. Nordschow, the Rev. J. C. Buthman, Supt. H. J. Williams and H. J. Luick, provided ample entertainment at the Odd Fellows and Rebekah hall Friday night in Belmond's fifth anniversary celebration. Mrs. A. C. Lieuwen read "The Old Cabinet Organ." The Rebekahs gave the play "An Old Fashioned Party." The program was followed by a lunch and old time dance.

Louis wasn't the only Luick asked to be on-hand as Belmond celebrated its own creation. As reported in the historical society's *History of Belmond, 1856-2006*, the observance took place over two days in October 1931 and

> featured a program the first evening sponsored by the Rebekahs and Odd Fellows, followed by a dance. The next evening featured H.C. Engelbrecht's four Belmond bands. The girls' band was dressed in old-time costumes and the German band was dressed in old-time band coats and white trousers. The oldest pioneer at the party was Sylvester Luick. He gave a short talk about the old times, using a microphone installed on the platform by Hill Radio Service. The oldest woman pioneer was Mrs. Fred Meacham, who was born here in 1857.

> The following items were on display: Ox yoke used by Fred Luick; two hand-made walnut beds made 150 years ago; spinning wheels; brass candle sticks and snuffers; old guns; hair wreath; key-wind watch; flag of 1862; tomahawks; first suit worn by Fred Fulton's father; pictures of some of the Tammany gang and other old timers; and old books and Bibles.

Fifteen years later, the popular press of what once had been "Franklin Grove" heralded the life of one of its oldest residents—as featured in the *Belmond Independent* on 29 August 1946:

„I think a man has to work hard if he wants to live a long time" said Louis Luick. Born in a log cabin, this Belmond citizen gives readers a glimpse of a time when frontier life was for the stalwart men and women who dreamed a dream and overcame the challengers of the environment to build a home for themselves and those of us now. At the age 90, Louis Luick tended his own garden, a garden free of weeds and a model for younger gardeners. He possessed a well of energy and talked with animation. His mind sharp, he could recall memories as though it were yesterday.

Names, faces, and dates came to him as easily as he recalled tales that entertained those that had the privilege to know him! Louis' greatest love of his life was music. He played the violin and snare drums. He was a member of the Drum Corp and with his fife, played for the July 4th celebration. He danced at Pierce's Hall. Later on, there was a famous Felt Boot Orchestra...

The article went on to review how

Louis' family history in Iowa began in 1853. Louis' father and Uncle Overacker, living in Michigan, joined the dauntless line of men who set their faces toward the West. They rode the stages, when they could, but walked for the most part. Their destination was Iowa and they decided on some land in this vicinity. Mr. Luick bought his acres near Franklin Grove. He returned to Michigan to get his wife. They drove two covered wagons with their possessions to Iowa. Jake Waltz, father of Mrs. Corie Smith drove the dozen cattle for them. They built a raft of logs, held together with wooden pins, to cross rivers.

Louis told of how the neighbors helped Mr. Thompson build his gristmill so the cornmeal could be ground nearer home. One day Louis was spearing fish by the mill when he watched Joseph Fulton trying to free a big water wheel at the mill from the ice and the following tragedy as Joseph was killed under it. This made a deep impression on his young mind.

When Louis was 16, his family moved to California to a sheep ranch and in 1881, he married Mary Hunt. They lived in the West for eight years and Louis and Mary moved back to Belmond. They had a family of 9 children, 18 grandchildren, 19 great grandchildren, and 2 great-great-grandchildren. It is good that a man who lived long and worked hard, cherished most fondly the good things he had known. He spoke of bad times, but his eyes shone as he remembered music, dancing, and priceless friendships. This was no moving picture tale, but a strong man that came before us to build Belmond.

Frank, Sylvester, Mary (Luick) Packard, Michael, Charles and Louis Luick; Belmond, likely mid-1910s

Not all media mention of Louis Luick and his venerable, founding family, however, bore such happy messages. On 19 June 1943 the *Globe-Gazette* tracked the movements of

Mr. and Mrs. [Charles and Mable Brooks] Luick, 202 North Fourth Street [in Clear Lake, who] are in Belmond where they were called Monday night by the illness and death of the former's mother, Mrs. Lewis [sic] Luick, 85, who had been ill some time. Mrs. Luick is survived by her husband and eight children. [...] Funeral arrangements are incomplete pending word from relatives at a distance.

With family present, Mary quietly passed from this Life. The subsequent obituary spoke of the exceptionally esteemed position she held in her family—as recorded a short time later in an undated, unaccredited newspaper:

Mary Louisa Hunt, daughter of Melissa [sic] and Curtis Hunt, was born in Calaveras County, California, May 16, 1858, and passed away at her home in Belmond, June 14, 1943 at the age of 85 years and one month.

Her early years were spent in the state of her birth where she was married to Louis Luick in the fall of 1881. Fifty five years ago, with her husband and three small children, she moved to Iowa, living in the vicinity of Belmond since that time.

Mother Luick was a quiet, home-loving woman, loved by all who knew her well. Her greatest pleasure in life was serving her family. She was a devoted wife and mother, a loyal friend, and a good neighbor. She enjoyed nothing more than having her children and grandchildren around her, and her love for them was reflected in their devotion to her. The end of a long, useful life came peacefully, surrounded by her loved ones who so willingly ministered to her in her last illness as well as in her declining years.

She is survived by her aged husband, eight children, sixteen grandchildren, twenty-two great grandchildren, and one great great grandchild.

The following verse by an unnamed author is so fitting it might well have been written especially for Mrs. Luick:

A noble life, but written not
In any book of fame;
Among the list of noted ones
None ever saw her name;
For only her own household knew
The victories she had won;
And none but they could testify
How well her work was done.

Louis Lee and Mary Louisa (Hunt) Luick with a descendent; Belmond, circa 1940

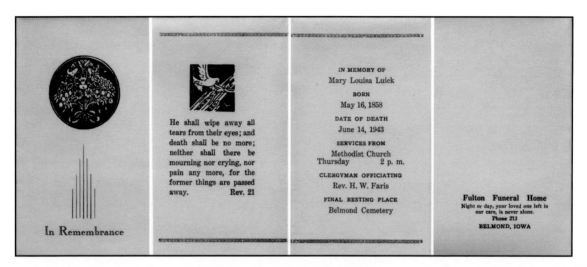

In Remembrance

He shall wipe away all tears from their eyes; and death shall be no more; neither shall there be mourning nor crying, nor pain any more, for the former things are passed away.   Rev. 21

IN MEMORY OF
Mary Louisa Luick
BORN
May 16, 1858
DATE OF DEATH
June 14, 1943
SERVICES FROM
Methodist Church
Thursday   2 p. m.
CLERGYMAN OFFICIATING
Rev. H. W. Faris
FINAL RESTING PLACE
Belmond Cemetery

Fulton Funeral Home
Night or day, your loved one left in our care, is never alone.
Phone 213
BELMOND, IOWA

For half a decade Louis lived on, without his partner of sixty-two years, before passing from this Life himself in May 1948—as announced by the *Belmond Independent*:

Louis L. Luick, son of Henry and Melissa Luick was born July 4, 1856 [sic] and died at home in Belmond Iowa, May 31, 1948 at the age of ninety-one years, ten months and nine days.

Mr. Luick was born in a log cabin located on the farm now owned by Ira Studebaker Jr., better known as the Fred Luick farm, and lived there until he was sixteen, when he with his family moved to California, where he married Mary Hunt in 1881. In 1889 with his wife and three children he returned to Iowa and has resided in the vicinity of Belmond since that time.

His father was one of Belmond's earliest pioneers, having come here in 1850 [sic], and it is doubtful if anyone knew more of the developments and early history of the town and community than he did. One of his favorite pastimes was comparing modern transportation and conveniences with the days when Franklin Grove was full of Indians camping there. Cedar Falls was a four-day trip by team. Belmond was just a few houses grouped together, and tallow candles furnished light. Nearly ninety-two years is a long time to live when so much history was in the making.

For many years he was Supervisor of roads for Pleasant Township and made many friends throughout the entire township. Up until two years ago he was active and industrious and took great delight in his large garden.

He was a good friend and neighbor, a loving husband and father and devoted grandfather. Nothing gave him more pleasure than having his children and grandchildren around him. His son Henry and daughter and family, Mr. and Mrs. Levarne [sic] Smith, resided with him at the time of his death, and with the other children gladly cared for him in his last illness.

He was preceded in death by his wife and two children, Ethel and Annie (Mrs. Harry Forrestall). He is survived by seven children, nineteen grandchildren, twenty-five great grandchildren and five great-great grandchildren. Mr. Luick was the last of his immediate family [with] four brothers and two sisters. Many relatives and friends join his family in mourning their loss. The sincere sympathy of their many friends and neighbors goes out to the bereaved family in their sorrow.

We cannot feel that he is far
Since near at hand the angels are.
And when the sunset gates unbar,
Shall we not see him, waiting, stand,
And white against the evening star,
The welcome of his beckoning hand.

With the loss of Louis Lee and Mary Louisa Hunt Luick, North Central Iowa lost some of its last surviving pioneers. And, my family lost what might have been in our direct lineage one of the last genuinely contented and happy generations. From appearances, those exceptionally long-living Luicks realized on the Iowa prairies The Good Life as heralded for centuries before them by pharaohs, philosophers, poets and alewives alike. They left an enduring counterweight to much of the wickedness as well as subsequent suffering among the generations that would immediately follow them. Somehow, over the course of decades of living together—of slipped tongues and loose fists, of shared tears and relieving laughter, of embracing babies and facing death—those eleven people eventually established equilibrium. Ultimately, they struck a sustained, satisfying balance between the personal and the familial, the material and the intangible, the sensual and the spiritual, the eternal and the temporal. Drawn together by visible tenderness, affection and empathy, Louis, Mary and their children appear to have often—if not always—succeeded in realizing what Epicure had, long ago, praised as

> modest, sustainable "pleasure" in the form of a state of tranquility and freedom from fear and absence of bodily pain through knowledge of the workings of the world and the limits of our desires. The combination of these two states [constitutes] happiness in its highest form […] obtained by knowledge, friendship and living a virtuous and temperate life [of] simple pleasures.

———

postscript: whose "Good Life?"

Tony Luick and I have never met in-person. In fact, we "met" less than a year ago, as of this writing. We've conducted our entire "relationship" via first terse emails, later frequent, far-scoped trans-Atlantic phone calls. As we worked closely and, subsequently, grew closer, our early fact-laced exchanges morphed into philosophical hypothesizing as we speculated on the character and careers of mutual ancestors or shared kin. And, we swapped views on if, for example, the Louis and Mary (Hunt) Luick family had "amounted to much" or not; if they and their children were "successful" or "simply satisfied."

Like beauty, "success" lies in the eye of the beholder. As Tony and I waded further and further into weighing any worldly indications of Louis & Co. having "made it," we struggled to find acceptable standards to measure "making it" in the first place. In the end, humility led us to grant them reprieves from our ruthless scrutiny. And, we abandoned our subjective searching in favor of factual comparisons.

We didn't have to look far. For one, Tony's analysis of census records revealed that Louis had accompanied his jolted mother, Melissa (Overacker) Luick (later Arnold), to Michigan once it became clear that Louis' father, Henry, had forsaken her for another, forever. In Ann Arbor, Louis would have encountered myriad Luick and Overacker relatives—including Gottlob, who, with his brother Emmanuel (two of their family's twelve children), co-founded Luick Brothers Lumber in 1873.

Luick Brothers Lumber in Ann Arbor, Michigan—shown here in 1895; an ad for the company

Besides later serving as mayor of the up-and-coming university town from 1899-1901, in the 1910s Gottlob held the vice-presidency of Huron River Manufacturing and was an officer of the Star Motor Car Company. When the Luick brothers ceased millwork in 1930, Gottlob donated their land as the site of today's still-extant Ann Arbor Farmers Market. In the process of all their business activities, the two men made a great deal of money over the course of their (at least outwardly) "successful" careers.

But, to consider a second example, from even earlier in the Luick family's new life in the New World: As family historian Albert Lea Luick wrote in the late 1950s,

Arriving in New York, [Heinrich's brother] Jacob and his family decided to sojourn in western New York state near Niagara Falls [in 1832, and] later to migrate to Milwaukee, Wis., as early pioneers, there to become a successful businessman in the building of that community, where many descendants now live—and operate Luick Ice Cream, or "Sealtest."

images from the "Wisconsin Luicks'" dairy empire, which included "Sealtest" bottled milk and ice cream

While his cousins, who stayed firmly nested in the former Big Woods of Michigan or went on to Wisconsin's largest city, notably thrived, Louis Luick drifted from Iowa to California and, some fifteen years later, back again; from gig to gig—literally, as a fiddling musician—and from job to job: cowboy, sheep shearer, farm hand, tenant farmer, drayman, road-grader driver, day laborer, truck gardener, etc. The fun-loving family man seems to have never had much money in the bank; we know he lived later in life with his adult children and their families, and that "confirmed bachelor" son, Henry, nursed his elderly parents as they ailed. Like their father, the five sons and three daughters held an ever-shifting hodge-podge of typically temporary jobs, or dabbled in stints of short-term self-employment. All in all, in worldly terms, Louis and Mary's family "didn't amount to much"—or did they?

As noted elsewhere, excepting for their half-sister Anna Leora and full-sister Ethel (who died at age 18 from typhoid fever), the remaining Luick offspring of that generation lived on average to be almost 90 years old. Don't those long lives hint at a harmonious (co-)existence, as well as represent another kind of "worldly wealth?" It seems so to this observer, who sees in their collective familial story a degree of cohesion and authentic affection for each other not visible in, for example, the families of Louis and Mary's son George and his wife Lorena, or their grandson Donald and his wife Charlotte, or...

The half-dozen group photos of Louis, Mary and their children clearly convey a genuine joviality. One senses warm, loving feelings independent of bank accounts or the number of vehicles owned per household, of the square footages of the houses awaiting the various family members back home or the title(s) their resumes sported—or not.

Their Luick relatives further east who, in contrast, had amassed much greater earthly fortunes were not immune to the unexpected cruelties that the world can deliver, despite the degree to which those same families had flourished in material terms. All the money in the world can't shield us when society unravels and social behavior degenerates to deadly levels—as my Luick cousins in Wisconsin learned:

Tattooed biker on trial for murdering police woman and her boyfriend after she pinched his bottom at a bar

By DAILY MAIL REPORTER
UPDATED: 05:11 GMT, 31 October 2010

A tattooed biker is on trial for the murder of an off-duty police woman and her boyfriend last December after the single mom allegedly grabbed his bottom in a Wisconsin bar during a night of partying with friends.

Andrew Wirth, who has a neck tattoo that reads 'Nothing to Lose,' did not appreciate the pinching from Jennifer Luick.

After Wirth glared at the blonde, she went and told her boyfriend Gregg Peters.

When Peters went to confront Wirth, Wirth pulled a gun and shot him three times at close range. One bullet passed through Peters and struck Luick, killing them both. Luick was 37, Peters was 40.

Wirth, an unemployed 25-year-old welder, had recently moved to Wisconsin to be near the Los Diablos motorcycle gang.

Andrew Wirth was not please when a partying Jennifer Luick grabbed his behind

He is claiming self defense, saying Peters lunged at him, causing him to pull the gun.

Luick, a police woman and mum, was off--duty when she pinched Andrew Wirth's behind

At the trial, witnesses to the fatal shooting recalled, with pain and tears, the night their friends were killed.

Angela Honkan was at the Rock Bottom bar in Jefferson with Luick and Peters. She described Luick as fun loving and testified Luick pinched Wirth on the bottom. Honkan says Wirth became angry and Luick told him to relax.

WITI-TV reports Alicia Koehler testified she saw Wirth with a gun to Peters' neck outside the tavern, went inside to have someone call 911, then saw Peters stumble back inside, asking her for help.

Another witness, Laurie Phillips, remembered Luick as 'she was dancing and having fun' and because 'she was laughing, she was tall, pretty and smiling.'

Phillips remembered Wirth because of his tattoos and because he was drinking the odd combination of vodka and Mountain Dew.

The trial will continue next week.

Jennifer Luick and Gregg Peters in happier times, before they were killed last December while partying at a bar

In trying to understand an event such as committing the murder of two unarmed people—as if there were any "sense" to be found in the whole, senseless matter—I combed numerous on-line articles. In the process, I learned a bit about what became of some of the Luicks who came to Wisconsin from Swabia, looking for the "good life." Jennifer Luick's mother, Karen, reported that, combined, their family had served some 42 years in various police departments. The articles I read suggest that the family is solidly middle-class, actively community-minded and deeply religious: in short, typical Midwesterners.

I have to think of other Luicks, of "my" Luicks out on the Iowa prairies, of Louis Luick & Co., who also were "typical Midwesterners" of their time. For me, however, a disconnect occurs when I try to jibe images of the world those Luicks inhabited with the discordant one we contemporary Luicks traverse on a daily basis. According to his grandson Gary Luick, Louis "would play his violin at the corner of 3rd and Main in Belmond." As I picture warm summer evenings, with Louis' lilting refrains wafting through the streets from over in front of Ralph and Mabel Jenison's place... my mind is then jarred by images of a cold, dark parking lot well after midnight, as a cousin I never met, Jennifer Luick, and her boyfriend exchange words with some stranger over some silly trifle... until shots ring out; two bodies slump, then fall to the ground, lifeless—leaving a 12-year-old boy orphaned and a young man to fester behind bars.

Bud & Phyllis with (top left) Debbie & David at Ashlawn Farm, 1960; with Michael & David (top right), circa 1975; at Jack & Eleanor (Thrams) Hunts' home, with Phyllis' Uncle Willard & Aunt Bernice, & kids

The world I grew up in the 1960s and '70s was much closer to those flickering moving-picture show scenes of a mythical-yet-lost Victorian heaven, of a cozy, carefree small-town life, than to the lonely, shallow existence many moderns endure at present. Trying to integrate, if possible to reconcile these conflicting worlds, I'm left wondering what happened to that world where money often took a back seat to matters of family, community and living in the moment at hand. No sum of cash can buy such moments, but they constitute the "Good Life" most of us say we seek, more than the physical trappings which constantly try to steal our attention and vie for our loyalty, or the rush of "extreme experiences" such as (with Jennifer's killer) riding "hogs," taking drug trips, etc.

As we moderns navigate between the pursuit of happiness—the Good Life "promised" to Americans in our national charter, in the Declaration of Independence—on one hand, and assorted "hedonisms" of contemporary culture, we are well served to meditate on the possible consequences of achieving each.

———

PART IV a

Root-Sinking Settlers

Section 6:
William & Annie (Shupe) Jenison family

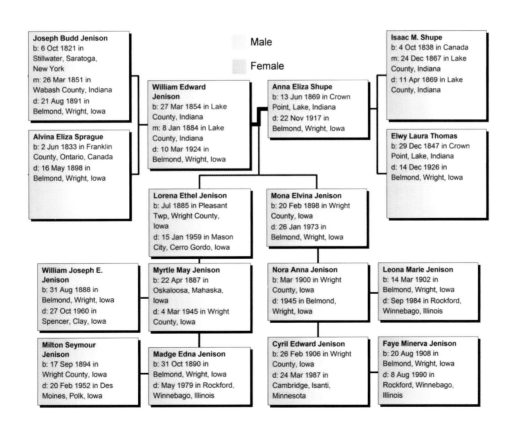

Joseph Budd Jenison
b: 6 Oct 1821 in
Stillwater, Saratoga,
New York
m: 26 Mar 1851 in
Wabash County, Indiana
d: 21 Aug 1891 in
Belmond, Wright, Iowa

Male

Female

Isaac M. Shupe
b: 4 Oct 1838 in Canada
m: 24 Dec 1867 in Lake
County, Indiana
d: 11 Apr 1869 in Lake
County, Indiana

**William Edward
Jenison**
b: 27 Mar 1854 in Lake
County, Indiana
m: 8 Jan 1884 in Lake
County, Indiana
d: 10 Mar 1924 in
Belmond, Wright, Iowa

Anna Eliza Shupe
b: 13 Jun 1869 in Crown
Point, Lake, Indiana
d: 22 Nov 1917 in
Belmond, Wright, Iowa

Alvina Eliza Sprague
b: 2 Jun 1833 in Franklin
County, Ontario, Canada
d: 16 May 1898 in
Belmond, Wright, Iowa

Elwy Laura Thomas
b: 29 Dec 1847 in Crown
Point, Lake, Indiana
d: 14 Dec 1926 in
Belmond, Wright, Iowa

Lorena Ethel Jenison
b: Jul 1885 in Pleasant
Twp, Wright County,
Iowa
d: 15 Jan 1959 in Mason
City, Cerro Gordo, Iowa

Mona Elvina Jenison
b: 20 Feb 1898 in Wright
County, Iowa
d: 26 Jan 1973 in
Belmond, Wright, Iowa

**William Joseph E.
Jenison**
b: 31 Aug 1888 in
Belmond, Wright, Iowa
d: 27 Oct 1960 in
Spencer, Clay, Iowa

Myrtle May Jenison
b: 22 Apr 1887 in
Oskaloosa, Mahaska,
Iowa
d: 4 Mar 1945 in Wright
County, Iowa

Nora Anna Jenison
b: Mar 1900 in Wright
County, Iowa
d: 1945 in Belmond,
Wright, Iowa

Leona Marie Jenison
b: 14 Mar 1902 in
Belmond, Wright, Iowa
d: Sep 1984 in Rockford,
Winnebago, Illinois

**Milton Seymour
Jenison**
b: 17 Sep 1894 in
Wright County, Iowa
d: 20 Feb 1952 in Des
Moines, Polk, Iowa

Madge Edna Jenison
b: 31 Oct 1890 in
Belmond, Wright, Iowa
d: May 1979 in Rockford,
Winnebago, Illinois

Cyril Edward Jenison
b: 26 Feb 1906 in Wright
County, Iowa
d: 24 Mar 1987 in
Cambridge, Isanti,
Minnesota

Faye Minerva Jenison
b: 20 Aug 1908 in
Belmond, Wright, Iowa
d: 8 Aug 1990 in
Rockford, Winnebago,
Illinois

Isaac Shupe's and Elwy Thomas' immediate or extended ancestors

John George Shupe
b: 1759 in Lancaster County, Pennsylvania
m: 05 Oct 1784 in Dauphin County, Pennsylvania
d: 08 Nov 1812 in Freeport, Waterloo, Ontario, Canada

Marie Elizabeth Diefenbach
b: 19 Dec 1763 in Paxtang, Dauphin, Pennsylvania
d: 21 Mar 1825 in Waterlo, Ontario, Canada

Benjamin Shupe
b: 1808 in Canada West
m: 31 Dec 1835 in Kitchener, Waterlo, Ontario, Canada
d: 1865 in Lake County, Indiana

Sarah Ann Master
b: 23 Jan 1816 in Chester County, Pennsylvania
d: 04 Dec 1881 in Lake County, Indiana

Isaac Master
b: 23 Jan 1787 in Chester County, Pennsylvania
m: 11 May 1809 in Pennsylvania
d: 21 Jun 1853 in Waterloo, Ontario, Canada

Mary Clemens
b: 27 Jul 1793 in Chester County, Pennsylvania
d: 26 May 1870 in Puslinch Twp, Wellington, Ontario, Canada

Isaac M. Shupe
b: 04 Oct 1838 in Canada
d: 11 Apr 1869 in Lake County, Indiana

William Cummings Thomas
b: 29 Dec 1817 in Monroe County, New York
d: Dec 1880 in Hebron, Porter, Indiana

Elwy Laura Thomas
b: 29 Dec 1847 in Crown Point, Lake, Indiana
d: 14 Dec 1926 in Belmond, Wright, Iowa

Elizabeth A. Vandercar
b: 1816 in New York

tagged with inscription "Yeoman's Club"

72

William Edward and Anna Eliza (Shupe) Jenison

born:	27 March 1854	13 June 1869
where:	Wabash, Indiana/USA	Crown Point, Indiana/USA
married:	8 October 1884	where: Lake County, Indiana
died:	11 March 1924	28 November 1917
where:	Belmond, Iowa/USA	Belmond, Iowa/USA

When this sepia image of so many initially-unknown faces first landed in my adolescent hands in the late '70s, I found it quaint yet felt unmoved by this motionless scene. Until, that is, I discovered that seven ancestors of mine are pictured on it, as well as the woman who, years later, shoved a shotgun barrel into my racing heart and—with finger on-trigger and hammer cocked—threatened "Take one more step an' I'll shoot ya backwards 'cross this house yard!"

(back row, on porch) Emma (Arends) & Seymour Jenison, Cloe Jenison, unrecognized, Lorena (Jenison) Luick, a Jenison relative, Madge Jenison, Anna (Shupe) Jenison, Mary Hunt Luick; (front row) Louis Luick, William Jenison, Curtis & Myrtle Jenison Luick—the three boys in front of them, Cyril Jenison, Myrle & Leslie Luick—Faye & Marie Jenison, Marion Luick, Nora & Lola Jenison, Esther Forristall, Mattie Luick, Mona Jenison, unknown, Charles & Mable (Brooks) Luick, with son Lee; in the front, crouched George Luick holds baby son, Donald; summer 1913.

As a beginning student at Iowa State I first majored in anthropology. Later, when "they" tried to force me to shift my focus from dissecting human sociality to fooling around with dusty bones, I jumped on the (for me) safer history-studies ship. Given my social-analytical inclinations as the eager teen handed the above photo, my interest in this crew of unknown somber figures was primarily that of a budding anthropologist—the kind who studies humans, past and present—even though I then lacked subtle discernment skills or familiarity with scholarly research.

I did know, I wanted to know about how the people shown as a "family" related to each other:

> Who exercised more power in the extended group—the matriarchal or the patriarchal figures? How were decisions that affected more than one person made? How was decision-making and how were material

resources distributed, as well as passed from one generation to successive generations? What lingering feelings did the various family members affect in each other? With what accents or distinguishing lingual markings did they speak; what messages did they convey through their body language?

Charles Andrew, Lee Wesley and Mable Omega (Brooks) Luick in Cerro Gordo County, Iowa; late 1920s

As relationships between people who see themselves as "family" unfold in daily-life contexts:

How did heads of families earn the means to feed their mates and children? What did members of the family eat and drink; what did they wear; what did they like to do in their free time? What roles did music, dance, play or sports have in their familial as well as individual lives? In what ways were the various art forms* present in their daily lives? How much contact did the family as a whole have, and in which form, with which media: text- or other books, newspapers, magazines, maps, church bulletins, posters or phonographs?

*The visual arts include ceramics, paintings and drawings, prints, photographs, or architecture and design; textile arts include beadwork, embroidery, knitting and crocheting, rug or lace making, quilting, sewing or weaving; and performing arts include concerts, theater, puppetry, the circus, recitation, public debates or oratory.

calendar from State Bank of Belmond, co-owed by Albert Lee Luick; masquerade in Belmond, early 1910s

74

transporting sugar beets via mule power, circa 1910: Notice the church and cables in the background.

As so much activity—the essential and practical, as well as elective or abstract—required fuel:

> What energy sources did the people shown tap: coal, cobs or wood (e.g., to cook and heat), wind (to pump water), solar (to dry food or clothes), petroleum (to create light or fuel engines)? How was fuel gathered or delivered, and stored? Did the town dwellers have reliable access to electricity or telephones, if not in their homes then at least at their workplaces? At what point did churches also have utility access?

an office with a wall telephone run on a hand-cranked magneto generator, and pot-belly-stove heating

Developments in technology and health care are some of the most revolutionizing forces in the modern world. To what degree and with what rapidity did they, already a century ago, alter the lives of those photographed? For example:

> How and to what degree did they practice sanitation? Who provided them with health care, where and in what forms; how did they pay for it? How effective was that health care? What diseases did they suffer

then that could be healed or premature deaths delayed today? How was death dealt with as a topic—both in the abstract, as an eventuality, and concretely, in specific cases? What forms of birth control or family planning might they have used? To what degree did the emerging telecommunications of their day (telephone, phonograph, radio) facilitate or erode their abilities to effectively communicate with others?

telephone switchboard office, likely early 1920s: note bed in back room for night shifts; program cover

Any time two humans share resources or exchange worldviews, conflicts unavoidably arise, so:

How, through what means did they attempt to resolve personal as well as public ("legal") conflicts? How did they see their place in the world; what was their relationship to governmental bodies and functions—local, state and Federal; to what religious, secular or civic bodies did they belong? What sacred as well as temporal holidays and traditions did they observe; how did they mark birthdays, rites of passage, anniversaries, etc.? To what degree were they openly demonstrative, physically?

exterior and interior of Clear Lake's Methodist Episcopal Church, circa 1900

No generation has to completely "re-invent the wheel" as systems exist to relay information, so:

How was knowledge, both from within the family and from without it, transferred from one generation to the next? What stories—fictive or factual—did grand- or parents relay to their (grand-)children? What formal education did family members undergo? How informed were they of larger social, economic or political events—and the underlying dynamics—around them; how did such developments affect them?

8th grade of 1907 (left) and senior class of 1910 at Belmond's public school

Of course, no family lives in isolation; each thrives to the degree it fits its local environment, so:

> What were their attitudes towards individuals or groups hailing from other ethnic or religious backgrounds, or with different shades of skin color? How often, how far and for what reasons did they travel? Did they move goods or people between points by wagon or buggy; did they utilize trains or bicycles; who among them had the means to afford one of the first local automobiles? Who among them owned a tractor? Who was the first to travel overseas via ship or ride in an airplane?

early automobiles in Belmond, driving over the Iowa River via Elder Bridge;
man in left car is Perry Loomis, driver of right is H.N. Hill, with son, Stan Hill

When I learned from the would-be assassin, that I not only was blood-related to all of the thirty souls shown but one, and that every day wear in my body genes directly passed to me from seven of them, the realization changed my entire perspective. The instant I comprehended that "those" people captured on film—in that long-forgotten frame, forever frozen in one suspended moment out of a gazillion moments that together comprise a single given human life—were "my" people, then any cerebral interests in them immediately gave way to probing emotional investigation. First of all:

> What did the people who passed on to me the most precious, rarest resource in the universe—Life— make out of the existence that had been afforded them? Were they kind to others—and, to themselves? Or, did they flunk Life's School of Hard Knocks and pass the fallout of their failures on to others?

Donald, George, Luwarren "Lil' Buddy" and Louis Luick, circa 1938:
My father later told his future wife that he felt "taken aback" by Louis.

Each mortal struggles with a Self—just as I do, every day. Thus, in my brokenness I wanted to know:

Did "my" people feel loved—and, in turn, love others—or were they trapped in self-loathing and its subsequent, debilitating sense of unworthiness? When they acted out of neither kindness nor love, were they capable of later at least *trying* to make amends? Were they capable of saying "I'm sorry" or "I don't know" to those closest to them? For themselves, were they able to find comfort and joy in their families—or more often unease and distress? Did they feel affirmed by their contact or interactions with their wider community—or devalued, even rejected by it? Did they seek social contact—or avoid it?

George Luick, 1950s, likely in Missouri; Lorena (Jenison), Donald, Debra and Bud Luick, 1955, in Iowa

At all times I wonder to what degree "my" people have found keys to The Good Life. Thus:

Did they know moments of meaning in their work—or did they find it mostly mind-numbing and vacuous? In states of repose were they able to still their minds, or did any restlessness from other areas of their lives, which they could not dodge or discard, deny them a chance to truly recharge their souls? Did they evolve during the course of living—or choose to stay static, too afraid to risk choosing a path that might lead to the unexpected?

Lorraine, Bud and Mardelle Luick in their family's farmyard, circa 1940

To think, that all this exploration, this endless digging into my family's roots, all began with an Iowa farmboy's simple question "Who were my Grampa Donald's mother's people?"—the Jenisons and Luicks captured together in a group photo, on some crowded prairie farmhouse porch. I strove to see them not just as faces frozen at one point in time, not just as birth and death dates, but as people whose diverse, ever-changing lives intertwined, with moments worth recording as well as darker influences left behind, passed on to my generation and beyond. Their shadows haunted me for years.

That my quest to uncover telling information about my paternal great-grandmother's, Lorena Jenison Luick's parents—William and Annie Shupe Jenison—would lead me across two continents, over three and a half decades, to such significant finds... in large part, to answer questions generated by one photograph, handed to me as a rash act. Who would have guessed? Not me—but, my search continues. As it does, I offer the same questions I posed myself about my family, to others, so that they might search for deeper truths in their own. I do so, that others might see themselves and those closest to them in a new light, illuminated by answers to questions they might not have even known they had.

———

chapter 29: a distant mirror

Modern youth might find it odd and maybe morbid, but when I was a teen, in the Seventies, our rural-Midwest family—like many—routinely visited local cemeteries where our deceased closer relatives lay buried. On one such outing Dad and Mom took Dave and me (Deb had already married and moved out by then) on the relatively long drive from Ashlawn Farm to the Belmond cemetery, where my brother and I had never before been. While cemeteries typically have something subtly eerie about them, both of us boys felt (in the latest adolescent language of the day) "creeped out" that late morning to see not just one, but several looming versions of "David Luick" or "Michael Luick" spread across gravestones of different shapes, sizes and colors.

Belmond Cemetery, 1979—site of the Luicks' first home on the prairie, overlooking the town they founded

After we at last fled the cemetery, we stopped by—unannounced—to call on Aunts Mattie and Marion, Great-Grampa George's widowed younger sisters who then were living in separate small apartments in the same tidy, brightly-painted retirement center on the edge of town. (Their nieces, Gary's sisters Donna and Mary Luick, referred to the complex as "Wrinkle City on Luick Lane.")

Marion hung in the background; although polite and receptive, she said little in the shadow of her commanding, two-year-older sister, Mattie. The latter welcomed us warmly and asked what we'd like to drink and if we'd seen "all the sites of big Belmond yet," about how our dozen horses were doing during the last months of the foaling season and, well, certainly we got the corn and beans in on time despite the soggy spring—didn't we? Would we go on a vacation: If so, where? "There's a cute little ol' river town jus' across from Dubuque" Mattie tipped us off, "called Galena, and it's got the best darned…"

For me, the sisterly pair seemed semi-ancient. Both pushing eighty, they *looked* like relics from a time long ago. Marion's face seemed somewhat shrunk, her lips tight as if she didn't keep them that way a small secret or, worse, a silly story might slip out. Mattie, on the other hand, embodied the stronger, decisive big-sister role that obviously served them both. Basically talking for the two of them—with devoted Marion only slowly nodding an affirmative "yes" or slightly wagging her petite head from time to time to mimic the negative with a muffled gasp— lively Mattie spoke stereo.

"Oh, Bud, your granddad, my brother George—now *he* could tell stories!" Mattie then slid her rather big butt back into the well-padded chair. She spread both feet out, locking her knocked knees into a frozen, stabilizing triangular position, as if assuming a cozy tale-spinning post for many ensuing hours. Clearly, the woman had a trove of treasured tales to tell.

friend with Mattie & Marion, 1910s

Mattie (Luick) Farmer and Marion (Luick) Smith, 1930s

"Say, isn't your name 'Mike'?" Mattie asked rhetorically as she turned my direction. Although I'd already pried my jaws open to offer a quiet affirmative, before I could answer Grampa Donald's whirlwind of an aunt rushed on with "Ya know, you're not the first 'Mike Luick,' don't ya?" As I began to slowly wag my little face from side to side, she barreled into a breathless accounting of "Listen up, then! Ol' Mike Luick opened a roadhouse up north of town on Highway 69 back in—"

Mattie interrupted herself to look at otherwise silent, mostly motionless Marion, who then quietly whispered "'38" before slipping back into safe obscurity.

"—or so, up there jus' south of Triggs Corner. He called it 'Dine an' Dance.' Oh, yes, sir—it was all quite fine! He had a gas station—ok, so it was jus' one pump, but in those days that was enough—and a café as well as a dance hall. But, oh, how we liked to go up there, Ross and me, and dance on Friday nights! We swung to the tunes jumpin' outta the juke box an' sipped soda pop an' had a high ol' time."

"Gee, Aunt Mattie" I finally squeaked, "that sounds great."

"Well, it was a family affair—don't ya know. Dora Wilcox, Mike's mother-in-law, cooked for the café." Then, Mattie's smile deflated and she shook her head sadly—"but Lucille Luick, Mike's pretty-young-thing daughter in law? He didn't allow her to go near that place at night—*no*, sir!"

Mike Luick's roadhouse and filling station, 1930s

Larger-than-life Mattie fascinated me so I could have sat at her knee for hours and simply listened, but just then Marion's oldest son, Ron, also unexpectedly appeared. We out-of-town kin rushed out the center's steel-and-glass double doors, lest we fell "too deep" into the unending morass that is extended family. Before we diaspora-displaced Luicks left "our hometown," however, Dad made a point of driving us down Luick Lane so we could swing past the high school's newish Luick Auditorium and Luick Gymnasium, as well as briefly admire what he told us was the "Luick-built" hospital and swimming pool, before finally heading out of Belmond and driving back to "The Lake." We sped past the site of Mike Luick's landmark diner that Aunt Mattie had crowed about, then bombed our way across the endless, late-spring cornfields (it being Memorial Day weekend). I sat in the back of our white-vinyl-topped mustard-gold Catalina Pontiac and meditated on who and what we had just seen.

"Who exactly were those people in that graveyard we saw?" I drilled the folks from the broad back seat. "Why did some of those old stones have Dave's and mine names on 'em?"

Dad replied over his shoulder "Those are our people—goin' way back." Without looking at me, not even in the rear-view mirror, he offered "There's been lotsa 'David' and 'Michael' Luicks."

"But why are there *so* many of them buried *there*" I wanted to know as our family's lumbering four-door strained to gain speed, "all in one place?"

"Because the Luicks founded Belmond, back when there was still buffalo an' elk roamin' round here." As Dad spoke I watched unending cornrows fly past the car window: The faster he drove, the faster the rows seemed to whirl by, until they made one big, verdant blur on the near horizon. "We were the first ones here; we opened the prairie. Back when it was nothin' more than a big ol' empty sea o' grass, waitin' ta be plowed."

I hadn't cared much for staring at "my" gravestone back at Belmond's spooky burial ground, but seeing

C. P. Luick, Belmond's benefactor, dies at 86

BELMOND — Chester P. Luick, 86, a pioneer resident of the Belmond community, died at the Belmond Community Hospital Tuesday following a stroke suffered five days before. Funeral services will be held Friday at 2 p.m. at the Congregational Church. The Rev. William Hill will officiate. Burial will be in the Belmond Cemetery with Johnston Funeral Home in charge.

Surviving are his wife, Grace; four stepchildren, Mrs. Evan Parry, Cedar Rapids; Mrs. George Price, Brownsville, Tex.; Mrs. Donald McNulty, Belmond, and William H. Luick, Webster City.

MR. LUICK'S philanthropies to the town of Belmond have earned him public affection and respect such as few men gain in their lifetime. Over a period of years he has given a total of more than a half-million dollars to the people of Belmond.

In 1952 he set up a trust fund of more than $100,000, known as the Chester P. and Vida Luick Memorial Hospital Trust, with proceeds earmarked for hospital improvements.

In 1956 another trust fund was set up for providing the town of Belmond with a swimming pool. By the time the pool and its grounds were completed there had been between $85,000 and $100,000 spent on the project.

HIS GIFTS HAVE also included $10,000 toward the build-

CHESTER P. LUICK

ing of the hospital and $25,000 for the Congregational Church Youth Center.

Mr. Luick's last benefaction to the town of Belmond was a third trust fund called the Fred and Alice Luick Memorial Building given in 1959 in memory of his parents, who were among Belmond's earliest settlers. Funds for this trust are provided from a 354-acre farm with an estimated value of $150,000; two city lots in Belmond and other securities to bring the total to about $300,000. The community building is to be incorporated in a new high school building in Belmond.

Chester Luick's obituary in Mason City Globe-Gazette, *5 May 1960*

"Luick" so prominently plastered all over so many big public structures did leave me feeling both excited and reflective.

"At one time" my noticeably proud father continued to lecture, "there were four banks sittin' on each corner of the busiest intersection on Main Street—an' they were *all* owned by Luicks."

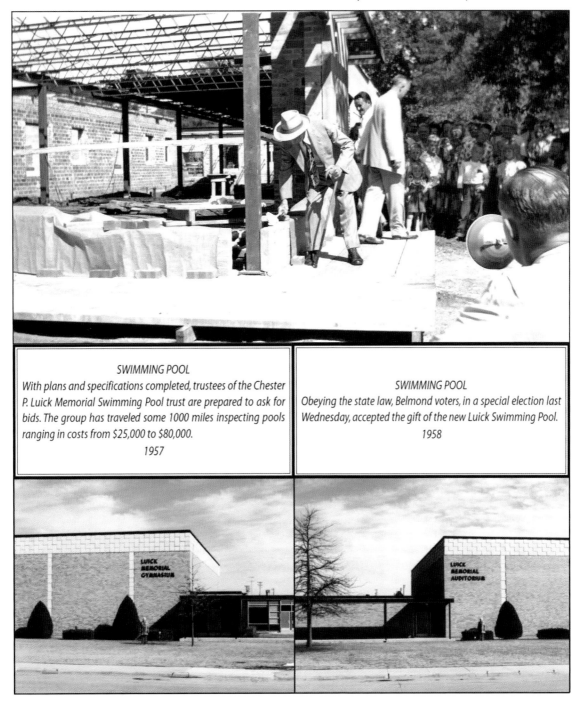

Chester Luick (top photo) laying ground stone of new community hospital, 1952; two newspaper notices about donated swimming pool; Belmond High School's Luick-funded gymnasium and auditorium, 1979: Since 1952, Chester P. Luick Trust has invested millions of dollars in Belmond, returning to the community some of the wealth Luicks have stewarded since coming from Michigan and founding a town on the prairie.

"Really-y-y? How could that be?" I quizzed, staring at the abundant foliage filing by past the lowered window, picturing how the same landscape would look had we Luicks *not* "opened the prairie" and, now, buffaloes still roamed free o'er beds o' bright flowers an' tow'ring grasses.

"Easy" Dad quipped. "Ol' Henry Luick from Germany came out to survey the prairie all around the area before anyone else got here—and he grabbed all the fillet pieces while he still could."

"Wow! He was pretty clever—Ol' Henry Luick from Germany was," I rejoined.

"Well, he liked what he saw. Before he returned out East, he met a trapper named Beebe livin' in a cabin on the Iowa River but packin' up his supplies, his squaw an' gittin' ready ta head—"

"Why was the trapper leaving?" I interrupted, filled with images of a greasy, half-toothless wild man wearing a coonskin cap and soiled buckskins. "Had he trapped out all the beaver or otter?"

"—further West 'cause he saw the smoke of a new neighbor's cabin."

"Well" I chimed, "he was sorta selfish!" I closed my eyes and imagined a faint plume of smoke begin to listlessly rise up on the distant horizon, then the wild-haired trapper, Beebe, spying it and beginning to jump up and down in a livid, headless panic. "But, *then* what happened, Dad?"

Iowa: blue skies, verdant Earth

"Ol' Henry stood up on the wagon wheel—'cause the prairie grass was too tall to see over, standin' on the ground—an' he made that trapper a deal: Henry'd buy all of the land that he could see from that wagon wheel, in every direction—"

Already worrying if his squaw would have enough to buy some fabulous new beads or fresh deerskin for clean drawers for her frontier family, I wondered "How much did he give Beebe for so much land?"

"—and then he headed out, back ta Michigan."

"Wow" I hummed, not knowing I'd hear the same tale numerous times from other sources, too. But instead of atop a wagon wheel, other versions would have 'Ol' Henry' hanging around, up a nearby "big walnut tree"—an impressive detail, given that there were so few trees there, then.

———

Belmondites in the process of constructing (top) St. John's Church & the public school, circa 1900

No one ever built a school or a church alone, or laid a municipal sewer or paved a road as a solo project. Every civic building, flood dike, park, etc. ever created in America was the result of shared visions and group efforts. The public coffers were not always flush, but the funds always found.

chapter 30: setting bells ringing

So simply, so innocently began my fascination with "my" people's primal connection with Belmond, that cozy little town in the middle of the big, open, wide prairie, smack in the heart of North America. As time went by, however, that fascination wouldn't be "so simple." In fact, it'd become literally almost lethal—but first things first.

The summer after that crawl through the bowels of our familial bastion of Belmond, lasting impressions gathered on that trip down Luick Lane lingered inside me. One morning during "fair week" in August, out of aimless interest I wandered into the Little Red Schoolhouse (which was, like almost all such structures I've ever seen, stark white) on the grounds of the North Iowa Fair. Shoe-horned into the midst of a blaring carnival mile run by honky-tonk characters drifting through from Florida or Texas, and tucked off the main drag, barely visible for all the gaudy signs hawking cheap trinkets and expensive eats, I almost strode blindly by the school.

Once inside, however, I met a slightly-bent, wizened old woman who I immediately sensed was still admirably full of piss and vinegar. Draped in an ill-fitting floor-length dress of an alarming shade of candy-pink meant to suggest Victoriana but failing to accurately do so, the woman introduced herself as "Ethel Tuttle, an old school teacher of short temper an' long repute but" she added, winking, "still young at heart." She cast a sparkling eye around the haunted building's single room, crammed full of old, initial-carved wooden desks fronted with collapsible bench seats, faded maps covering flaking walls, and dusty, forgotten books with busted bindings. "I spent many a year" she attested nostalgically, "teaching in schools just like this one—yes, I did!" At that, crusty ol' Ethel lustily rang the big brass school bell she'd been fondling with her gnarled hands the whole time we talked.

Ethel Luick, mid-1920s in Belmond

Her sole-but-captivated audience, I listened as the white-haired, sharp-tongued sage spoke of endless spelling bees and tasty box socials, of giggle-pierced Christmas pageants performed to wall-to-wall crowds, of cold winter days when the ladle irretrievably froze in the water bucket at the back of the room. "The kids carried coal for the pot-bellied stove in from the shed in the yard, out by the one swing and teeter-totter. In the winters, their mas took turns bringing hot lunches—pots o' bubblin' stews of meat, with home-baked bread and pies—for all to share." Visibly lagging, Ethel stepped back and leaned against the robin-egg-blue wall behind her. "In good weather, some of the kids rode their ponies to school and tied them to the plank fence out by the coal shed. In bad, their pa might drive 'em over with the ol' buggy before going back home to do fieldwork. Oh, my!" Ethel paused, gazed out the tall, wavy-glassed windows, then repeated wistfully "I spent *many* a year teaching in schools *just* like this one."

PTA Group Will Appear on Forum

Mrs. Floyd Wade, president of the Harding school Parent-Teachers association, will lead a group of women from that district in the monthly sponsored PTA talk on the KGLO Forum Monday from 5:15 to 5:25 p. m. The general title of the discussion is, "Keep the Home Fires Burning." Those to take part with Mrs. Wade are Mrs. Ted Leaman, Mrs. H. H. Boyce and Mrs. Adrian Ringold.

Lake Township #5 rural school during recess; Erma (Falcon) Thrams long coordinated the district PTA.

Stirring her arthritis-stiff, garden-stained fingers in the air, Ethel recounted how "her" charges barely survived the Depression, then too many of "her" boys "marched off to hit Hitler in the nose—but never came back. They're still lyin' somewhere over there in Normandy, under mowed-over turf." She told how the post-war boom lured "folks from the farm. They all wanted what they thought they didn't have or couldn't get here. They wanted their damned idiot boxes and big sleek cars—'Dallas' and Las Vegas. They forgot all those pageants an' bees an' socials—those many happy hours we spent together. They drifted off, one by one, an' chased their stupid loneliness." Herself sliding into melancholia, Ethel asked "What do we have to show for all our fancy crap an' fast-paced busy-ness, all our rushin' about, doin' nothin' of lastin' value?"

Just then, the mesmerized stupor I'd fallen into burst when Mom popped her head in the door and declared with an air of disgust bred with betrayal "Oh, *here* you are! Come on, will ya! We've got to pick that pie up over at the 4-H building." As I jerked back to life and dashed for the door, Ethel asked warmly "What'd you say your name is, young man?" As my odd, for most mortals unpronounceable surname tumbled over my lips I assumed the old lady'd stumble over it like everyone else. But, she didn't. "Oh, I'm a 'Luick,' too" she sang out with complete credibility. I'd have to explore that connection, however, after rescuing a melting meringue pie.

———

Serendipitously discovering cousin Ethel happily coincided with novice family-history research projects that I began in junior high, inspired by the approaching Bicentennial.

David & Phyllis Luick celebrate Michael's book, Christ Lewis Thrams: An Individual in History, *winning first place at the state-level History Day held in spring 1980 at Iowa State University in Ames; the prize was a trip to Washington, D.C., to compete at National History Day. Soon thereafter, Michael published two more books of family history, one about the Luicks, the other about the Mooreheads, Kews & kin.*

Michael "Thomas Jefferson" Luick, dressed for a school event commemorating the U.S. Bicentennial

Besides appearing in a school play as a wigged Thomas Jefferson, flaunting frill-laced sleeves billowing out of a tight gold-velvet vest with bulky metal buttons, and boasting knee-length britches with tight white stockings and silver-buckled shoes, I launched a self-assigned project of interviewing all of the relatives and collecting all of the family photographs I could for what would become a half-dozen thin, self-bound books about the Luicks and Thramses in North America. Not able to know beforehand that the project would win me four first-place local and state awards, as well as two expense-paid trips to compete in National History Day, I pursued my passion with not a shred of regard as to where my investigations might lead or what tangible rewards they might bring me.

In the fiery figure of Ethel Mae (Luick) Tuttle ("The 'Tuttle' is a leftover from my disaster with that damned Norwegian farmer from Eagle Grove who I shoulda never married!" she liked to repeat), I found an eager and infinitely entertaining collaborator. Ethel and I—who had just earned a driver's license and bought a Mercury Comet—spent many afternoons charting Luick history and once ventured per duo to Belmond to scour the cemetery, as well as poke about the town, digging for clues to our shared roots.

Marion (Luick) Smith, Ethel (Luick) Tuttle and Mattie (Luick) Farmer; Ethel at sign near high school: 1979

89

As Ethel enjoyed once again seeing relatives from vanished days of yore, we happily used the excuse of "conducting family-history research" for a ruse to meet with compelling Mattie and her docile shadow, Marion. When I mentioned to Aunt Mattie the many "Jen[n]ison"-marked gravestones Ethel and I had just seen in the cemetery, she belted out "Oh, yes! The Jenisons came out here at just about the same time we did. Your great-grandfather, my brother George, married that Lorena Jenison, and our brother Curtis married Rena's sister, Myrtle." As she began to stack the coffee and tea cups and saucers onto a crowded tray, Mattie noted "Lorena's cousin, Cloe Jenison, lives on Meachams' road, you know."

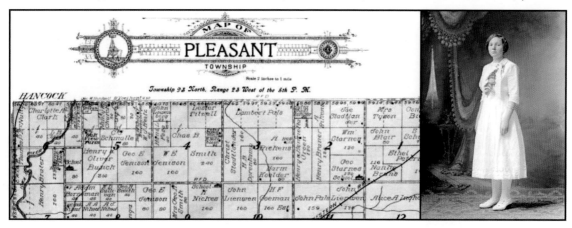

Cloe Jenison, perhaps in a confirmation pose, early 1900s: Jenison-family farms appear in #4, 5, 8 & 9.

"Why, that crazy ol' bird!" Ethel protested, then dropped her head and looked me in the eye. "If you wanna interview *her*, kiddo, you're on your own. I am *not* puttin' myself through *that*."

———

chapter 31: dance with death

A short time later, as soon as I could wrestle the Pontiac from my then one-car parents, I sailed o'er the prairie and returned to Wright County. When I reached Cloe's place, overgrown with scrub trees and volunteer hemp left over from The War but still sprouting up all over the place, I parked the car near the stump of a once-functional windmill. Then, with notepad and pen in hand, I made my way across the rain-soaked farmyard towards the antique house-yard gate.

"Hello" I called softly, "anyone home?" After a moment's wait, I walked through the sagging wire gate, strolled up the sinking sidewalk, then scaled the creaking steps—at which point the kitchen door flung open, a stocky woman in a floor-length skirt popped out and the end of a long-barreled shotgun poked me square in the chest. As my heart raced, I heard the scowling old crone threaten "Take one more step an' I'll shoot ya backwards 'cross this house yard!"

Seeing her finger on the trigger and the hammer cocked, I froze.

I pose with the rifle Cloe once threatened to end my young life with. She is shown in a childhood portrait with brother Oscar, circa 1905.

Only after a few eternity-like seconds was I able to offer a meek "Hi. I'm your cousin, Michael."

"My co-o-ousi-i-in?" she tested, her one eye closed, the other still fixed on zeroing her weapon's front sight straight at my heart. "Which 'co-o-ousi-i-in' might *that* be?"

"Lor... e... na... Jen... i... son's... great... grand... son" I whimpered in staccatoed syllables.

"*Which* kin o' poor Lorena's?" she drilled.

"Mi... Mich-ael" I stuttered, "Michael Luick."

"*Luick!*?" she repeated.

"Lu-ick" I confirmed, at which point she opened her closed eye and lifted her stiff, round head.

"Oh, *those* people" she rumpled her nose, dropped the shotgun, turned around and headed through the open back door. I awkwardly hesitated. Then, uninvited, I cautiously followed.

Inside the dusty farmhouse, the dank warren of what today is labeled a "messy" but we knew then as a "hermit" or "coot," I gingerly treaded down tight paths between towering mounds of books, groves of painter's easels splattered full long ago, dozens of unfinished oil landscapes leaning in unison against a slanting walnut-wood secretary. I quietly trailed behind the mysterious, plodding figure draped in bolts of dusky cloth, between long-unused settees and carved-backed chairs buried under tattered magazines or folders bursting with dog-eared documents.

Although not once inviting me to sit down or offering a glass of water, at least after a few more minutes the old loon did lay her trusty shotgun on a shelf in the middle of the main room and thus relaxed—at least for the time being—the threat of my imminent death. Finally half-turning to me, Cloe asked "So, did you want somethin'?"

"Well, thanks for askin' as I actually did wanna—"

"Did you say you're Lorena's grandson?"

"Oh—no, no" I carefully corrected her, "he's long gone. Lorena was my father's grandmother."

"She married that George Luick character, didn't she?"

George & Lorena (Jenison) Luick's wedding, March 1907

"That's right"—and so began our cat-and-mouse exchange. Assuming that I "want[ed] somethin' like all the rest" Cloe didn't exactly warm up, but she stopped being only icy, as my obvious dedication to genealogy at least partially rehabilitated this fiendish boy, this scheming agent in her midst who'd risen from the groin of "*those* people."

At first Cloe let me believe that she hardly knew or had ever had anything to do with "my" people, but during a rare moment of generosity she inched near me, close enough to drop a creased, soiled postcard in my palm—sweaty despite her house's frigid interior temperature—then swiftly scooted away, backwards.

"You recognize any of those characters?" the old bun-haired schoolmarm huffed in my direction, having reached a safe distance from her unwelcome guest.

"At first glance" I admitted, shaking my head slightly, "can't say that I do."

"See that brat in the front row—on his sporty daddy's lap?"

"In the front row you say?"

"You deaf, boy?"

I looked at her, afraid that I might start to cry and, if I did, that she might relish her victory.

"Yes!" Cloe then snipped as she leaned back, shrugged her shoulders and looked in the direction of the yellowed, frayed shades permanently rolled down to block the windows facing the gravel road that passed in front of her gloomy house. "That baby's your grand-dad, Donald."

"It is-s-s?" I gaped. "Gos-s-sh, I've never seen a picture of him so young!" After studying the large assembly of souls gathered on and in front of that long farmhouse porch, I guessed "So one of these young women on this picture must be my great-grampa's wife—"

"Lorena's in front of the window, the right one of those two" Cloe snapped.

"Oh, really?"

"Of course" Cloe barked. "If it were not so, I would not say it!"

"Of course" I acquiesced. "So" I tried to bait her away from her hate, "you knew Grampa Donald's mother?"

Donald and George Luick, summer 1913

"What a *stupid* question!" she barked again, then turned, dug into the corner of a nearby drawer and took out a yellowed card. As Cloe handed me the lifeless relic she quipped haughtily "So, now do you think I knew your grand-daddy's mama?"

program for funeral services held for Lorena Ethel (Jenison) Luick in Thornton on 18 January 1959

"Of course" I echoed spinelessly, wondering if she could see that I was finding it hard to breathe, mainly due to the small boulder stuck in my dry throat. *Can the ol' bat hear my heart race?* I wondered.

"I jus' meant, you were, indeed, close—not estranged or sompthin' like some families become."

"'Es-tra-a-ang-g-ged'?" Cloe mouthed the word at a just-audible whisper. As she let the word float through the room, she reached up, poked a hooked finger through her pulled-up hair and scratched her muddled head.

"Well, you know" I backpedaled nervously, "these days—"

"'These days' is 'these days'!" she retorted. "What does anyone alive today know about keepin' a family together?"

For a moment I simply stared at this odd, sullen creature, completely unsure what to say or do next. And, I did wonder briefly if my body would ever be found: if not, what would Mom think ever happened to her bookish son who'd snuck away with the family car one rainy fall day and...

"If they was all 'es-tra-a-ang-g-ged' do ya think my cousin Mona, Lorena's younger sister, hadda so spoiled that lil' brat o' a grand-dad o' yours?"

My insecurity giving way slowly to angered resentment of her offensive rudeness, I asked so boldly with "What you mean by that?" that I surprised myself.

Again turning to the magic drawer in an ancient buffet not far behind her, Cloe pried open the dust-covered lid, pulled out a photo and another, buff-white postcard, then handed them to me.

"Does this look like 'es-tra-a-ang-g-ged' to you?"

"I jus' thought—"

"Just what *did* you 'jus' think'!? Isn't it clear as ink on the page, that lil' buster-boy Donny used to stay with Uncle Bill and Auntie Annie sometimes? You think that his mother, that Rena sent him to them if they was 'es-tra-a-ang-g-ged' or sompthin'?"

"I jus' thought that, maybe, after Lorena and George got married in Clarion, moved to Goodell, then Hampton, back to Goodell, and then on to Thornton, that her Jenison relatives and she might have lost contact over the—"

"We was *cousins*, weren't we?"

"Of course" I repeated meekly.

Cloe looked at me, clearly waiting for a meatier explanation.

"After Great-Grampa took up with Olga, my dad and Grampa Donald didn't seem to have that much to do with Lorena anymore. I mean, our family never really spoke about her much after that or—"

"That's nothin' new! Luick men was *always* leavin' their womenfolk, in thought or in deed—like most men, everywhere, every time. We Jenisons stuck with *our* people—so jus' 'cause George ran off with that Danish trash from next door didn't mean we forgot Lorena's name!

Halloween card Mona (Jenison) Hanson sent her nephew, Donald Luick

That was a Luick tactic, boy. We Jenisons—we's cut from better cloth!"

Perhaps also seeing her extreme behavior as unnecessarily harsh and undeserved, Cloe stepped in my direction and pushed our shared focus back to the sepia postcard. Pointing a dangling index finger at it, she asked "See that man on the left?"

"With the white-felt hat?"

"*Yes*, for damnation!" Just as Cloe's look threatened to burn a hole right through my battered soul, she continued. "That's your George's dad, Louis, and"—sliding her pale claw across the picture—"that slouch of a woman over here, with the idiot bow tie, that's his mother, Mary."

Louis & Mary (Hunt) Luick, summer 1913

"Wow" I marveled, "I'd never 'ave recognized either one of 'em!"

"I'm not surprised" she snarled.

By the time it seemed as if she'd finished throwing names at me, Cloe had identified all but three of the thirty people crammed into this packed scene. Aware that she'd overlooked naming a few, I asked "And the other three?"

Hesitating for a visibly uncomfortable moment, she conceded "Those are Lorena's parents, William Edward Jenison, second from the left, an' the woman in the middle of the door's his wife, Annie Eliza Shupe Brooks."

For moment I savored the novelty of seeing faces of ancestors for whom just minutes before I didn't even have names.

"Was Annie married to a Brooks before she married William Jenison?" I wondered as I re-emerged from my short-lived reverie.

"No" Cloe shook her head hard, "but her widowed ma of Welsh stock, Elwy Laura Thomas had been."

"Elwy?" I echoed softly. "What sort of weird name is 'Elwy'?"

"She was named for a small river in Wales, which flows through a village with a primeval tree."

William & Anna (Shupe) Jenison, summer 1913

River Elwy in 1860; the yew tree in nearby Llangernyw is 4,000 years old: Note Celtic cross in cemetery.

When she saw that I wasn't following her, Cloe fairly shouted "Oh, never mind!" then added "Look here—it's like this. Elwy'd been married to a handsome Mennonite, Isaac Shupe—on Christmas Eve, eighteen-hundred-an'-sixty-seven. They'd met in Crown Point, in the northwest corner o' Indiana. He came from Canada, but his people, they'd come from Lancaster County."

"In Pennsylvania?"

"*Where* do you *think*?" Cloe dropped her narrative for a moment to glower at me. "Well, his grandmother's line went way back—the Diefenbachs to the Hudson Valley before seventeen-hundred. Their people was fighters—in the French an' Indian War as well as the Revolutionary."

"Were they—what was it you called 'em—'Melonites'?"

"That's 'Men-non-ites' for god's sake! That's a denom'nation, *not* some sortta fruit!" Cloe shuddered a bit, shifted her considerable weight, then resumed with "Anyway, those Diefenbach offspring was buried all over the place—in cemeteries belongin' ta Presb'terians an' Luth'rans an' Congos, so who knows what their family really was."

"Yeah, who knows" I parroted.

"What we *do* know is, that the oldest girl, Marie Elizabeth, she married a Mennonite—then lived the rest of her life 'plain' as the night."

"What do you mean, 'plain'?"

"Sortta like the Amish live."

"Like the Amish?"

"Well, the Mennonites are sortta cousins to the Amish—the way they live an' dress an' all."

Mennonite cemetery in Salm, France; a "plain" teacher and class in one-room Pennsylvania school, 1942

"What do you mean?" I repeated.

"It's all in Elizabeth Diefenbach Shupe's obituary, that's what I mean." Cloe again consulted her faithful drawer and produced a long strip of aged paper, unadorned and bearing no date nor hint of source. "Here, you can read it for yourself." Among other things, it stated that:

> Elizabeth Shupe was an inhabitant of the township of Waterloo, Upper Canada, where she resided with her family until her death. The time of her living in that place was twenty-four years, which about one-half, in latter life, she lived in a state of widowhood with her children.

> The following is a true and short history of her holy life and death. The late Elizabeth departed this mortal life March 21, 1825; and [these] remarks were made a few days after her death by an intimate acquaintance with her person, life, death and character, who had the great satisfaction to preach her funeral sermon to a numerous concourse of people, from the following words:

1) Ye nations of the earth give ear
to what I here relate;
Your Maker learn to love and fear,
Prepare to leave this state.

2) The Lord his messenger did send,
The Widow Shoop hath died,
She was the poor, the orphan's friend,
Likewise the Pilgrim's guide.

3) Religion is a glorious prop,
Surely it is the best:
We have a consolating hope,
Her soul has gone to rest.

4) The place of praise, the house of prayer,
It was her chief delight;
She was a constant member there,
She kept the end in sight.

5) That hateful sin, call'd dressy pride,
Her soul it did abhor;
Such vain and foolish sins as these,
She kept at open war.

6) What others took to paint their clay,
And dress their bodies fine;
Unto the poor she gave away,
To cheer the feeble mind;

7) The lame, the sick, naked and poor,
They were her constant care—
Were always welcome at her door,
With her they had a share.

8) She often borrowed of the rich,
To give it to the poor:
Her love and charity was such,
She gave them all her store.

9) Third of March she was taken ill,
And to her bed confin'd;
Yet to her heavenly Father's will,
Appeared to be resigned.

10) While she could use her feeble tongue,
Her Maker she ador'd;
By exhorting both old and young,
To seek and serve the Lord.

11) Twenty-first of March, on that day,
She bid this world adieu;
Her longing spirit left its clay,
The age of sixty-two.

12) Oft at her tomb, my heart shall rove,
To drop a sacred tear;
In token of that Christian love,
While she was with us here.

13) Whatever we may count our loss,
Shall be her greatest gain;
She now can say, farewell to cross,
Farewell to grief and pain.

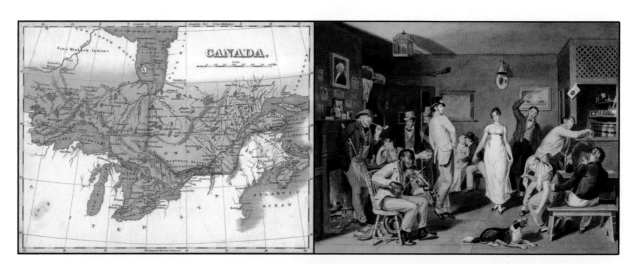

1827 map of then-extant British Upper Canada, with Mennonite area in Ontario peninsula; dance in a bar, 1820. In the rhyme, "paint" is a euphemism for "makeup" and "clay" for human flesh, for the mortal body.

As I finished reading the poem I looked at Cloe, who cocked her head and squinted one eye as she confided "Ya know—she mighta married a Mennonite man, but Elizabeth's people had money."

Tired of being constantly chided, all terrorized me could allow myself to utter was a blank "Oh?"

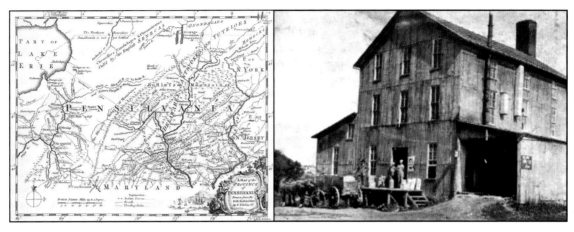

1756 map of "The Province of Pennsylvania;" the mill in Belmond

"Ya, sure—200 acres an' a mill, there in Dauphin County, in southeast Pennsylvania. That's where they was when ol' Johan Georg Diefenbach served in the militia during the Revolution. Maybe it was his early death—at forty-seven—that led young Elizabeth to marry John Shupe, go plain an' move ta a Mennonite settlement in Ontario."

"If the Shupes were Mennonites, then why did they leave Lancaster County an' go to Canada?"

Again wizarding a relic from her yielding drawer, Cloe said nothing, but simply produced an article:

> Among the early pioneer settlers of this county was old John Shupe, a native of Lancaster County, Pennsylvania, to which place his grandparents had moved from the Palatinate, Germany, as early as 1715 if not earlier. Mr. Shupe was born in 1759. When a young man, he was married to Elizabeth Diefenbach. In 1801 he, with his wife and family, moved to Canada and settled in Waterloo County, on the east bank of the Grand River, near Freeport, where he died November 8th, 1812, and she died March 21st, 1825. To them was born a family of seven children.

> As third generation in Pennsylvania, John Shupe had probably established a prosperous farm. He and his family had survived the terrible years of the Revolutionary War which had driven others of our ancestors out of the county. Peace had returned. Yet in 1801, John at about age 40, uprooted his family, his wife Elizabeth (one wonders if she wanted to go), and many children: Daniel the eldest, John 17, George 13, Adam 8, Jacob 6, David, Benjamin, and Catherine 3. At least the older children could help with the younger on that long, rigorous journey north. Two young Pennsylvanian Mennonites, Joseph Sherk and Samuel Betzner, had scouted out good virgin land for settlement in Canada in what was to become Waterloo County. What motivated John Shupe and others like him to leave behind home, relatives, and friends, and doubtless some of their possessions, and set off on a uncomfortable, tiring and dangerous 500-mile journey in order to start from scratch a new, unknown life in a wild, unknown country?

> Ezra Eby suggests two reasons; land hunger and faith in the British. The population had increased so dramatically in Pennsylvania since the first immigrants that it became more and more difficult for the prosperous farmers with their large families to find enough good farm land to purchase. Two generations before, the English [Quaker] William Penn, had offered sanctuary from military and religious persecution, and under the British government, the Mennonites in Pennsylvania had been exempt from military service and the taking of oaths. These rights were not guaranteed under the new American government. The new masters did not treat kindly those who had not supported them under arms during the war or who refused to take the oath of allegiance. Also, the Mennonites who had preserved their German language since coming to America were now forced to send their children to English-speaking schools.

> They made their way to Harrisburg and hence north to Upper Canada, starting out along the east bank of the Susquehanna River and following whenever possible, pioneer roads and Indian trails. All their possessions would be packed into a heavily-laden Conestoga wagon. The wagon would have been pulled by four or six horses or perhaps oxen. Most of the family would have had to walk, the wagon being too full of possessions and supplies. The bodies of these wagons were made waterproof so that they could be

taken off their wheels and floated across a river where there was no ferry; horses and cows had to swim. The scenery of forests, rivers, and the Allegheny Mountains must often have been breath-taking but the trip must have been exhausting and frequently terrifying: It could have lasted four, six or eight weeks.

We always pushed ever onward...

When the long weary journey ended, and John had chosen the site for his homestead, he had to face the pioneer's task of finding food and shelter for his large family; of struggling little by little, to make a home in the wilderness. When, eventually he grew enough grain for his own family and had some left to sell at the head of the Lake, he and other farmers along the Grand could not take their grain out the way they had come in. They waited until winter when the river was frozen and the grain could be taken by sleigh on the ice to Dundas Street and then east to Lake Ontario.

After working my way through that dense text, I looked up searchingly at Cloe, who finally replied to my original question: "Mennonites is pacifists, an' they had hopes of avoidin' the worst of all that war goin' on between Americans and our former keepers, the English" Cloe explained impatiently. "Queer thing is, Elizabeth an' John's grandson, Isaac Shupe, fought in the Civil War anyways, got wounded an' limped back to Crown Point."

"Is that so?"

"Yes! If it weren't—"

"You would not say it" I finished Cloe's sassy sentence for her.

The old crone froze, tilted her head, glared at me down her nose and asked "You mockin' me?"

"Absolutely not—wouldn't think of it" I lied. "But" I confessed, "I don't understand: Why would pacifists fight at least one war, maybe more—and why would Canadians fight the U.S. Civil War?"

Instead of offering me an answer, Cloe rewarded my critical thinking with a chilling glower.

Elwy (Thomas) Shupe Brooks, 1920s; Isaac Shupe's grave in Crown Point, Indiana; Isaac Shupe, 1860s

"As I *was* sayin'" she huffed on, "he'd fought in the Civil War and come back to Indiana, where he married Elwy. He died later o' his wounds, though—almost two months to the day before Annie was born, June thirteen, eighteen-hundred-and-sixty-nine. Isaac Shupe was only thirty when he died" Cloe *tsk-tsk*ed, "so Annie never knew her daddy. An' Elwy? She never got over it—but she did get a new husband, three years later. It was with old man Brooks that she came out to Ioway. But, wait" Cloe sighed, then—noticeably bothered—ordered as she turned again to that mysterious, apparently bottomless drawer, "read this yerself. It's not *my* job to educate *you*!"

Burying my nose in the disintegrating newspaper clipping she handed to me in short jerks, I began to read an obituary from the 27 March 1907 issue of the *Belmond Herald* for

> James Wesley Brooks [born] in Canada March 14, 1841. When a small boy his parents moved to Illinois where his father died when he was about 16 yrs. of age. After the death of his father, his mother with a family of 7 children, of which he was the eldest, moved back to Canada.
>
> When about 19 years of age he walked from Canada to Carroll Co. Illinois, where he worked on a farm 1 year. In Aug. 1861 he enlisted and was mustered into the U.S. service Sept. 7 as a private in Co. I, 31st regiment Illinois Infantry Volunteers. He was wounded in the left leg June 23, 1863, and was discharged Dec. 23, 1863. By reason of re-enlistment as veteran in the same company and regiment was promoted to Corporal, Duty Sergeant, Orderly Ser't., and 2nd Lieut., and was honorably discharged at Louisville, Ky, July 12, 1865.
>
> He married Elizabeth Shupe in 1866. They had lived together about 4 yrs. when she died of quick consumption leaving two children. […] He was again married in Oct. 1872, to Elwy Shupe of Crown Point, Ind. They came to Hancock County, Iowa, in 1874 where he resided, with the exception of a few years' residence in Wright Co., until his death March 9, 1907. Seven children were born to this union […]

"What?" I balked. "Does this mean that ol' man Brooks married his dead wife's widowed sister-in-law, Elwy?"

"Don't wrinkle your nose like that, boy" Cloe demanded. "Marrying a deceased spouse's sibling or single in-law wasn't thought 'bout twice back then. It was a duty, not an oddity."

"Really?"

"Ya—an' folks married their siblings' spouse's siblings, too."

"They did?"

"Why, sure—all the time." Tapping her cane's pointy tip on the floor, "Elwy married her dead sister-in-law's widower—an' *her* daughter Annie's daughters, Lorena and Myrtle, married those Luick brothers, George and Curtis. And *their* brother, Charlie, married Annie's twenty-years-younger half-sister, Mable Omega Brooks. That's jus' how things worked back then." As she began to tap her heavy cane, ever faster and harder, in quickening tempo with her own accelerating cadence, Cloe reeled off "Life was hard. Folks died. Families had to go on or the whole crew'd be gone. They was-n't all a ga-ga with ro-mance or oth-er silly notions; those peo-ple *had* ta be prac-ti-cal!"

Emil Bock Lumber, Belmond, circa 1915

Taken aback by Cloe's unexpected musical performance, it took a few resounding beats before I could muster the straight face to ask her "So, three of the four out of five Luick brothers who ever married, got hitched to two Jenison sisters or their half-aunt, Annie's Jenison's half-sister?"

"Oh, jus' go ahead" Cloe commanded, pointing to the limp obituary like an oracle, "an' keep readin'!"

For a couple moments I deferred to my disinclined informant and dutifully read how James Brooks, Annie Shupe Brooks Jenison's step- and Mable Brooks Luick's father, had been

> in reasonably good health until Wednesday preceding his death when he was stricken with an attack of heart trouble while at Goodell. He was not confined to his bed at any time after the attack and on the day preceding his death [on the following Saturday] he seemed to feel much better and ate quite a hearty supper. About 12 o'clock he called to his wife and complained of a pain around his heart and of a choking sensation. She ran to the telephone to summon medical aid and before she could reach his side, life had departed.

At that point, however, I set down the clipping and complained "I don't see what's this got to do with…" but just as my eyes locked with Cloe's I realized *she* was baiting *me* this time, stubbornly trying to lead me away from something on that group photo that she didn't want me to notice. So, I picked the picture postcard off the table and held it in the air like a lost shred of evidence.

"Okay—and the woman to the right of the man with the straw boater hat" I pressed, "the sharp-lookin' young man you said was Lorena's brother, Seymour? You didn't say, Cloe, who *she* is?"

Seymour and Emma (Arends) Jenison; Cloe Jenison—both photos taken by Martin Thoe in the mid-1910s

As if caving in to hours of exacting questioning after days of merciless torture, Cloe sighed, then granted her inquisitor dejectedly "That's me"—before absently adding in the next breath "but, *say*: Aren't your folks wond'rin' where you are?"

————

Cloe LaVerne Jenison, mid-1910s

chapter 32: shared ancient roots

Cloe LaVerne Jenison was a force to reckon with. But, then, so is Michael Luick-Thrams, then still known as "Mike Luick."

"No" I answered softly but sternly, avoiding her locked gaze, "my folks don't need me right now—this mornin's rain left the late hay all wet anyway, so…"

Seeing she'd met her match, Cloe unexpectedly capitulated to a commensurate albeit younger force. "So" she surrendered with a sigh, "what else ya wanna know, kid?"

Without asking I cleared some floppy magazines from a saggy caned chair and took a seat as I invited "*Anything* ya wanna tell me, I wanna hear."

Then, for the next couple hours, Crazy Cloe held forth over the Jenisons, ancient and modern, per spoken but mostly written word.

————

Right away that eventful afternoon I learned that most Jen[n]isons in the world—our diaspora has spread us from Texas to New Zealand—come from one once-landed family in County Durham, the last English hold before the land of the Scots rises on the other side of Hadrian's Wall, the Romans' ruined attempt to keep raiding Celts at bay. Two descendants of the Jennisons of County Durham's Walworth Castle were Robert (born 29 September 1594 in Keddington, in the English county of Lincolnshire) and his year-older brother, William.

The two had attended privileged Cambridge University, then practiced law at venerable Gray's Inn in London in the early 1600s. With roots dating back to at least the 1370s, its early notable patrons included Queen Elizabeth the First and it boasted practitioners such as Francis Beacon. The young brothers had done well to land coveted places there. Still, their prestigious posts didn't last. The politics of the time, as well as their religious convictions, wouldn't allow them to.

At some point, in the course of sharing the story of mutual ancestors she'd spent decades tracing, in spite of herself Cloe haltingly handed me an account she had researched and written about why the Jennisons left England, how and with whom. It consisted of hand-typed notes on yellowed onion paper, with frequent scribbles and arrows throughout, in barely legible ink. She titled the piece—excerpted here, with her peculiar capitalization intact but most spelling mistakes edited except where they suggest her speech or level of education—as

Charles I of England, after 1636 original by van Dyck

Massachusetts Bay Colony.

I have spent considerable time Studying the Pilgrims at Plymouth in 1620, especially the life of Miles Standish [and] how ten years later in 1630 there is another Colony only a short distance from Plymouth being settled. It is much larger because of the nine ships in the harbor. The ship I am mainly interested in is the *Arabella*. The ship was named after Lady Arabella Thompson from the house of Lincoln. Why she and her husband were aboard I have never been able to find out but there were others of Nobility aboard and again why? I don't know why, but they were non-conformists and many had been asked to leave England because of their beliefs. Some had been threatoned by the King and left without his knowledge before he found them and put them in jail or worse cut their heads off or hung them.

I paused from reading Cloe's tome to ask—as inoffensively as I could for fear of raising her inflammable ire again—"How in the world could you find all these fine details?"

After a moment of non-response, my unwilling host lifted her head and challenged back with "Ya think I got nothin' better ta do than hang round Belmond all the time?" Unsure whether or not one was expected, I didn't give her an answer—but luckily she continued with "I've spent more than enough of my time buried in archives in Des Moines, New York an' Boston. I've even" Cloe leaned forward a bit and lowered her head as well as her voice, "made the trip to England. An' anyway" she asked in a suddenly loud voice, grandly, "see all them books over there?" Cloe turned slightly in her chair and made a sweeping gesture in the direction of a bowed shelf full of worn volumes, "I track down what I need."

"I see" I exclaimed noncommittally, then inquired gingerly about her intentions in writing the text.

"Oh, I don't know" Cloe pokered, "maybe I'll publish it someday, along with my paintings and poems. But, then again" she leaned back and clutched the crook of her cane, "maybe I won't."

I only blinked a time or two, staring at her dumbly, then continued reading aloud:

> What ever they had done to displease the king, among the passengers were Sir William Jenyson, his brother Robert, Sir John Winthrop and Sir Richard Saltenstall, [the last two men's] two daughters and three sons and some servants. Those mentioned were Attorneys, graduates of Cambridge and good friends. Sir John Winthrop of the gentry was of a highly esteemed family and was one of the separatists, the Protestants, and because of his faith had been asked to leave England.

> In 1626 Winthrop had became an attorney and a member of the Inner Temple. At the same time the Jenysons had graduated and had established themselves in Colchester as attorneys. They had not been satisfied with King James I but when he died in 1625 and his son Charles I took the thrown things were much worse, as Charles had professed to be Protestant but at once married a Catholic and to do so he had to promise the father, the King of France, he would persecute the Protestants and make England a Catholic country again.

> It was in 1629 Sir John Winthrop, Sir William Jenyson and his brother, Robert, and many others showed their discontent with conditions in England with intimations of what they intended do. Conditions worsened as the new Queen and the King of France were threatening the new King Charles I. To men like [them] England was becoming a place no longer fit to live in. The settlement at Plymouth had not been too successful but the English still claimed the right to America because of the discoveries of John Cabot. Two companies had been formed to settle America, the London Company and the Plymouth Company. The first settlement had been made in Jamestown in 1607, the second at Plymouth and the third at Charlestown, Boston Harbor and Watertown.

1850 depiction of John Winthrop arriving in Salem in 1630; the first streets of early Boston, mid-1630s

Even though just an inexperienced teen, as I read Cloe's narrative it struck me how fascinated she was by royalty or noble title, by position, wealth and religion. There was no gray in her story, only black and white. And, few descriptors. Or feelings. Looking around her shabby house cum archival library cum art studio, crammed full of chaos, the contradictions confused me.

> Just where the ship the *Arabella* joined the other eight ships to sail to American I'm not sure but think it was the Isle of Wight in the English Channel south of the town of Southampton, the inland port. The Jenysons, Sir William and his brother Robert, went overland from Colchester to Gravesend on the Thames where they sailed through North Sea and the English Channel to the Isle of Wight. There they boarded the *Arabella* with Sir John Winthrop and Sir Richard Saltenstall and family. They sailed to lands end, the last

sight of England. When they bid farewell to England a Mr. Jiggens said "Farewell, dear England, farewell the Church of God in England and all our Christian friends. We donot go to New England as Separatists from the Church of England, though we cannot but seperate from the Corruption in it, but we go to practice the positive part of the church reformation and to propagate the gospel in America."

The ships arrived about the same time with Higgens as pastor and Skelton as teacher. At once there was intolerance. Some wishing certain forms and another group a different. The quarrelling was so bad certain ones were sent back to England. Sir Richard Saltenstall was fined twice for "Prelacy." The Church of England demanded some people be returned to England. A Mr. Morton went to England because of mistreating the Indians. Another ship arrived from England with Sixty well passengers but half the cows dead.

1850 depiction of early Boston; "Plan of Boston showing Existing Ways and Owners of December 25, 1630"

At that point I looked at Cloe—who by now sat motionlessly, looking at me like a hungry hound at the edge of a table waiting for crumbs to fall or scraps to fly—and wondered why her text suddenly became terse and read like disjointed complaints.

> Watertown was made a fortified town. Very cold weather, rivers frozen. Food scare. Many dead of scurvy, but women recovered when a ship of lemons came. Indians came offering Indian corn. At one court a servant was convicted of officenses against the church and was whipped, another had his ears cut off. Another ship came with hogs, cattle, goats and provisions. They had a celebration day when they ate fat pigs, venison, geese, and partridges. The weather was wet and cold. There were many worms to eat the corn. Many mosquitoes and rattle snakes to worry the people. Wheat and oats not good but plenty of eel and lobsters. There were many oysters to be had as well as hemp and beavers. Small pox very bad, many people dieing. The land was poor and the crops bad because of the poor soil, draught, birds and insects. Families had to depend upon fishing and hunting for most of their food. Sickness was always prevalent and many dead. There was much bickering over religion and church affairs. Indians uprising kept the people in a constant unsettled life. Life was hard, life was full of evils, stealing, adultry, murder, hangings, cutting off ears, cutting out tongues, whipping, putting in the blockade [all errors: sic].

———

After reading eight single-spaced pages sans margins, I found those following to consist of a stream of taped-together pieces of paper, three yards [almost three meters] long, at points tacked together with straight pins dulled by age. Even for me, Family-History Mega-Nerd Extraordinaire, wading further into and digesting Cloe's *Lebenswerk* seemed daunting. At least all that effort—both hers and mine—yielded a comprehensive account, which her notes suggest to be based on credible, documentable sources. It seems:

"Sir Robert" had sailed to New England in 1630 and after an initial stay in Boston made his way up the Charles River to Watertown, where he established a family tradition of pushing ever westward—an impulse that nudged his descendants across a continent until, two centuries later, they landed in Iowa in the mid-1850s. The Jennisons' route to the American Heartland, however, would be circuitous and full of adventures, mishaps and restless, short-lived sojourns.

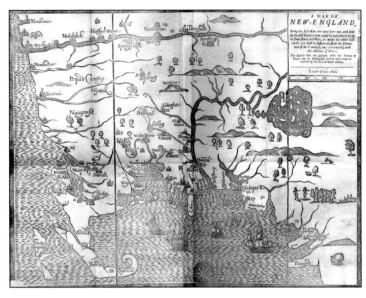

William Hubbard's 1677 "Map of New-England," with west on top

Already in 1634, for example, "Ensign [Robert] Jenyson went to Bermuda as a ship's pilot"—reportedly a trip he had made in that position before emigrating to New England on the *Arabella*. According to Cloe "He said there had been great changes in the way the people lived as they had become Christians." She also claimed that while away from Watertown "Robert met and became friends with Lord Baltimore," the frustrated founder first of a failed "papist" colony in near-Arctic Newfoundland, then of an enduring haven for Roman Catholics in Maryland.

Once back in Watertown, Robert Jennison found himself in an uncomfortable position. Although it omitted reference to killing Quakeress Mary Dyer, Cloe's narrative includes Massachusetts Bay Colony's banishing dissenters such as Roger Williams or Anne Hutchinson over differences of religious belief. "The people of the colony were divided" Cloe's account claims, and many

> would not vote against [the dissenters.] William and Robert Jenyson (Jennison) refused to vote [for banishment] though they had been very friendly with Governor Winthrop. When they refused his will he was very much against them [and later] wrote in his diary that William was a very capable man but that he was too easy for his own good. The Jenysons went on serving Winthrop and the colonies as attorneys, settling quarrels, surveying boundaries and laying out towns but little is mentioned of their work as it is likely Governor Winthrop did not forgive them for opposing him. He was considered a very stubborn man.

John Winthop (left) had Quaker Mary Dyer hanged at Boston Neck.

"Do ya know that the Jennisons were in Massachusetts at the time of both the Pequot Wars *and* the Salem Witch Trials?" Cloe baited me as I turned the pages of her seemingly endless tome. When I returned her revelation with a blank look, she asked "Don't you know what those was?" When I shrugged sheepishly and said nothing, she complained "Don't they teach you kids *anything* these days!?"

Since Cloe was neither a patient teacher nor positive enough as a personality to inspire real learning, I only later discovered that between 1634 and 1638 the Jennison brothers had fought in an alliance of New England colonists and their Native-American allies (the Narragansett and Mohegan) against a third local tribe, the Pequots—with disastrous results. Ultimately out-gunned, under-fed and overpowered, the Pequots lost, with some seven hundred of them being killed or captured in the process. The English sold hundreds as slaves to be shipped off to the West Indies, and dispersed the rest so successfully that it took the tribe more than three and a half centuries to regain a polity in their traditional homeland along the Pequot (now "Thames") and Mystic Rivers in present-day southeastern Connecticut.

Though English colonists slaughtered the "bothersome" Pequots, their colony's seal featured a native.

What particularly caught my attention were the contradictory moral standards tucked amidst the unsettling details of the event. According to Puritan thought, because the Old Testament condoned slavery, that wretched institution did not constitute sin or a violation of "God's will." Samuel Maverick, an Anglican vicar's son, for one, brought African slaves to Massachusetts and Governor Winthrop supported that commercial practice. Indeed, Winthrop not only headed the council which approved the sinister action, but kept Pequot slaves himself—a male and two females. As the colony had deemed warriors dangerous, at the conclusion of the Pequot War native men were shipped to the West Indies, whereas their distaff and children were divided among the colonists as enslaved laborers. As Massachusetts Bay Colony's heavy-handed leader, John Winthrop, later reported, the defeated warriors exported into bondage were traded for "salt, cotton, tobacco, and Negroes."

In Cloe's black-or-white world, however, a different story unfolded, along less differentiated lines:

> In 1636 John Oldman was killed by the Pequot Indians. They long had been the troublesome tribe. The near by colonies decided to each send a company of soldiers to fight the Pequots. Plymouth sent forty men under Captain Miles Standish; ninety men were sent from Massachusetts Bay Colony under Captain William Jenyson [as one of four in command.] The colonists lost few men but most of the Pequots were destroyed and sent into hiding, never to bother the colonists again.

"Enemies" of the Puritans' fragile foothold in the New World, however, did not come only from without but also from within—or, at least, so some colonists thought. Of all the accounts I've encountered since that rainy fall day in Cloe's damp, dumpy farmhouse outside Belmond, Iowa, I find that of my fellow, history-minded Upper Midwest writer, Garrison Keillor, singularly concise and honest.

While writing this chapter in my sun-soaked living room in Dresden on 2 June 2014, I happened to hear his daily "Writer's Almanac" and immediately smiled, thinking of grumpy old Cloe's indictment of my alleged historical ignorance. Much gentler than my brutalized and brutalizing great-grandmother's cousin could have done, Garrison explained in his melodious, lulling voice, that on that date

> in 1692, the Court of Oyer and Terminer convened in Salem Town, Massachusetts, beginning what would become known as the Salem Witch Trials. The hysteria had begun in Salem Village (now Danvers) in

January of that year; a few preteen and teenage girls, including the daughter of Samuel Parris, the village minister, began acting strangely and having fits, insisting that they were being poked and pinched. The local doctor was at a loss to explain the behavior, and concluded that they must be bewitched[.]

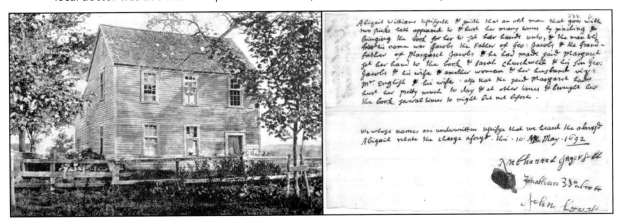

1892 photo of "House Where Witchcraft Started;" deposition of Abigail Williams vs. George Jacobs, Sr.

Within a matter of weeks, warrants were issued for dozens of accused witches, and the jails were full to bursting. Governor William Phipps ordered the formation of the Special Court of Oyer and Terminer—which meant "to hear and determine"—to try the backlog of cases. [Ultimately] 19 executions took place over the next four months. A 20th victim, Giles Cory, was tortured to death when he refused to enter a plea. The hysteria spread to nearby towns, and feuding neighbors began to see it as a handy way to get revenge. Many of the accused people confessed to witchcraft to escape execution, because confession meant you were repentant, and it was up to God to handle your punishment. Those who refused to confess—either on moral grounds or because confession meant they would forfeit their property—were executed.

In October, Governor Phipps abruptly dissolved the [trials] and prohibited further arrests, maybe because Puritan ministers were calling for an end to the trials, or maybe because the afflicted girls had accused Phipp's wife of witchcraft. Over an eight-month period, more than 200 people had been accused and imprisoned, and several had died in jail. Some of the judges and examiners later expressed remorse. Examiner John Hale wrote in 1695, "Such was the darkness of the day, and so great the lamentations of the afflicted, that we walked in the clouds and could not see our way."

William Phips, first governor, Province of Massachusetts Bay, circa 1690

Cloe's narrative refers to the Jennisons' experiences with witchcraft in both Olde and New England, but paints a simplified black-and-white picture, topped with heroism and rewarded virtues. She held that

> Captain Jenyson was sent on many missions among both whites and Indians. There were many accusations of witch craft and many put to death. The Jenysons were very much against witch craft and often spoke up. They spoke their minds on many issues. They believed in being honest with the people and if they felt they had made mistakes they were willing to say so. They had lived in Colchester England where witch craft was much in use and they did not believe in it in England, nor would they in America. Captain Jenyson was considered a very able man and was much consulted on all issues. Much land was given to him for his services to the colony.

Indeed, between them, the Jennison brothers accumulated and sold at a profit "much land." As the *Giles Memorial Genealogical Memoirs* (published in 1864) recounts, William alone

> had a homestall [piece of property in the form of a town lot] of fifty acres, on the north side of what is now Mount Auburn Street, between Common and School Streets, a little to the south of Strawberry or School-House Hill. This was much larger than the average of the homestalls or home-lots, assigned to the first settlers by the freemen of the town. Few of them exceeded sixteen acres. Probably, Capt. Jennison had at first a small lot, afterwards increased by grant or purchase to fifty acres. We find, indeed, that he was grantee of eleven lots, of which he had sold seven before 1644. Besides his homestall, he had 220 acres of land in Watertown. The Court also granted him, Sept. 3, 1638, two hundred acres of land, in what was afterwards Framingham.

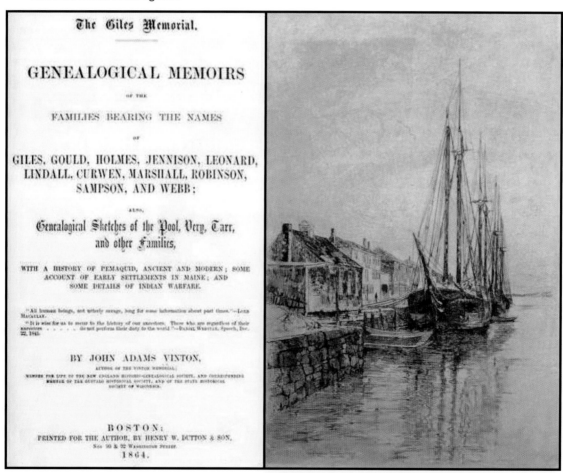

title page of the Giles Memorial, *1864; Derby Warf, Salem, etching by Charles Herbert Woodbury, 1889*

Cloe obviously had spent much time looking for proof that our people came from honorable, esteemed individuals of means and ability. As evidence, she repeated the findings of Victorian scholars, such as those printed in the *Giles Memorial*, claiming

> Sir William, the elder brother, was envested freeman at once in 1630 [on 18 May—the first man to be so designated in the new colony.] He was a leading man in the settlement and chosen selectman from 1634 to 1644 [with the exception of one year.] He was one of the three commissioners from Watertown and held that office until he returned to England in 1651. He didnot bring a wife or children but he did have a wife, Elizabeth, who remained in Colchester.

According to the *Giles Memorial*,

> The prefix "Mr." was commonly attached to [William Jennison's] name; it was then an honor sparingly bestowed. He was Deputy, or Representative, of the town in the General Court, from 1635 to 1645.

Cloe's own, amateur research bore out such scholarship. She wrote:

> Sir William and Robert were both attorneys having been to Cambridge University and [...] colonial records show that the court had great confidence in their integrity. They received numerous appointments for determining boundaries between towns, laying out new towns and settling Indian affairs and contested land claims. William was chosen Captain of the Watertown Train-band. He was an original member of the "Great Artillery Company" incorporated in 1638.
>
> Governor Winthrop said "the Jenysons were staunch friends of civil and religious liberty and sometimes suffered for their causes." They refused to vote for the condemnation and banishment of Roger Williams and Ann Hutchenson in 1637 because they had different views on religion. It was said [...] the Jenysons did not believe that people should be burned at the stake or hung or beheaded with out a fair trial. Governor Winthrop did hold it against them for not believing as he did.

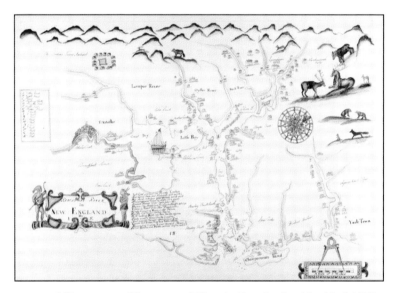

map of "Pascatway [Piscataqua] River in New England by J.S.," 1670

The most rabid religiosity of even the most pious polity, however, could not shield even the most faithful from one's own body determining one's fate. As Cloe's chronicle testified next,

> William was ill for some time and had to cut down on his work relieing on Robert to carry on. In 1651 he was too ill to work and decided to return to Colchester England to be with his wife. He gave most of his land in America to his brother Robert and nephew Samuel. He didnot overcome his illness and died in 1657. He was buried in the church yard of Saint Mary's Church in the wall in Colchester. His wife, Elizabeth, lived several years longer and in her will she asked to be buried beside her husband [who] always preferred to be known as Captain rather than Sir. Williams brother Robert in America went to Colchester as an attorney to settle his brother's estate. He and his son inherited Williams property in America and Elizabeth got the money and property in England. The wills of William and his wife are on file in Chelmsford, the county seat of Essex County not far from Colchester. I have both copies. I donot find the name of Elizabeth ever mentioned again.

———

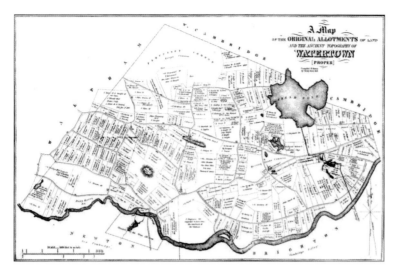

"Original Allotments of Land & Ancient Topography of Watertown," 1860

But, what of Robert's life, back in the New World? Cloe had ferretted out much about him, too. She cited, for example, two histories of Watertown (published in 1855 and 1878) that she had acquired. According to them, when the Jennison brothers arrived in their adopted homeland

They could not live with the awful water of Charlestown. They found good water and started a plantation or settlement [on] some fertile land along the Charles River which had many freshwater brooks and many springs. Just why they named the new settlement Watertown is not exactly known. The name first given was Pequest. It was an Indian name. It was later changed to Watertown […] probably because they found so much good fresh water and that was what they were lookin for. They had one thousand, five hundred acres. It seemed to be a fruitful place with its fresh water. Soon other settlements were started near by at Sudbury, Weston and Waltham.

The Charles River of the town was wide and deep, the tide waters from the sea extended to three miles above the town making the river navigable for small vessels. There was a water fall at the head of the tide water which furnished power for the first Grist Mill near the town, one of the earliest of the colony. By 1634 they were raising grains to supply their needs and had out grown the rock pounding of grain for meal. The same water power furnished power for a fulling mill built a few years later and a saw mill. […] There were several brooks leading to the river [and they] played a great part in the settlement for supplying the water as they dug no wells for many years. Fish were the main source of food. Other wild life was at a distance such as deer and bears and wild hogs. Soon they were busy building roads and bridges to cross the streams.

Money had been paid to the Indians to get them to move further west. At first they seemed to have little trouble with the Indians but too soon the Indians began to bother them.

According to the chronology of Cloe's tale, once the early New England colonists' earthly needs were set, they shifted their attention to their heavenly ones.

[After] every settler had been asigned a piece of land and built his cabin they met in a congregation to make and sign a covenant for rulling their settlement. No one had a right to vote unless he was a freeman. None could be admitted a freeman unless he were a church member and that church had to be congregational. Then all affairs were managed by votes of the members. The first three men chosen as freemen for ordering the civil affairs of the colony were Mr. William Jennison, Brian Pembleton and John Eddie [who] made the divisions of the land and the division of trees to the individuals.

As Cloe alluded, the church remained omnipresent in colonial New England. In her text she said

No records are left of the type of home life that the early settlers enjoyed or suffered but what few that are left show that all their activities beyond making a living were directed toward the church's relation to there home life and their community. All their activities in the home and in public were based on their relation ship to their church and that influence extended through the many generations to follow. Every head of a family had to own a pew in the church. The location of the pew in the church and the number of pounds paid were very much an indication of a man's wealth and his social prestige.

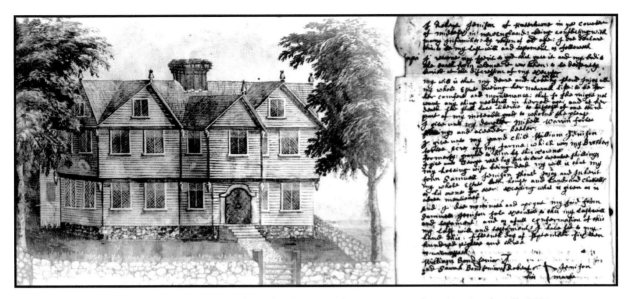

1642-built home of Salem-witch-trial judge, Jonathan Corwin; Robert Jennison's will, 1683

Both the wealth and prestige that the Jennison family enjoyed seemed considerable. After William returned to England, Robert

> took up the work of his brother in civil and religious matters of the Colony for his brother had been his teacher and the people had faith in him as they had had in his brother[.] His home was east of the lowest falls on the Charles River, Cambridge Road, now Mount Auburn Street. He was never made a captain as his brother William had been[.] His will gave his wife, Grace, his whole estate during her natural life. After which it was devided between his children.

A harbinger of significant dates in the family's history to come, Robert Jenison died on 4 July 1690 at the astonishing age (for that high-mortality era) of 95. His sole son, Samuel—born on 16 October 1645—inherited much land and thus stayed in Watertown until he died on 15 October 1701. Listed in a "sundry deed [as] yeoman and gentleman and Mr.," Cloe noted that Samuel had married the "belle of the town" Judith Macomber "of a very well known family [and] highly esteemed in the community" on 30 October 1666. The father of ten children who survived to adulthood, Samuel earned the title of "freeman" in 1682, allowing him the right to vote in civil matters, and became town clerk in 1691. An ensign like his father, Samuel also held offices in the Congregational Church.

By the time Samuel died, he came to oversee a considerable fortune—as revealed in the following inventory, dated 31 October 1701, about a fortnight after his death:

> house, &c., £95; farm, 50 acres, £90; farm, 20 acres, £60; 12 acres in lieu of township, &c., £5; one acres of meadow, £10. Total, real and personal estate, £383.1. As the currency was not then depreciated, the whole amount was equivalent to 1270 [1864] silver dollars [about $20,000 in 2014], which in those days entitled the possessor to be considered a rich man.

Indeed, as so many accomplishments suggest, already by the second generation of being in the New World, the Jennisons had built a life in New England that would have been the envy of many still struggling back in the hierarchical, hamstrung Old.

———

chapter 33: leaving New England

A century and a half after Sir Robert Jennison sailed aboard the *Arabella* into Boston Harbor, his descendants left the Massachsetts Bay Colony—at the time of their departure, circa 1780, not yet a state in a not-yet-established nation—and spilled westward, into the great American frontier.

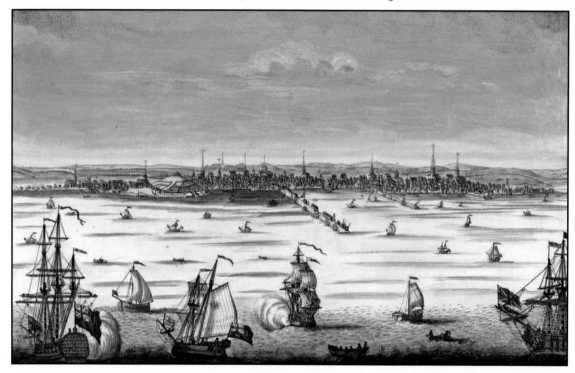

titled A South-East View of the City of Boston in North America, *by J. Carwithan, circa 1730*

It was Sir Robert's grandson—his son Samuel's son, named Robert after the boys' grandfather—who actually resumed the Jennison family's historic westward push in earnest, some ninety years after the founding of Massachusetts Bay Colony. After marrying well, to widow Dorothy Thomas Whittemore, young Robert and his bride moved to Framingham and had five children.

As an adult, the middle of Robert and Dorothy's three sons, Elias—born 23 September 1724,

> was wealthy and owned a great deal of land. Much of the land had been passed down from one generation to the next, land acquired from the estate of the first Robert Jennison. Elias was well educated and held many colonial positions. He married Hannah Twist of Salem in 1748 [parallel to Elias' brother Joseph marrying Hannah's sister, Martha] and moved to Sudbury, then Sutton where he had land. His health was poorly and he died [6 March] 1760 a fairly young man.

> Hanna was young and with six small children, the youngest a tiny baby, she soon married [five months and eight days after Elias' death] as the third wife of Ebenezer Gould who had children by his two former wives. Hannah Twist Jennison Gould had no more children but with three families to raise she had a hard life. Her sister Martha, married to Joseph Jennison, brother of Elias, moved to Vermont and on to New York and to Michigan, where their family was of the very wealthy Jennisons who built the town of Jenison.

Elias and Hannah's oldest of three sons, Elias 2nd—born in 1756 on an auspicious date, the 4th of July—would serve in the American revolt against the British crown. As Cloe wrote, "Even though his father died early in his life," the native of Millbury, near Sutton, Massachusetts,

> stayed near his mother Hannah Twist Jennison Gould[. She] had lost all of the Elias 2nd's [inherited] money but he was known to have been interested in farming. It was said Hannah and the Goulds did not give their children much education. Elias 2nd went to serve his country when [he] enlisted in 1778. [His

younger brothers] Robert and William were in Maine, then a part of Mass. [Cloe] found records that say they all married but [she had] no records that tell what became of Robert and William after the war. But they must have been in touch with each other for a time because even though Elias 2nd was married he met with William some years later to visit their mother and got to Philadelphia on horse back to witness the first Fourth of July.

1777 map The Provinces of New York and New Jersey

A woman of limited and modest formal education, Cloe spent almost all her austere life in the middle of the eastern Great Plains—most of that pre-Interstate and before affordable airline service reached North Central Iowa. Despite geographical isolation and a thrifty purse, by the time I met her Cloe clearly had perused a host of widely scattered records and harvested a wealth of details about our ancestors. From Elias 2nd's military service records, for example, she learned

He was 5 ft. 10 inches tall. Dark hair and eyes and complexion. He was a good looking young man [who] served less than a year when he was seriously injuried in the right leg which left him with a limp. He could not go back into service. July 1, 1779 he married [nineteen-year-old] Betty Gage often called Betsey. They were married in Sutton as the records show the posting of the marrage intentions. Where he met Betty Gage is not known but later Elias 2nd and Betty moved by wagon train to Stillwater New York. The place was then called "the limit of the far west." It may be that he had met her when he was serving in the war near White Plains and Saratoga where the most important battles of the war were fought. Perhaps it was up

there that he was injuried and met the Gage family. Betty was the daughter of Jabez and Elizabeth Gage. Jabez was the son of Amos Gage. Several of the Gage men served in the war. Amos Jennison son of Elias 2nd and Betty died as an infant and was buried beside his grandmother Elizabeth Gage in the Congregational church yard.

Much of the three yards of taped-together scraps of paper bearing Cloe's chronic of what she titled "The History of the Jenysons, Jennisons, Jenisons and Jenesons in America" consists mostly of the same notes, recorded repeatedly, with only strands of new information woven into ever-recycled information from previous pages. Although likely mirroring her own inner muddle, disjointed excerpts do provide shards of mostly lost family lore that, despite the passage of four hundred years, leave a colorful mosaic. And, periodically,

view of Troy, New York, as seen from Mount Ida, circa 1820

her saga peered into the nation's soul—as well as into her own.

"Every body was very poor" Cloe reflected, as the war between England and its former colonies

> had taken its tole in all families, in lives, in ways of living and in property. After the war the Jennisons lands and wealth were gone as most of the other colonial people had suffered and lost. It is true men had to furnish their own clothes and weapons and much property was confiscated for one reason or another. There had been many differences of oppinions in regards to the war. Some whose ancestories could be traced back hundreds of years into England knew there were people still living in England by the name of Jennison. They had strong thoughts on the war and independence from England. Some Tory blood there was and some there would remain. Elias Jennison was of the opinion that he had fought in the Revolutionary War to make the colonies free. He had seen his relatives and friends die for the cause of freedom. He had learned to fight, to think and stand on his own two feet with no money or property and only a wife who believed in him and thus he would seek a new world to conquer.

"How much of this did Cloe find in books or other places" I wondered, even as a teen sitting nervously in her poorly-lit living room, *"and how much of this did she spin herself?"*

————

As she followed the Jennisons' post-war lives, conservative Cloe seemed to continue to liberally interpret their biographies. "It was a pioneer trail" she wrote, that Elias 2nd

> took to what was then called "the Far West," a little settlement called Stillwater. It was a beautiful country but at that time not a productive country. The land was good for dairying but few could afford the buying of the cows [so] Elias 2nd farmed and lumbered. He had been there only a short time trying to improve some land and building up his property when he was killed by a falling tree [in 1792]. Betty Gage Jennison was educated and did the best she could to educate her four children. [She] died there many years later never remarrying but raising her two daughters and two sons [one being Elias 3rd, born 1785].

> Because of his father's early death Elias 3rd had to help support and raise his younger brother and sisters, and care for his mother. He stayed in Stillwater until after both sisters had married [one to a man named Barker of Brooklyn, the other a Green of Albany] and both his mother and brother William had died [per *Giles Memorial* "of consumption, July 18, 1827"]. Elias 3rd married Sarah Bagley a neighbor girl.

> They were unhappy with the rocky land and had heard of the good land to the west so with some neighbors [by] 1830 they made up a wagon train to go west. Not knowing where they were going, they passed through western New York and around Lake Ontario, passed Pennsilvania into Summet [sic] County, Ohio, the very north east of Ohio, where they found good land. They had not been sure where they were going but the land in Ohio looked good for forming. A small village was being started and there were a few people already settled so the Jennisons decided to stay. A school was started so the children got a country school education. They farmed and Elias did a great deal of building.

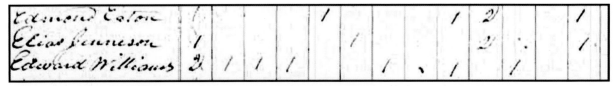

For the first time, Cloe's hot pursuit of the Jennisons' centuries'-long trek across the northeast quarter of today's contiguous United States leaves contemporary researchers cold. Despite her repeated references to the family being in Summit County, Ohio—around Akron—1830's census shows an "Elias Jenneson" family enumerated in southeast Indiana's Ripley County, near Cincinnati, Ohio.

plan of Akron, 1825; view of Cincinnati from the north towards the Ohio River and Kentucky beyond, 1841

In her jumbled tale, Cloe maintained that her great-grandfather Elias Jennison 3rd

> was always wishing he had gone further west where he had heard that the land was very much better. There in Summet County his oldest sons [grew] to maturity and wanted to get out and find land for themselves. They had given them the best of pioneer education but it was not as good as he had hoped.

Any sleuths' confusion aside about exactly where the family was at what point for about a decade around 1830, as of the Jennisons' removal from Upstate New York to the Old Northwest, the family's chronicle as recorded by Cloe shifted from the foggy realms of handed-down lore or later sifting through dry documents, to the vivid, colorful recounting of personal memories by people who either Cloe once knew or who the people around her personally had known. Of her and my great-grandmother Lorena Jenison Luick's grandfather, Joseph Bud Jennison, she wrote that he

> was born October 6, 1821 in Stillwater, New York the son of Elias 3rd and Sarah Bagley. He was seven years old when his parents moved to Summet County, Ohio where he grew to manhood. He was reared a farmer and received a good country school education.

> When Joseph Bud was twenty two years old, about 1843, he went with his brother [William Edward] on horse back to Lake County [in the extreme northwest corner of] Indiana, where they did building work. They stayed and worked for some time but land was too expensive as it was too near Chicago.

When Joseph and William arrived in Indiana they found, in part, a primeval forest falling to the ax and flint stone literally before their eyes. Once the southern flank of the densely wooded Northwest Territories, Indiana was filling quickly around the time they had come, above all with immigrants from the exhausted farming regions of Upstate New York and New England, as well as crowded Pennsylvania, with some settlement by European newcomers—although nothing like the Old World masses that

1847 ad for farmers to the Northwest; 1852 plat for Medaryville, Indiana

would flood the Upper Midwest a few years later.

Wanting to grab what they thought the best to be had before it was all gone, forever, the two Jennison brothers

wanted to buy land and heard that the land was very good around Wabash so again they set out on horse back and went south. It was a very pretty place and plenty of cheap land for sale so Joseph Bud and William bought 160 acres of raw unimproved land. They built a shanty to live in and broke up much land, payed money for their seed and planted a crop. The land was low and [had] poor drainage. The first year was very rainy with a flood so their first crop drowned out and they had no money to buy more seed.

The clearing the Jennisons hacked out of the woods of Indiana would have been a crude affair, as they did not remain there long enough to develop it into a highly developed home and farm.

four from a series of scenes from frontier life in Indiana in the 1860s by D.H. Roberts, per the original titles: (top left) Stereoscopic views of Indiana, Farm in Indiana, Sheep on pasture *and* Starting to town *(lower right)*

Attempting to cultivate crops or graze livestock amid remnants of ruined, charred trees—often in what for millennia had been treed bogs—proved too much work for too little rapid reward. So, the Jennison brothers took work on the Wabash-Eric Canal which was being dug [so] they hired out digging. When it was complete and water flowing in the canal they continued to work on the Canal by driving mule teams and horse teams to pull the boats up and down the Canal hauling freight on some boats and passengers on other boats. The canal was a great help to the country and many people used it [who] were going west to settle in the new lands being opened for settlement in the mid-west and the west.

Problem was, those giddy, migrating hordes seemed to give little thought to the cruel fates of the quiet thousands who had occupied the land before it had been "won," then "opened" for Euro-American settlement. If they did, too many settlers blindly supported ridding the land of those pitiable souls who no longer possessed a meaningful degree of say over their own lives.

———

Non-native peoples first began arriving in what today is known as "Indiana" at the end of the 1600s. First the French, then the British vied for influence and territory—less for the sake of land per se than for a determining hand in the lucrative beaver-fur trade. The natives—mostly splinter groups belonging to the Algonquin-speaking realm of tribes—found their fates first disrupted, then dictated by the outsiders' ensuing fray. So, too, did the land—their only home.

Cutoff River Arm of the Wabash, *by Germanic painter Karl Bodmer, 1832*

Few Americans or Europeans filling the frontier, though, thought about what the impact their recent arrival and long-term dreams would mean for the region's aboriginal inhabitants or its ecology. They looked at the natives and saw competitors for food and shelter; in the land the natives occupied, they saw jobs and a future. That future, however, would be formed more by force than by wisdom or charity.

One by one, the arriving Americans deported tribes that had lived in the area for generations—the Delaware in 1820, the Potawatomi in the 1830s and, finally, the Miami in the mid-1840s. Ironically, the deportation of the natives took place both *because* of dreams to transform the wilderness into a canal-connected agrarian and manufacturing landscape, and *aboard* the very barges later floated—in parts of the dual river-canal system—on what had been wild rivers, plied by free peoples in canoes for centuries.

According to Huntington County historian Terry Pepper, the systematic deportation of the Miami began in fall 1846 in Peru, Indiana, on October 6. Three canal boats were loaded with baggage, Indians, and white officials. On the second day, the three boats reached Fort Wayne, where the remainder of the tribe was awaiting the conductors; two more boats were added to accommodate them. The party followed the Wabash & Eric Canal to its junction with the Miami and Erie Canal in Ohio, then passed through Dayton to Cincinnati, where the entire party was transferred to the steamer *Colorado* on the Ohio River.

The expedition reached St. Louis [two weeks later] on October 20, 1846, transferred to the *Clermont II*, and three days later steamed up the Missouri River. The Indians and baggage were unloaded at Kansas Landing (now Kansas City) on the first of November and reached the Osage sub-agency reservation eight days later. Many Miamis carried with them handfuls of earth taken from the graves of their loved ones.

signing of the 1837 treaty which removed the Pottawatomi from Indiana; Miami chief Mi-A-Qu-A, 1827

A Quaker-born native of Upstate New York, Benjamin Gue moved to Iowa with a younger brother in 1852. Late in life, over seventeen years, he researched and wrote the illustrated *History of Iowa*, which he published a year before his death in 1904. In his exhaustive chronicle of his adopted state, he wrote:

> When the time came for the departure of the Indians they were sad and sorrowful. They lingered around their old homes reluctant to leave them forever. The women were weeping as they gathered their children and household goods together for the long journey to a strange and distant country. The warriors could hardly suppress their emotion as they looked for the last time upon the beautiful rivers, groves and prairies that they had owned so long and were so reluctant to surrender. As the long line of the retreating red men silently and sorrowfully took its way westward, the booming of guns and the light of a hundred bonfires gave evidence of the advancing hosts of white settlers who hastened in to occupy the vacant places. In the progress of years, these once powerful and warlike tribes became listless and enervated, losing the energetic characteristics which distinguished them in former times. The excitement of war and the chase having long ago died out in their changed environment, they became degenerate, intemperate and lazy.

Gue's fellow immigrants to Iowa, the Jennisons, had played a role in deporting aboriginal peoples occupying land coveted by land-hungry whites. Over several years, Joseph and his brother William had helped build, then operate the Wabash and Erie Canal—so much we know. And, that boats on which the Miami rode stoically into their involuntary exile passed over sections of canal dug by my ancestors. Were Joe or Bill some of the hands driving the mules that pulled those boats on that day in October 1846 to Fort Wayne, where pitiable natives were transferred to the next leg of their final journeys?

It is plausible, but undocumented. But, if so, I find it unshakably sad.

———

With the "Injun threat" extinguished as of the deportation of the last natives and with canal construction in full swing, a quintessentially American-style land grab continued to draw thousands into the new state—which had joined the union on 11 December 1816. Between 1820 and 1840 population of Indiana (cynically, its name means "Land of Indians") doubled, then redoubled. Ten years later, by 1850, the population had increased by another forty-five percent, then between 1850 and the start of the Civil War by another third. With such exponential growth, the possibilities seemed infinite.

For their part, the Jennisons seized the choicest of the opportunities their adopted home and newfound work offered them. Cloe's older family members later told her as a rapt little girl,

> Joseph Bud Jennison liked meeting the many people and learning what the different parts of the country were doing. He liked the horses and mules and became an authority on the care of those belonging to the Canal company. Soon the managers of the canal noticed his care and interest so he was made an overseer with much more salry. It was his job to keep the animals healthy and looking good and to trade, buy and sell for replacement.

Good-paying jobs and steady work lured thousands to central Indiana in search of a job on the Wabash-Eric Canal. Each *arrivée*, however, brought his (or her) own personality and resume along—and their baggage wasn't always pretty. The spewing contents both appalled as well as entertained the reportedly teetotaling Jennisons:

> Much drinking was done by canal workers but Joseph B. didn't use liquor so he was respected. During those years on the Canal he learn[ed] much of life and people and he learned how to get their stories and how to retell their stories. It was hard work walking the tow paths but it was interesting. The two brothers liked the work and it payed better than farming so they sold their farm hoping to buy a better farm later when they could save more money.
>
> Where most of the men were interested in "Fire Water" the Jennisons were interested in earning money to buy better land. The owners of the canal were unmindful of the life of their men and didnot care what they did as long as the work was done. But they soon found out that liquor didnot make progress so when they found they had some men who were not interested in liquor and were capable of leading their men and getting the work done faster and better it was not long before both Joseph Bud and William had been given overseer jobs and much more money.

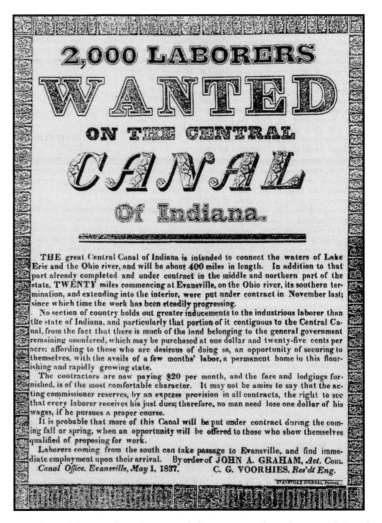

1837 broadsheet calling for 2,000 laborers on Indiana's Central Canal

119

At that time, much money was to be had. During the canal-building rush of the early 1800s, millions of dollars flowed freely. Vast fortunes were made—and, later, lost—overnight, all built more on promise than on productivity, on what could be rather than what was likely or sound. Further east—in New York and Europe—the canal boom had provided a sustainable boon. As its Midwest backers would painfully learn, however, replicating that sensational success only a couple decades later and a thousand miles further west would prove but a short-lived dream.

In the 1810s lacking both steamships and railways, in the United States of America before the opening of the Erie Canal, the growing country could claim no waterways between the eastern seaboard's Atlantic coast and the western interior's Great Lakes that did not require slow, costly portage. Once it opened, however, the Erie Canal provided shipping of goods and passengers much faster, at far less cost.

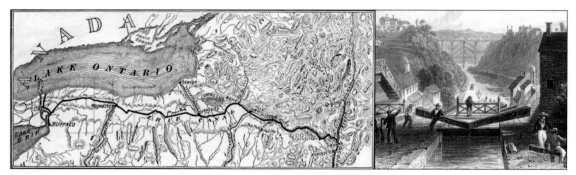

1840 map of the Erie Canal's route and axillary canals; view of locks on the Erie Canal near Lockport, 1839

The Hoosier boosters of the Wabash and Erie Canal hoped to sow a comparable boom in their nascent state as its prototype had in the Empire State twenty years earlier. As the Erie Canal had fanned a population surge in western New York and opened regions farther west for settlement, the men behind the W & E saw only halcyon days ahead for their state—and their own fortunes.

The actual construction of the arteries meant to deliver their dreams, however, would be hard work. According to Cloe,

> The digging of the canal [was] a dangerous job. It was said that the work was so dangerous that a life was lost every six feet of progress. Many workmen had to be brought in to work. They were Irish workmen that had come from Ireland to work on the Chesapeake and Ohio Canal. There seemed to be two factions among the workers dating back to old disputes in Ireland. The canal boss knew about the bitter hatrids and tried to keep the two factions apart. But occasionally some members of the groups met and terrible fights took place. Both groups did plan one battle to take place using picks, shovels, scythe blades, knives, hoes and the few guns they had. The bosses found out the plan and called out the state militia to stop it.

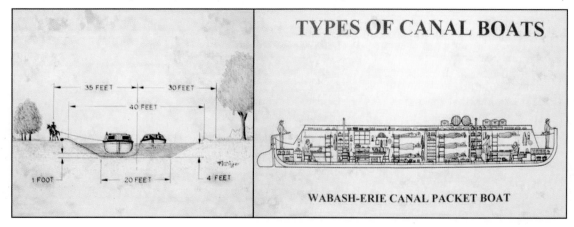

cross-section view of Wabash-Erie Canal bed and towpaths; diagram of interior of "packet" canal boat

Lingering resentments that the workers dragged along with them from previous worksites or, even, the faraway Emerald Isle were only one factor affecting the canal-construction project for which the Jennisons increasingly were responsible. As Cloe testified,

> The work was terrible. Joseph B. and William Jennison had helped to stop the fight so the bosses had confidence in them. Joseph told the bosses that things would not get better until they made things easier and better for the workers. The bosses believed him and asked for his help in knowing what to do. He told them the men had to have better food, shorter hours and better working conditions. Joseph was made the head man and allowed to put into effect the conditions he suggested and immediately life on the canal improved.

The experiences the Jennisons gathered while helping to build Indiana's canals, however, did not involve work alone. Those they had during their freetime also stayed with them a lifetime, and inspired following generations of both excited story tellers as well as eager story listeners.

> The Jennisons had some days off from work so became acquainted with many people in Wabash [which] was a pretty place and made more so, for many Quakers came and they liked to plant trees. Joseph B. and William led an interesting life away from the canal in Wabash. They met many nice people and attended their social functions. They liked Wabash so well that they encouraged their parents, Elias and Sarah, and their brother Charles and sisters Mary, Louisa and Sarah to come and live in Wabash. There was a lot of building going on in Wabash at that time so Elias and Charles had plenty of work.

With the whole immediate Jennison family—elderly Elias and Sarah, with their young-adult offspring—now living in one place, they got to know other pioneer families. According to Cloe,

> The Jennisons met the Spragues and became great friends. It would seem they came from New York not too far from where the Jennisons had once lived. Solomon Sprague, the father, had once been in Canada where he had met his wife Lavina Fargo, a French Canadian. The story was that her family back many years had been Hugunut [sic] in France. The Hugunuts were protestants who had broken away from the Catholic religion and they were very much persecuted in France. Some rich noble man had helped them flee to America. No records were left of them in France and none kept in Canada so the name could not be traced. Solomon Sprague married the beautiful Lavina and returned to New York. For the safety of Lavina's family no contacts were made and as time went on Lavina's family was forgotten. [Some time later] Solomon Sprague took his family to Wabash Indiana hoping to buy better land. There they met the Jennisons [who later held that] Lavina had been a very beautiful woman. Her daughter Alvina was a beautiful girl.

Confluence of the Fox River and the Wabash, *by Karl Bodmer, 1832*

In newly-opened Indiana, newly-arrived settlers truly could thrive—even if on land that only a few years before had been the wilderness home to ageless, tribal peoples. After the arrival of the Americans, both the pristine wilderness and its original inhabitants were gone, forever.

Be the historical facts as they may, the European Americans had come—including the extended Jennison and Sprague families. Having established the whole clan on the banks of the Wabash River, the various members had to work. Ironically, even as the Jennisons settled into the lives they'd just transplanted to Indiana, they already—if inadvertently—began tugging stakes upward yet again, as yet another station on their westward trek across North America sparked their imaginations.

As the Jennisons traveled up and down the canal driving their horses or mule teams and making stops to pick up cargoes of wheat and other grains, hides and furs, wool, salt, sugar, spices, tea, coffee and many other commodities they continually met up with people going west and some returning east for supplies and to get their families. There was much talk of the new land being opened by the government in Iowa. The stories were wonderful, no red blooded young man could resist listening and getting the wander-lust fever. Many times a rider came from Iowa and told of the beautiful land being sold for almost nothing. Land that was far more wonderful than anything they had ever seen.

For the time being, however, for the Jennisons the work in front of them trumped thoughts of the days ahead of them.

The hours on the canal were long and tiring and many times true drudgeory. Walking the Tow-path until the stops were all made and the heavy cargo lifted and loaded. After the loading and the teams were rested there was a chance of hearing the news and some stories of many kinds, singing, cussing and drinking with plenty of food, sometimes the best and sometimes not too good.

According to Cloe, the Jennison brothers' efforts on behalf of the men to improve working conditions yielded results. Even with such advances, however, the work remained grueling.

The life of a driver on the Erie and Wabash Canal was hard work and long hours even though they had been shortened. They not only had to drive the teams but they had to teach them how to work, like a fast pull would not budge the heavy cargo but a slow pull would gradually get it moving. There were certain rules that were recognized on the canal. The teams starting slow would go faster and faster as they got their cargo on the move. Cargo boats always move slower than the passenger boats so it was necessary for the cargo drivers to honor the rights of the passenger boats to move faster and have the right of way. That made ill feelings and many fights. There were no written laws but infered rights. Sometimes the life seemed impossible to law abiding men and their families.

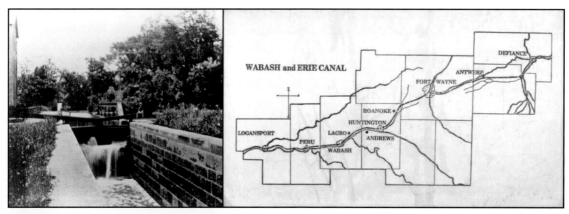

Peninsula Lock at the Cuyahoga River; map of Wabash & Erie Canal, from Defiance to Logansport, Indiana

It took a certain kind of man to both fit the requirements of such a job, then be able to endure it.

If a man did not like mules and horses he could never be a good driver. Joseph B. not only liked the animals but he knew how to keep them in good health but that was not true of all men so he was often sent to tend and doctor the mules and horses on the different runs. Many of the drivers were forced into the life for a way to make a living but their only interest was the wage they collected. Many of the men had been salt water sailors who had come inland hoping to get some of the new cheap land opening up in the west. Too often they had drank up and caroused away their savings by the time they got to the canal and had taken jobs to exist. They were often sullen and cruel with little respect for any one but they did have many interesting stories of their lives at sea and the many countries where they had made port. Many had commited crimes and had been in prisons.

Mississippi Boatman *(1850) and* Jolly Boatmen in Port *(1857), painted by George Caleb Bingham*

Cloe clearly saw her and Lorena's grandfather, Joseph Jennison, in a certain light. Regardless of the degree to which it was truth, she claimed

> Joseph B. Jennison was a quiet, unpretentious man so he listened to their stories as well as the stories of the people he met in the towns where the boats on the canal stopped to leave cargo and gather cargo of every sort as well as the passengers. The life the drivers led was pretty much a man's life so they had to make their own intertainment which was made up of drinking, cursing, singing and telling stories. Because Joseph B. was not interested in their crude living all he could do was listen and thus he became a wonderful story teller as well as a fine singer. He not only knew a host of stories but he had a way of telling them so true to life that any one having heard him tell one always asked for more. Nature had endowed him with a friendly, kind manor as well as the ability to talk but his years as a driver on the canal in Wabash gave him many stories.

Well, at least something somewhat durable would last—for after thousands of men (and beasts) had worked tens of thousands of days on such a massive project, its backers' worst fears unstoppably materialized. The largest construction project undertaken in the Old Northwest till that time, it all just went bust.

As an aging Cloe tersely noted over a century later,

> The Jennisons in Wabash had promised that if the Wabash-Erie Canal closed down because of the railroad going through Wabash that they would go to Lake County to join their parents […] the town being Crown Point. In 1852 the rail road did get to Wabash and the Canal was closed.

Once touted by its advocates and believed by even its detractors to be *the* cutting edge in transportation technology, seemingly overnight, with the arrival of what Native Americans called the Iron Horse, King Canal was all wet.

And, the Jennison brothers suddenly were left without a job.

drawing showing train overtaking riverboat at Baltimore, Indiana, 1870

America would not, after all, become a nation laced with canals, moving millions of people and billions of tons of goods cheaply but slowly, gliding silently along at a mule's pace, leaving behind only (well, mostly) fresh air and compostable "horse apples." No, instead 19th-century America would race up mountains, down river valleys and over the endless prairies at breakneck speeds, behind smoking, belching engines stoked by filthy coal. Entire industries would spring up to service Iron Horses—and whole, pop-up towns would spring up in the wake of its sprint across the country. In the process, the lives—and fates—of millions would be decided by…

————

chapter 34: leaving Old Northwest

Changing technology meant changing lives—it did then, just as it still does today. Thus,

When the railroads came through Wabash there was no use for the canal so the Jennisons and Spragues went back to Crown Point Indiana where the brothers had lived a short time after leaving Ohio to which the family had pioneered from New York when Joseph Bud was a boy of 7 years.

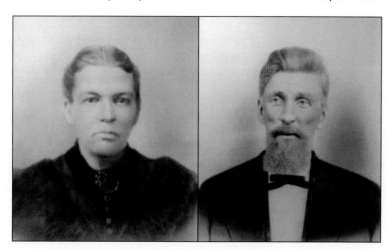

charcoal portraits of Alvina Eliza (Sprague) & Joseph Bud Jennsion as drawn from photos, decades after marrying

Since leaving Upstate New York twenty years earlier, much had changed in the Jennison clan. At almost thirty no longer a boy, Joseph Bud had proven himself to be a self-reliant young man—and, he had married. On 29 March 1851 he had taken as his bride Alvina Eliza Sprague, the seventeen-year-old girl of Yankee and French-Canadian blood mentioned earlier. The couple wasted no time in beginning a family: Already that October they gave birth to Charles Earl, the first of what would be seven sons. Around the same time, Joseph's brother, Charles Platt Jennison, married Alvina's sister, Deborah, and soon thereafter Joseph's sister, Mary, married Alvina's brother, Charley Sprague.

Even as new faces and lives were expanding the circle of the extended Jennison family, some would soon leave it. Elias 3rd was now over sixty-five, his wife, Sarah (Bagley) Jennison, over sixty, making it difficult for Joseph's parents to move yet once more. As for the Spragues, what Cloe later called "a terrible sickness in Wabash at that time" claimed the lives of Alvina's father, Solomon, and those of her and Joseph's second- and third-born, little Harry and baby Elick. The same ruthless plague claimed a sister of Alvina's, as well as a child of another sister, "Debby"—five family members in a matter of days.

With so much dramatic change, the surviving Jennisons and Spragues decided the time had come to leave both the Northeast and Old Northwest forever and, hopefully, also for good. Once the Jennison brothers' jobs on the canal had evaporated, little remained for the quickly growing clan to do but to start their lives over again—likely farming, likely further west, where land was cheaper and more fertile.

> In 1852 the Jennisons and Spragues tried to find work in Crown Point and tried to buy land. The land being so near Chicago had increased in price so much they felt they could no longer afford it. While working on the Canal they had met up with many men coming and going west to get some of the very good farming land they had heard of. Every one seemed to think that Iowa with its fertile land and newly opened territory was the place to go. Especially did they hear of Spirit Lake, Iowa, with its good land, good timber for building and fuel, its good hunting for buffalo, deer, elk and many wild animals as well as good fishing was the very best place to go. Indians were mentioned but they were led to believe that the government had forced the Indians to move west and north so they would not be a problem.

Well, so they thought.

Erroneously assured they'd be safe on the wide-open prairies, the little band set off. As Cloe recounted,

> Great grandfather Elias Jennison came to Iowa in 1856 in oxen drawn covered wagons with his three sons. Mama Sarah Bagley had died on the trail to Iowa some where in Illinois. It had been a great shock to Elias to have to bury Mama Sarah in a lonely grave along the now forgotten trail. Great grandfather Elias did not get over that shock and the bad cold he took during the terrible blizzard of 1856-57 and the Indian scares and Spirit Lake Massacre he did not survive and died in the late summer of 1857 and was burried on the hill north of Franklin Grove where he had often walked to view the country side and see the buffalo and deer grazing in the distance. It was the first funeral on the new Cemetary Hill of Belmond.

Before he died, however, Elias Jennison saw to it that his family had shelter in remote Ioway.

> The first home in Iowa was a log cabin in Franklin Grove in 1856 and 1857. There they lived with the David and Henry Luicks, the Anthony Overackers, the Grays and a Mr. Wilsey.

Having left their homes back in Indiana, in Iowa the Jennisons anxiously awaited roofs of their own. As they would discover, however, building one's own fortress would not assure the place to be impenetrable from outsiders. As the retold almost a century and a quarter later in fuller detail in the *Belmond Independent* on 4 May 1978,

log cabin in Clay County—the Jennisons' original Iowa destination; a 19th century drawing of a crowded cabin

> In summer 1857 the Jenisons and Spragues acquired land and were very busy building cabins. The cabin of Joseph Bud had been completed and the men, with their friends, had gone a short distance to build a cabin for his brother, William, leaving Alvina alone in her new

cabin with her two children. She had a riding horse by her door and there was a choice horse in the corral some distance from the cabin.

Alvina heard a dog barking, so with gun in hand, expecting an Indian, she ran around the cabin to see what was happening. Three men riding horses had taken the horse from the corral. She yelled and shot, but the men rode off. Alvina, with her children in tow, rode to where the men were working. The horse was eventually recovered.

For a family that had been so transient for so much of its North American career the previous three hundred years, when the Jennisons finally sunk deeper roots in North Central Iowa's rich soil, those ties proved to be lasting. Nothing if not a local patriot, Cloe later boasted that

> Most of the children, 12 in all, of Joseph Bud and Alvina Sprague Jennison were born in Iowa, 8 here in the old Jennison Home, 2 miles north of Belmond. All of the children lived their lives in Iowa and are burried on Iowa soil.

Originally, as they set off from Crown Point, the Jennisons intended only to winter in Franklin Grove, then after the snow melt of spring 1857 to push on to a much-touted New Canaan called "Spirit Lake." With the coming of the news that starving, renegade Sioux had massacred some forty settlers and dragged four young women with them into Minnesota, however, they changed their plans.

(standing) Joseph, Oscar, Edgar, and Russell; (sitting) William, Charles and George Jen[n]ison; 3 May 1904

The prairie lay open and ready. When Europeans took "dominion over it" we changed it forever—and ourselves.

Having been kidnapped at age 14 by the attacking Wahpekute Sioux and held captive for three months,
as an adult Abbie (Gardner) Sharp marketed her biography. After marrying and years of living elsewhere,
in 1891 she returned to Spirit Lake, bought the cabin where her family had died, and sold souvenirs, such
as a drawing reproduced on framed rawhide, "The Killing of Mrs. Thatcher." The late-19th-century History
of Iowa *depicted a fictitious* Sioux Indian Scalp Dance, *which represented widespread non-native angst of*
the time rather than historical reality. The corner image is "real" but staged—a stereoscopic view sold by
(per the caption) "Abbie Gardner Sharp in Front [of the] Log Cabin Where Family [was] Murdered in 1857."

Staying in Wright County, after all, meant the Jennisons would need to settle in. And build homes, then farms. And roads. As Cloe retold it,

> In the spring after the waters had gone down from the Blizzard of the winter and the Spirit Lake Massacre, the Joseph Bud Jennison [family] with Grandfather Elias had moved up the river a mile where they had built a cabin on an eighty acres he acquired. Within a few years when a saw mill was built he built a very fine two story home to the east side of his land beside a road which had just been surveyed for the locations of farms and roads. He still could not get water other than the river so he built beside the creek which at that time was large and plenty of water, known as Jennison Creek.

Joseph Bud Jennison must have fared well in North Central Iowa. Other than shaving the second "n" off his surname, most other indications were that his fortunes swelled, not shrank with his final frontier move. The *Biographical and Portrait Album of Hamilton and Wright Counties, Iowa* (1889) entry about him, for one, sung of his celebrated accomplishments. Calling him "one of the well-known pioneers of [Pleasant] township," it said

> He came to the county in 1856, just as the buffalo and elk were leaving, and he has witnessed the wonderful growth and improvement of the county. [...] He was one of the first to settle on this wild prairie and to brave the blizzards and hardships of this county. He has a good house, barn and other farm

buildings, all surrounded by a fine grove. Mr. and Mrs. Jenison are the parents of 10 children [who] all live at home or near Mr. Jenison. In politics he is a Republican.

It was only by having ventured onto Cloe's creaking porch and risking death by shotgun blast that I learned that my father's grandmother's father was the son of one Joseph Bud and Alvina Sprague Jenison. The same busted-binding copy of the *Portrait Album* that glowed with the heralded biography of Joseph Bud also featured his son, William Edward Jenison, my great-great paternal grandfather,

born in Lake County, Indiana, March 27, 1854 [who was] two years old when his father removed to this county. Here he grew to manhood on his father's farm and received his education in the public schools near his home. He was married February 21, 1878, to Miss Romanda Church, a daughter of Orick and Nancy (House) Church, who located in Hancock County, Iowa in 1854. Mrs. Jenison died [1 April 1881, one week after giving birth to Mable, who did not survive.] On the 8th of October 1884, Mr. Jenison was married to his present wife, Miss Anna Shupe, a step-daughter of [Civil War veteran] James Brooks. Mr. and Mrs. Jenison have two children: Ethel Lorena and Myrtle May [both of whom later married Luick brothers, respectively George and Curtis; William and "Annie" eventually had a total of ten children]. Mr. Jenison moved onto his present farm in 1875; it was at that time wild land and contained 160 acres. He has a good house and barn, a fine grove and everything about the place shows the thrift and prosperity of the owner. He is engaged in general farming and stock-raising. He is a member of the I.O.O.F. No. 265 of Belmond. Politically he is a Republican and has served on the school board.

As a group, the longer the extended family lived in Wright County, the more it let its presence be felt in the local community. According to the *History of Belmond, Iowa 1856 - 2006*,

Many of the Jenison descendants were farmers and school teachers in the Belmond area [including, for some years, Cloe Jenison.] Joseph and Alvina Jenison were among the organizers of what is now known as the United Methodist Church.

By this point in telling her version of our family's (hi-)story, Cloe had reached events that she herself had, in part, either personally experienced or as a young person directly felt their repercussions. And so, my periodic posing of questions about her ever-more-intimate narrative led her to shift in her seat on the sagging sofa and swallow swelling knots down her dry throat.

"The rest here" she motioned towards the pile of paper of my lap with a flap of the back of her hand against the house's stale air, "they don't have to do with your Luicks or Rena, ya know."

Edith Sandberg, Thelma Carpenter, Hazel Sandberg, Fannie Christie, Dorothy Hubbard, Maude Griggs, Anna Rust, Iva Christie & Leora Allabin

"Oh, but it's all so interesting" I stalled, trying to delay the forced conclusion of my audience with crazed cousin Cloe that I could smell brewing around the dusty edges of the dank room.

Ignoring increasingly uneasy Cloe as best I could, I read on.

As the years went on and marriages and deaths took place, most of the families remained near each other. In the early days the families seemed to get along fairly well. If one family had sickness or death or family troubles or financial needs they shared but as the years went on some families moved away and got more independent. As the children grew up there was quarreling and bitter rows took place.

Even after they left and moved to Buffalo Center some of Charley Spragues family considered Belmond home. Nellie had taught school [pictured above] near Belmond and married George Bryant. She died soon after her marriage and George Bryant married Nettie Sprague, Nellie's sister. Now they are all buried in the Belmond Cemetary. To the east and south of my parents family lot. All the others of that family are buried near Buffalo Center.

two of Belmond-area's countless "Jennison boys"

"Say" Cloe protested as she swatted with a jabbing finger at the onion-paper scroll in my eager hands, "you've been here an awful long time. Your parents are gonna—"

"Oh" I fibbed, "they know I'll be back late. And besides, we're almost done."

"Look here, that there don't pertain to you" Cloe barked as I held her text out of her reach and learned that

William and Harriet Jenison had at least seven children. 4 boys and 3 girls. James a little boy died very young. The 3 little girls died young of dyptheria with in a few days of each other. It so affected their mother that she took to doing strange things like putting food through a trap door in the floor to the cellar where she expected the little girls to come back for food and she kept a light in the window at all times to let the girls know she was looking for them. Soon people began to say she was crazy and that they saw ghosts walking in the house at night. Harriet died of grief and William tried to raise his three boys. The boys spent much of their time with Joseph Bud's boys across the road. Grandma, Alvina, was always especially good to them and when their father, William died they moved in

with Grandma Alvina and Joseph Bud. Grandma didn't have an easy time with those boys and so many of her own. When grandpa, Joseph Bud died in 1891, Grandma's 3 girls were married but she still had 3 unmarried sons at home. Grandma really had a tuff time with all those boys.

Just then the splintery end of Cloe's cane came crashing down upon the brittle, bent sheets I was gripping so hard that they hung tautly between my stiff, curled fists.

"Ya think you can jus' camp out here overnight an' read about other folks' lives 'til the sun comes up? I got work ta do an'…"

Deciding to take her hint rather than a hit of shot in my butt, I packed up to leave, fast. Chary Cloe, though, wouldn't let me remove a single Jenison-family photo or portrait—of which she had myriad—from her jam-packed

an unidentified Iowa Jen[n]ison family

house. When Cloe rejected my offer to pay the studio of her choice to professionally copy them in Belmond, with her present during the job, I fetched my cheap Kodak from the car. Although it took poor pictures, I hastily made snapshots of yellowed charcoal portraits of her and Lorena's grandparents, Joseph Bud and Alvina Sprague Jennison.

As I left her at the end of what had been a bizarre but productive day, though, she did wave in my face the beat-up postcard we'd long sparred over to identify.

"Oh" startled Mike Luick asked, "do you mean to give this to *me*?"

"I have no use for those people" Cloe stated blankly as she turned back into her cluttered abode, then slammed the back door behind her with a resounding *BANG!*

I got into my folks' waiting land yacht and sped down the gravel road towards home. My knees trembling and my heart still racing, I let out a *Yippee!* as I now had not only new, earlier images of my father's most immediate Luick forebears, but also previously-unknown faces to put onto Jenison ancestors I didn't even know I had. Before risking having my chest blown open by some hoary, shotgun-toting recluse, I'd seen photographs of all of the other ancestors I've written about up to now, but neither had seen the faces nor knew the names of Lorena's parents or those who had preceded them.

For me, until that exciting, almost deadly day, the Jen[n]isons had been a complete Unknown. Ever since Great-Grampa George had left her at Mabb's Grocery & Mercantile on Thornton's Main Street, waiting literally for nothing, my father's family had effectively erased the woman who Gramma Charlotte habitually called "Ol' Sourpuss" out of our collective memory. By the time I came on the scene, it was if Lorena Jenison Luick had never existed. The only picture I'd ever seen of ill-fated Rena

was as an old woman, sitting on a blanket-draped Fifties sofa, pausing mid-sentence while talking to some off-camera soul, sharing a sweltering summer day with my short-sleeved "Gramma Luick" as Charlotte coaxed my brother, David, to nurse an unwanted baby bottle.

That her only son, Donald, and his only son, my father Bud, had immediately and without qualification sided with high-tailing George said everything about how all three men operated. But now, having collided with her cracked cousin Cloe, I began to get to know a great-grandmother about whom the men in my family made sure I'd know nothing about as a person. More than that, I now had an entire ancestral lineage that would lure my eager, adolescent imagination back eighteen generations to one "Thomas Jennison" living in the North of England in the 1500s.

Charlotte (Juhl) Luick holding David, with Lorena (Jenison) Luick, 1959

———

Appearances really *can* be deceiving. Initial glances might suggest that my Iowa farm-wife mother is, well, cut from homespun cloth, but, boy, can the woman ever drop sagacious one-line sayings—like "Life is what you get while you're planning something else." Certainly, in my case, after traversing Europe from Rome to Inverness for a month between my junior and senior years of high school, in summer 1980, my soul burned with the call of the faraway and exotic. So, I longed to be an exchange student—but outside of already-tasted Europe. As I didn't speak a word of lovely French, sexy Italian or romantic Spanish, and couldn't speak even half a sentence of intelligible German, the only possible countries that came into question were English-speaking ones. Dismissing Australia as "California with kangaroos" and New Zealand as "Canada with kiwis," I ached to spend a year in South Africa—then-reigning brutal Apartheid or no. I applied to a couple exchange programs and weathered several rounds of interviews—only in the end to be told by the Iowa division of Rotary International "*so* sorry, but there are *no* slots left open in South Africa. If you're willing, however, to consider living a year in Britain, we've just received an urgent, last-minute request for an exchange with North Yorkshire…"

1980s postcard of the Yorkshire Dales around Skipton, England

Once I got settled in Skipton, I had only two modest goals: experiencing as much as possible, while getting to know as many people as possible. As my heart would have it, as far as I could steer the plethora of experiences and people Life kept flinging my way during that exceptionally rich year, the most deeply-impressing manifestations of both goals were connected to either digging deeper into Quakerism or digging up my family's roots. Motifs and insights arising from both would change how I saw the world and myself in it, forever.

some of the author's 6A classmates at Ermysted's Grammar School; Michael Luick in Leningrad, 1982

Yes, during school breaks at Ermysted's I traveled to the Soviet Union (stupidly, in winter!), to Southern Germany and Northern Italy (humanely, in springtime) and both Irelands (wisely, in summer). And, true, I rarely spent a full weekend at the home of my patient hosts, the Gullys. When I wasn't in the classroom I constantly found myself in buses and trains, on canal boats and bicycles, up hill and down Dale, over the rivers and through the woods, in cities and around villages across Britain—above all, as the guest of Quakers whom I had encountered and at some point visited. However, time with "family"—regardless how distant—proved most memorable.

In her younger years, when she perhaps still possessed a shade of sanity, Cloe Jenison had not only contacted Jennisons in Britain but called on some of them. When I got to England myself, a couple decades later, I recalled her mentioning a "Roger Jennison in Canterbury"—so, naturally, one of the first things this Iowa farmboy did after unpacking my many bags was shoot a letter off to:

PROFESSOR ROGER JENNISON
c/o some department at
the University of Kent
Canterbury, England

The postal gods must have smiled, as my absurdly addressed inquiry not only somehow reached the many-lettered, much-awarded head of the Department of Electronics there, but resulted in the busy man actually writing back to some hayseed from Iowa pausing in the Pennines at the beginning of adulthood. And, he invited me to join his family "at Wildwood, our home in the Kent countryside, during the coming Yuletide holiday of nineteen-hundred and eighty-one." Until the moment that I received Roger's receptive reply and read his invitation, the world had never seen a more euphoric hayseed!

I'm not sure now what I expected, but the amiable, polished man who met me at the Canterbury train station stood in stark contrast to Will Jenison, Grampa Donald's cocky, cigar-chomping grandfather pictured on the tattered postcard that Cloe only too happily threw my way as I fled to the safety of my parents' well-padded Pontiac. While to my Midwestern ears the Roger Clifton Jennison family spoke with rather stiff "O-o-oh, yes-s-s, in-n-nde-e-ed" upper lips, its patriarch came from Grimsby, a thoroughly unpretentious, mid-sized coastal town near the mouth of the Humber. Already a North Country wannabe given the geography of my adopted home for the year, I felt even more connected to Roger when we discovered that the previous week, on the 18th of December, we'd both celebrated recent birthdays—his 59th and my 19th. As his little car jiggled and jumped its way through the narrow streets of Medieval Canterbury, he explained that he had

hayseed Michael Luick in Wharfdale, winter 1981-82

served the Royal Air Force during The War "developing magnetron-enhanced radar and microwave systems. After the defeat of Mr. Hitler," Roger recounted as we neared Wildwood, he researched "visibility phases in interferometers—that stage when delay errors called 'closure phase' are present—as well as optical or infrared wavelengths, but of course, necessarily, also relativity, self-calibration and radio interferometry…" The scientific minutiae that I mistook for Greek quickly left this boy from the prairies dazed. When Roger took pity and explained in lay terms that he'd also studied ball lightening and water diving, I felt truly inspired. When he then mentioned that for his advanced academic work he had been named an Officer of the Order of the British Empire, I felt duly impressed.

The intellectually accomplished Jennisons also proved to be flawless, sociable hosts. Their second-oldest son, blond and wiry Tim, was about my age and enjoyed showing me his alma mater, King's School. Originally an appendage of the cathedral in 597, it is the second-oldest extant school in the world. Having been evacuated to Cornwall during the Battle of Britain, it returned to the "Garden of England" after The War and, after receiving a new Royal Charter, in Tim's era admitted girls for first time in its almost millennia-and-a-half existence. On the same tour, Tim also showed me Canterbury Cathedral. With its cream-white edifice dating to 1070, it is one of England's oldest Christian structures. He spoke proudly of the cathedral's boys choir—"but having been founded *only* recently, in 1483..."

Tim Jennison showing off Canterbury Cathedral, late December 1981

After we saw the ancient pilgrimage site of the shrine to murdered archbishop Thomas Becket, "cousin" Tim took his bumpkin charge to see the rest of Kent, too, with its White Cliffs near Dover and rustic, kiln-based hop-drying oast houses, its endless orchards and busy harbors. The whole time, I had the pleasant yet disorienting sense of watching myself romp about in some Kodachrome film from decades long past, about some sappy, smiling adventure where country boy lives out unlikely dreams.

While Tim and I explored Canterbury and Kent by day, at night we either enjoyed intra-family festivities or were present as his parents entertained an array of guests, some of whom came from the local arts scene in which Roger moved widely and with confidence, given that his father, George Robert Jennison, had been an accomplished portrait painter back in Grimsby. Roger had brought his artistic sensibilities with him when he came to Kent from Manchester University in the turbulent Sixties as its first professor of Physical Electronics. In his adopted home, he co-founded the Canterbury Society of Art and, as a Fellow of the Royal Society of Arts, pipe-smoking Roger promoted the Canterbury Arts Council.

Besides those with local artistic and academic circles, Roger and his wife also cultivated contact with scientists and other great minds from around the world: the Soviet Union and the United States, Japan, Oceania and much of Europe west of the Iron Curtain. As my visit took place between Boxing Day and New

Roger and Tim Jennison, two sitting on the far right, December 1981

Year's Eve, it seemed a constant mill of intriguing guests kept Wildwood lively. I'd sit at the Jennisons' crowded table and listen to the loud, laughter-laced talk as long as I could, but then excuse myself, offering some lame excuse like a mild headache or some other purported, bogus malady, then retire to the guest room, lock the door and retreat from all activity downstairs.

Don't get me wrong: I found meeting and even briefly staying with English cousins truly grand, but at times I also found it to be more input than late-teen me could integrate. For starters, I felt like a poser. My father's people had done well to finish high school; here I was, hobnobbing with some of Britain's best-educated brains. Then, as much as I cherished sweet Tim, listening to him hold forth about his beloved 1,500-year-old This or his tolerated "only" 1,000-year-old That made me feel self-conscious, as if my family's having been (at that point) in North America for "only" 350 years and in Iowa for "only" a century-and-a-half constituted cultural pauperism. Feeling naked and fraudulent, I found it easier to withdraw to a darkened guest chamber than sit in a buzzing dining hall with Big Wigs and, in the scrutinizing light cast by their brilliance, betray my own, pathetic lacking. Twas easier to self-isolate upstairs than self-immolate down.

———

chapter 36: relief comes haltingly

Alone, miserable and helpless, I hid in the semi-blackness of a frigid night in quaint but alien Kent and... *suffered*. Lying there, I considered my options: In 1981 civilians in the Free World had neither cell phones nor internet—and most of us didn't even know that we didn't know what we didn't have! On my exchange-pupil budget, calling "my people" back on the prairie via trans-Atlantic telephone cable for something other than hospitalization or a military evacuation was inconceivable. Very-verbal Sheila Brunkhorst, my Rotary-exchange pal from Waverly, Iowa, placed in Derbyshire for the year, was spending the holidays at some undisclosed location. My closest Quaker friends, the Harlands back in Wharfdale, were visiting Elma's relatives in her native Scotland... and the Gulleys were in Surrey, visiting "Gram" and cousins... so *who* to call, and *where* to turn for spiritual relief?

"I'M SLOW-LY DY-IN' HERE!" I screamed silently inside my pounding head, to no one but my shocked self.

At the moment that I hit emotional bottom, I swear I heard raving-mad Cloe back in Belmond scream

Mike Luick, lost in space... um, make that "England," 1981

"No, *you* can't do it, kid! You're just a little Luick outta his lousy league! You sweet-talked your way into Wildwood, but you shoulda stayed back at Ashlawn..."

"That must have been a bit too much spiked Advocat *that I nipped down there"* I told myself, physically checking to see if I was really all right or not.

Then, just as I resumed my mental inventory of possible sources of psychological care, I saw in my mind the assemblage of Luicks and Jenisons strung across that postcard Cloe basically had thrown away as I scurried off the old Meacham place. It was at that point, as I pondered what inner repertoires my ancestors tapped as antidotes to despair, that I heard a faint older woman's voice ask "Well, what did you expect to find here?"

"Sorry," I called, looking around the Jennisons' guest room, "who's there? Tim—is that you?"

That voice came again, this time teasing "Did you really think the answers would be lying around like in some sacred book, open an' ready to read?"

"Who *is* that?" I shouted. "Tim, if this is a joke—"

"No, it's dead serious."

"Look, *who's* here?" I demanded.

"Me" the soft but clear voice replied.

"Who's 'me'—if you don't mind sayin'!"

"Me—your father's great-grandmother, Anna Eliza Shupe Jenison."

"Wait a minute" I reflexively questioned my unseen guest, "I thought you were a 'Brooks' when you married ol' Bill Jenison."

"You've been reading incomplete notes again!" The Voice sighed, then quickly fired off "So, it's like this: My father was a 'Shupe' but died from Civil War wounds later, back in Crown Point, in Indiana, two months before I was born, but then Ma—Elwy Thomas, a Welsh lass—married a 'Brooks' an' we moved with him out to Ioway, so..."

"Okay, okay—I remember that from my condensed family-history lesson with Cloe—"

"Who's 'Cloe'?" Annie wondered.

Curtis (on planks), Myrle, Myrtle (Jenison), Annie (Shupe) Jenison, Mattie, 4 unidentified women, Marion & Henry Luick; on the ground Esther Forristall, Louis, Gladys Forristall & Mary (Hunt) Luick; 1910s

"—but could we talk 'bout that some other time, please?" My throat grew tight. "Can't you see?" I pleaded. "I'm not doin' so hot here right now!"

"Then why'd you call me?" The Voice asked impatiently.

"'Call you?' I didn't call you."

"You must have—'cause I'm here with you right now, aren' I?"

I thought a moment as I peered around the darkened room, trying to pinpoint from where, exactly, the disembodied voice I heard was coming. "Well, okay" I granted, "I did kind of ask for some help."

"So, like I said, 'Why'd you call me?'"

"You see, I'm in England right now—and the people here aren't like the folks back home."

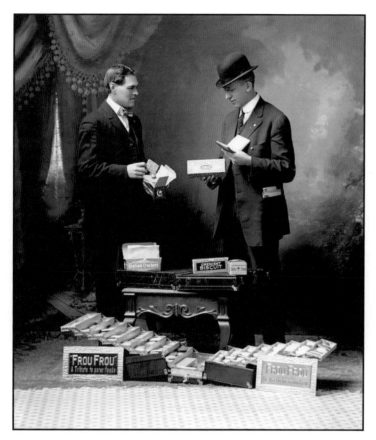

Martin Thoe's "Selling Crackers" studio shot in Belmond, mid-1910s

"Do you want them to be?"

"No, not exactly, but—"

"Then what's the problem?" my distant ancestor wanted to know, clearly piqued.

"—it's all a little bit more than I can handle."

"It seems like it's a little bit *more* than 'a little bit more' than you can cope with, dear Great-Great-Grandson o' mine!"

I rolled over and faced the wall, feeling rejected and pouty. "Hey, I'm *only* a teenager, after all!"

"When I was your age, I already had my hands full with a of mess o' kids to raise, a house to keep and a barn full o' cows to milk by hand. Then, there were the chickens to feed, eggs to gather, a garden to hoe and an orchard to..."

"I get it" I cut her off forcefully, "I get it already!"

"You do?"

"Ya, I think I really do—but at least you were almost an adult already when you had to cope with everyday life."

"Look here, young man: I was *fifteen* when I married William Edward Jenison!"

"Gosh" I back-peddled, "that *was* a bit much—a bit young and a bit soon, I guess."

"Did I have a choice?" ethereal Annie wondered. "Did *any* of us?"

Not knowing how to speak to that, I simply reminded my still-invisible visitor "Don't forget—at thirty-one your groom was more than twice your age at the time."

"Details, all just details!" Annie sighed, then softened her tone. "Times were hard; we *had* to eat. The men had the money and the say—*and* the land Remember: Women couldn't own land, other

later William Luick farm, Wright County, Iowa; circa 1910

than through our husbands or fathers. Land meant food; food meant life. Were there any means for us to make our way in the world, other than through massaging our menfolk and having too many children?"

"How many'd you have?"

"Eleven! An' I'm tellin' ya, a few fewer woulda been more than enough!"

"Sure, that makes sense" I conceded, "you sortta had your hands full in that world, jus' survivin'."

"You youngins have it *so* good these days, but you don't see it. You have dry, warm cabins and fancy buggies, fuss-less clothes, shifted flour in paper bags and all the toys you could ever wish."

"But, do you think we're really happy?" I turned my head and challenged the shadowy, empty room over my shoulder.

"Were we?" Annie snapped back.

I shrugged, even if I didn't know if anyone could see me do so or not.

"Ya" Annie added, "that's the ever-lasting question: What is it in a man—"

"Or a woman" I interjected.

"—that is hungry and sad, even when the stomach's full an' cozy?"

"I'm still just a kid: How can I know the answers to all this?"

"Isn't that why you're here?"

"What" I protested, although growing increasingly fatigued, "do you mean with"—I yawned—"that?"

"Why are you here?"

"In Canterbury?"

"No, you sassy boy: *anywhere!*"

Then, as my own body started to shut down for the night (or had it already?), Annie's speech began to slow, even to slur slightly. "What is this all about?" She

Kensington Ladies Club, circa 1910; Myrtle (Jenison) Luick 7th woman on ground, from right; Annie (Shupe) Jenison 3rd woman on porch, from left

continued, "What answers... are you chasing?" My head began to bob as she blathered on. "Why do you think... we who have lived before you... know any better... than you... how to... live... or... how to... find... hap... pi... ness?"

"Oh, that-t-t" I purred as my eyes drooped shut. "Ask me-e-e" I invited Annie amidst a deep yawn, "tomo-o-orro-o-ow..."

———

chapter 37: into the world

While I met a plethora of intriguing people on my travels around Britain, at times I found quiet, idyllic Skipton too conservative to be inspiring. So, sometimes Jenny and I left Craven purposely to encounter a few other interesting folks. One morning at breakie, quite unexpectedly, she sat across from me and, beaming, asked rhetorically if we should "go on two North-Country outings that might appeal to [me]?" Before I could parrot the answer she already knew, Jenny cryptically instructed me to be ready to go for a drive after school "to meet someone you surely know *of*, but do not yet know." When she met me at the bottom of Ermysted's lawn that afternoon, I had no idea where we were headed. Only as we arrived in Thirsk, a small market town in the heart of North Yorkshire, did she, the widow of a locally esteemed veterinarian who had been known across Yorkshire for his animal-surgical skills, announce that she'd "contacted Mike's old acquaintance, James Alfred—known among friends therefore as 'Alf'—Wight, and asked for a private audience."

"That's nice, Jenny" I absently replied, staring out the smudged car window at Thirsk's tall market-square clock tower, which the Michelin guide to North England that Jenny always kept in her run-down Volvo noted was "built in 1896 to commemorate the marriage of Queen Elizabeth's grandparents, the Duke of York, later King George V, to Princess May of Teck, the future Queen Mary." Stranded briefly in the seductive swirl of history, I then jolted awake enough to ask "So, who's 'Alf Wight,' Jenny?"

Playing her hand with coy relish, my host mother teased "Ever heard of 'James Herriot,' perhaps?"

"*Have* I?" I shouted. "Mom's one of his biggest fans! She's seen all the episodes of his series that Iowa Public TV's ever shown!"

"I thought you might have run across him somewhere" Jenny baited further, then added as she feigned looking for a turning place, "but if you already know all about—"

"Don't you *dare* turn this car around!" I sputtered. "If Mom knew I'd gotten this close to the man who wrote *All Creatures Great and Small* but didn't…"

Thirsk's Victorian clock tower, dedicated 1896

As Jenny pulled up in front of the famous author's unassuming veterinarian practice, my musings stopped short and I marveled at my good fortune. The shock disabled me briefly, rendering me a stunned, numb idiot.

"Well, shall we go in" Jenny blustered, "or just sit here and watch little grannies toddle by with big baskets, enroute to market?"

Jenny had had the foresight to sneak along in her bag that day the copy of *James Herriot's Yorkshire*, the photo book Phyllis had presented me when Sheila Brunkhorst and I were about to fly off from the Minneapolis-Saint Paul airport for London the previous August. As the world-reknowned author signed aspiring "Johnboy's" copy of his best-selling book, I wondered if I might not truly be the luckiest Iowa farmboy in the world that day—as I suspected I was.

James Alfred "Herriot" Wight being interrogated by Michael Luick, 1982

———

The second outing Jenny promised wasn't to see a person, per se, but rather to see a place connected to a *set* of people—to some of "my" people, about whom she had heard likely too much, too many times. What neither she nor I imagined before we set off for Walworth Castle, however, was that I'd have an encounter of the most surreal kind there, at that centuries-old hereditary seat of the Jennison family.

Before we packed our bags and Bramble, their black-and-white Border Collie, into the horse-loving Gullys' hay-strewn, old crimson-red Volvo and set off for a weekend of snooping around Walworth Castle, I scoured the Skipton library. I went to bone up on "a little history" about "my" family's home before combing the place for clues to why the Jennisons went to North America 350 years earlier. What I learned about the place—and the people who called it home—wasn't a trifle:

Walworth Castle seen from gardens, from a mid-20th–century postcard

Walworth Castle is a 16th-century Tudor mansion house near Darlington, built in the style of a medieval castle. Completed around 1600 for Thomas Jennison, Auditor General of Ireland, it stands on the site of a castle built as of 1150, title to which fell to the House of Neville after the 1349 Black Death, but was claimed by Robert Hansard in 1391. The estate passed through the hands of several families before the Jennisons' in 1579. King James VI of Scotland is said to have rested here on 14 May 1603 while travelling to his coronation as king of England, and that he knighted his hostess's son–in–law in return for bountiful entertainment at the castle. In 1605 Elizabeth Jennison died, so son William Jennison inherited the castle. It became dilapidated as of 1610, while he was imprisoned for being Roman Catholic. In 1679 Francis Jennison sold the estate's land and fled to Europe due to accusations of involvement in the Popish Plot to assassinate Charles II; he was arrested and thrown into Newgate Prison. The castle was searched for arms in 1689 on suspicion of rebellion against the Protestant royals, William and Mary. Ralph Jennison inherited the castle at the age of 10 years in 1704. He later renovated the castle at great expense, and died in debt, so that the castle was sold. In World War II it was a prisoner-of-war camp for 200 German and Italian officers. In 1950 Durham County Council bought the castle and it became a girls' boarding school. The building is used as a polling station during elections.

When Jenny and I arrived at Walworth Castle, its new owners had opened it as a hotel only a short time before. John and Jennifer Wayne said we were "among the first guests, so we bid you a hearty welcome! Please do note, however, that a few things are not quite set yet—like a fully functioning kitchen, for one—but we'll surely do everything we possibly can to make your stay a pleasant one... even if we will have to improvise a bit on having breakfast ready in the morning."

"You mean 'on-time,' do you?" I asked so loudly that Jenny cringed—as she often did when in public with me.

"No—at all" the castle's mistress quietly confessed, slightly biting the corner of her lower lip.

"Oh, fine—that'll be *lovely*" Jenny gushed with full propriety, then bolted onward with "but did you happen to see on tellie that *smashing* hat that the Queen was wearing this morning?"

"Oh, *yes*," Jennifer resounded empathetically, with the same very-British, talking-zombies-on-speed tone and gestures, "twas *lovely*, twasn't it!"

"Indeed, and those ado-o-orable little Corgis!" Standing straight, snapping her usually slightly hunched shoulders back and brushing her Maria-in-the-abbey bangs to the side, Jenny's high-pitched voice fluttered "Oh, my—and have you heard the la-a-atest?"

"Oh, *no-o-o*" Jennifer couldn't wait but likely also couldn't care to know, "but *do-o-o* tell, Love. Please, *do* tell!

"*Well-l-l*" Jenny began as the two very-English ladies strolled off, arm-in-arm, still talking *very* much about *very* little, with *very* many hand gestures flying through the *very* historical air.

Despite the handful of passing glitches at the newly-opened hotel-in-a-castle, I wandered off to enjoy a solo tour of the centuries-old site, both of the house and its grounds. The house fascinated me, with its limestone walls, squatty old towers and gun loops outside, and its 18th–century Palladian plasterwork, Rococo detailing and grand staircase inside. The parkland south of Walworth Castle was originally "enclosed" land belonging to the then-feudal manor, and north of the castle 19th-century brick-and-squared-stone garden walls, dressed-stone gate piers with pyramid–shaped tops and an elongated greenhouse completed the grounds. Makeshift huts to the east of the castle remained from the time of the World War II prisoner-of-war camp.

As I returned to the mansion from strolling round the extensive grounds, co-proprietor John Wayne appeared with an algae-green bottle of red wine and a crystal glass, tottering on a silver tray. "I say, ol' chap" he apologized, "*so* sorry for the cock-up with the kitchen—but please *do* accept this complimentary bottle of burgundy with our regret for the mess, will you? Such things..."

"Oh, thank you, John" I began to explain, "but—"

"Oh, no! We *insist*!"

"That's very kind of you, but, you see" I smiled, trying to tell him "I was raised—"

"Yes, of course! You were 'raised a proper young gentleman' so of course you'd like enough to offer your friend a glass or two, too—so" he grinned, reaching to a ready wine cart waiting behind him, "take *two* bottles! You and your lady friend will have enough to—"

"John, that's very sweet of you, indeed, but Metho—"

"Ol' chap, it's *no* problem. If two don't suffice" he offered, turning around to disappear behind a frameless servants'-passage door hidden in the wall behind him, "then simply pull the cord over there and summon us: We'll happily bring you two a third if two don't keep you both busy."

Before I could explain to kindly John that I had grown up in a tee-totaling Methodist household in the American Heartland, he had left… me… with two… bottles of the finest… Burgundy in County Durham. I stared at them a moment, then looked into the hallway in hopes that Jenny might be coming down the main stairs. Seeing no one, I assumed she'd resurface soon, so took the tray through the open door to the terrace and sat down to pour my first full glass of alcohol I'd ever consumed. *"If not now, when?"* I reasoned, for I knew that to live in Europe meant, at some point, facing the social obligation to at least toast, if not drink with others.

At first, the flavor of the tangy red fluid took me aback, but after a minute or two I decided it tasted

statue of John Wesley in Melbourne, Australia

"good enough, and did no real harm" so took another sip, then another—all the time expecting Jenny to appear and hold me to respectable restraint. When she still did not come back, however, I drank a bit more anyhow—then a bit more after that—until the bottle was almost empty! *"Well, there's still one left to open when Jenny comes"* I rationalized. What I did not consider, though, was that I had not eaten since that miserable lunch of baked beans and flakey fish sticks I'd somehow gotten down—"again"—at Ermysted's cafeteria. It also failed to occur to me, novice drinker that I was, that as I sat on the terrace a seldom occurrence was taking place: A bit of sunshine happened to be shining down upon the North of England at that very moment; even a weak beam o' sun-born warmth might make all the difference…

Walworth Castle's terrace from the south park

As it was, sitting there alone on Walworth Castle's quiet terrace, looking out over its south park, I felt truly *GREAT!* And, light-headed—as well as slightly dizzy. Sitting there, reveling in the rare sunshine, I honestly could not think of a single care or woe currently plaguing me or the planet. So, I simply sat—and sat some more—and savored the azure sky overhead—an' the sweet lil' birdies in it. Then, panning my swirling head slowly from left to right, I celebrated the deep-green grass—and smiled at the playful bunnies frolicking on the lawn just at that moment—and at the man who I then found standing right in front of me as I swiveled my head back, straight to center.

"Oh, pardon me!" I giggled. "Where'd *you* come from?"

No answer.

As I waited for a reply I looked the 30-something man over, from his long wavy locks that spilled over a stiffly-starched white-laced ruff collar to his shoulders, down to the floppy leather boots that reached mid-calf—and realized that he was wearing the clothes of an English man of means from, say, about 1630. If I had any doubt, the silver sword hanging from his hip tipped me off.

"Are you looking for the Waynes?" I innocently asked the man dressed all in black save for the white blouse that flowed out of slits in the chest and sleeves of his short-waisted doublet. When he still didn't respond, I pressed "Are you here for a banquet or a reenactment or sompthin'?" I then duly informed the speechless man "I think John just headed back into the house to—"

When I saw that the man hardly moved and reacted not at all to my Midwestern friendliness, my smile quickly faded and I stopped mid-sentence. "Sorry" I proceeded to defensively ask the dark-haired man not even a meter away, directly in front of me, "but was there sompthin' you wanted from *me*?"

To my surprise, the baffling bloke finally moved and, ever so slightly, nodded to the affirmative.

In rather rattled response I turned for the second bottle of burgundy and asked "Care to join me?" before commenting to myself *"Jenny's probably off anyway with Jennifer, still marveling over the Queen's pudgy Porgies!"*

The man's unbroken staring at me was making me feel exceptionally uncomfortable. As I began to pour him a glass I asked "So, do we know each other?" Again, the wordless man only nodded

A likeness of the man I saw in front of me...

'yes.' "We *do*? I'm sorry" I countered, "but I can't recall having ever met you"—at which moment the man finally moved his lips weakly, for a few seconds. Not a sound came out, but he did slowly lift his hand, point at me and jab it in the air in my direction a couple times.

"Look" I protested, "I'm quite sure that if we'd met I would—" to which the man nodded his head more animatedly and quickened his jabbing the air between us. I challenged him "If you're so sure you know me, then tell me where I'm from." Confident that the strange, silly man was a total nutcase, I sat back in the metal garden chair and smugly watched as he scratched the letters "I – O – W – A" in the terrace's beige, small-grain gravel.

Confounded, I looked to him and demanded "Jenny sent you, didn't she?" Casting a quick glance around the terrace, I grilled "Is she hiding behind one of those bushes? Is there a camera: Will we be on tellie later?" Seeing no one besides the weird mute and me, I goaded "Come on, *say* something! Be honest: She prepped you on what to do, didn't she!" I stood up, slapping my thigh with a flat, open hand and exclaimed "That devil! I'll get her! JENNY" I called across the lawn, "you can come out now! I'm on to you! *Very* funny, Jenny—but now you've had your—"

At that moment the man shoved me backwards (or did I just fall?), sending me into the chair with a PLOP!, then wagged his finger in my face like a metronome, with an expression like a schoolmarm scolding an errant pupil. I looked at him, wide-eyed, and wondered what in the world he was up to.

Poking his own chest with a stiff index finger, he shrugged, with his eyes clearly eliciting me to do something. "You want me" I guessed in starts and stops, "you want me to"—the man nodded 'yes' as his expression lightened—"to guess who you are?" At that, my unexpected visitor almost jumped with excitement and his reactions quickened.

"Oka-a-ay" I stalled as I pondered a plausible guess. "You are a history teacher on your way to a lecture about period clothing?"—at which the man's expression changed to disbelief and he shook his

head impatiently, as if I were the biggest idiot he'd seen that day. Shrugging, he lifted his forearms into the air and motioned to the house and grounds around us with a sweeping gesture. "Oh, you belong to Walworth Castle?" I ventured an answer that earned an immediate and enthusiastic 'yes' nod. Beginning to think that the man might mean me no harm after all, I sat back in the chair and took a sip of wine. "Let me guess" I yelled out, "you freelance here as an actor for murder mysteries or historical skits?" The man froze and glared at me in disbelief.

"*Or-r-r*, then again" I self-corrected, "maybe not."

Eventually, he moved once more, at first pointing stiffly at me and then himself, then ever more rapidly flapping his hand at the wrist like a fan, indicating some connection between the two of us. Not wanting to articulate the obvious, I said nothing—until he stamped a foot, shook his head a bit and let his hand buzz between us like a hummingbird. Feeling almost mesmerized, I found myself asking "Are you a Jennison?" to which the man's head bobbed up and down. "Oh" I mouthed, barely audibly, before adding "Might you possibly be a forefather of mine—Sir Robert Jennison?" at which he nodded 'yes' once, with force. "Oh" I responded blankly, wondering if I could still move my limbs, and if the wine-induced coma into which I'd obviously slipped meant total or just partial paralysis.

For a moment, neither of us moved. Finally, looking at the second bottle of wine, I asked "Are you sure you don't need a glass?" When Sir Robert declined without uttering a sound, I asked "Do you mind if I—" to which he bowed slowly as he smoothly drew his hand upwards in front of his finely-clothed chest, rolled it under his goatee-tipped chin, then stretched it outwards and down in front of him, ending it with an upward end curl as if drawing a graceful "S" in the air.

"*Jenny's never gonna believe this!*" I thought to myself, then sat and contemplated what to do next. For his part, Sir Robert simply went on standing in front of me, as if waiting for a cue.

After a few moments of mounting tension, I swept an open hand in a broad arch in the direction of the grand park, then pointed to the stony structure behind me and dared ask "So, why would you ever leave something like this all behind?" I sat up and looked the man closer in the eye. "You were landed gentry—no landless peasant: *Why* would you give all this up and sail off over unfriendly seas, for many weeks or more likely months, to a completely different, alien world?"

Sir Robert remained motion- as well as expressionless.

"I mean, the survival rate of the first settlers in their first years of life in New England was less than half—*and* you had to survive the ship's passage to begin with: the disease, the storms, the doldrums… thieving under-paid crew and pirates. What on Earth" I demanded, "*ever* made you leave all of this for all of that?"

Sir Robert only blinked—once—and listened.

"Don't get me wrong" I begged off, feeling a bit embarrassed by my brashness. "The decision to emigrate couldn't have been easy. I mean, you knew you'd most certainly never see your family or friends—or even England—again. Setting sail for 'America' was a life-altering decision."

…and this time, portrayed as white as a ghost!

143

The Mayflower in Plymouth Harbor, *by William Halsall, 1882*

Despite my display of empathy, the man still did not speak—which made me a bit testy. And, feeling full of myself—or at least the empty bottle—I inferred "You came from devout Catholics, but the moment you got off that cramped ship in Boston, you dropped the pope and embraced the Puritans: How—and *why*? Did your faith seem so cheap, or so interchangeable?"

The accused moved not a muscle, so I pushed on with my inquisition, charging "You arrived in 1630, when Boston was hardly a hamlet: no well-stocked shops or established inns, no amenities and hardly any institutions! I mean, you came"—I swung my chin and gestured behind me—"from a *castle* for god's sake, with servants! You had attended university: You were 'someone' here—but in Podunk New England, you were 'nobody!' And, I'm tellin' ya:Aall the degrees in the world wouldn't keep a man from starvin'." Sir Roger—or whatever this joker's name really was—remained motionless. "Didn't you sometimes wonder if it were all a big, foolhardy mistake?" I droned on. "Didn't you sometimes wanna get back on that boat in Boston Harbor and head back to England, with your baggy breeches neatly tucked between your cavalier's legs?"

Sir Robert looked down at his feet as if suddenly fascinated with his big, silver shoe buckles.

"You'd been a solicitor at Gray's Inn, in bustling London: What did you expect to do in the dreary backwoods of America? How did you think you'd feed or clothe a family? Success was by no means assured." Sir Robert looked up and studied my face. "Why'd you give up all this comfort and age-old privilege for all that hardship and endless toil? Didn't all of those unknowns grind away at you? Was the lure of the New World worth all its dangers and difficulties? What made it worth risking everything you'd ever known

Gray's Inn's buildings and walks in 1591; boots like Sir Robert wore

or had?" My eyes searched his. "What made likely losing your life—or at least, certainly, that of some of your loved ones—worth all of that?"

As my words hit their target, Sir Robert again slapped his chest. "What" I eagerly asked, "what do you have to say for yourself?" Patting his breastbone with one hand, the well-dressed man motioned towards me with the other.

"Me?" I asked, astonished. "What did your motivation have to do with *me*?"—at which he patted his own chest faster and harder. "Your heart? *Huh-h-h*?" He seemed desperate to make me understand. "You mean 'love'?" He nodded 'yes.' "Are you trying to say ya did it for 'love'?"

Sir Robert's hatless head bobbed forcefully several times as he confirmed my choppy induction.

"Wait a minute" I interjected, "that sounds admirably self-sacrificing, but there's a problem: When you set sail for North America, you didn't even know me—and you certainly didn't make life-or-death decisions for some unseen, unknown distant descendant!"

Sir Robert lifted a hand at the end of a stiffened arm, palm-side facing me, and motioned 'Stop!' Dropping his head a bit to the right, he shook it slowly but with visible consternation. My long-dead ancestor then stomped his foot and pointed an index finger to his forehead.

"Head" I guessed, then extrapolated ever faster, "conscience, thoughts, philosophy, politics… religion—you went to America for religious reasons?"

Again, he quietly but clearly signaled a solid 'No.'

"Ya" I muttered more to myself than to him, "you couldn't have gone to New England for freedom of religion: There was an official church there until the early 1800s—and you became a practicing Puritan, in any case."

I looked at Sir Robert searchingly, unable to follow. "All right, but what *are* you trying to say?"

Again, he rapidly patted his breastbone with one hand, but this time with the other he drew a big circle in the air.

"You're saying 'love' of" I surmised, haltingly, "love of—of what?" His circle-in-the-air grew ever bigger as Sir Robert's drawing motion grew ever faster and more emphatic. "Love" I resumed, "you did it for love of—of circles?"

'NO!' His exasperated look clearly communicated impatience even sans a decibel of sound.

"Love" I started over, "you went to America for love of—the sun." He again looked at me incredulously, nodding to the negative. "Okay—the planet!" Realizing on my own the unlikeliness of such a pre-environmental-movement motive, I expanded upon that theme anyway, theorizing further with "You went to America for the love of nature or the wilderness—or the exotic animals—" Again, his nod screamed a silent 'NO!' "Or, the noble natives lurking there…"

For a moment, he buried his face in his hands and shook his head. Then, as if a stroke of genius had suddenly struck him, the man fell to a low crouch before abruptly springing upward and reaching for the sky, stopping only when his arms were fully extended and he was standing on stretched toes. As he looked to me with a hopeful glare I shouted out "Of course! You went to America for love of adventure!" Standing again fully flat on his feet, my dead-serious charade partner's disappointment with yet another failed answer was palpable. "Okay" I punted, "for the love of change—or maybe a departure from boring routine?" Once again being met with a flat 'No!' I bid "You went out of love for—for danger." He shook his head sadly. "For the thrill of it?"

Sir Robert Jennison, my emigrating ancestor from three-and-a-half centuries earlier, then dropped his arms by his side, paused and looked at me leniently as a faint smile broke out on his softening face. Gesturing with his arms opening outward in either direction, then freezing, he gazed at me with a clear, tender look of love.

"You went to America… out of a love… for life?"

With that, the silent man who had implied that he belonged to the unending line of mortals who had passed life on to me reached out his hand, palm upwards, with uncurling fingers, and held it in front of me as if in offering—then gently closed his eyes and he bowed his head.

———

It had been a couple years since I'd last been stateside. Christian, my East-German-born boyfriend, had never been to "*Amerika.*" Thus, we were both excited as we boarded our first flight from Dresden.

No sooner than it had taken off, I discovered that one of the in-flight films offered on the second leg, from Munich to Chicago, would be a well-rated documentary, *Tim's Vermeer.*

"So?" Christian replied casually when I blurted out the name of the film. "The 'Vermeer' in the title?" he asked without looking up from the on-board-shop magazine spread across his disappearing lap.

"No less than renowned Dutch painter, Johannes Vermeer" I pitched.

"And, the 'Tim' in the title?"

"No less than my unknown-to-me geeky cousin from Belmond, Tim Jenison!" I beamed.

The moment Christian realized the film featured kin of mine as protagonist, he was in.

Luckily, as a historian, I had an excuse to not fully understand the technical minutiae behind Tim's theory about how Vermeer used a camera obscura to create his masterpieces—a premise that the film dissects with compelling finesse. Instead, as a trained chronicler of human and of our wider, social origins, behaviors and soul, what still excites me are the historical connections behind the larger story.

The Jennison brothers landed in Boston Harbor two years before Johannes Vermeer was born in Delft. Later, as the young painter experimented with daringly bright colors and a bold use of light in his work, Tim's and my common ancestors were daring to co-build a new culture, a bold new society in the wilds of North America. As the young country endured, passed milestones like wars or political growing pains, and spread westward, our people grew with America, pushing ever onward, chasing restlessly after elusive dreams, the assumption that Life not only could be, but would be better somewhere else.

Like me, Tim grew up on the windswept Iowa prairies in the middle and later half of the 20th century—a time, we were told repeatedly, overtly and subliminally, that was "the American Century." He pursued the sciences; I, the humanities. While he made millions with his patented innovations in video technology and improvements in computer hardware as well as software, I made the rent and a cup o' cheap coffee with my pay as a social historian. Still, in the end, we each found in Europe clues to the Western cultural framework within we each function, every day—nay, every hour... every *second.*

Sure, as someone with whom I carry common genes, I feel no small pride in being able to call him a relative: As an accomplished graphic artist, innovator, inventor and entrepreneur, Tim deserves all our admiration. In addition to his stellar career, though, I'm inspired by his roots. When Robert and William Jennison disembarked in New England, blue blood could be heard the moment they opened their red lips. In the leveling social climate of life on the frontier, however, they couldn't eat inherited privilege: Within a generation, their offspring had to prove themselves, just like anyone else struggling to survive in the New World. So, by the time the Jennisons reached Iowa, Tim's and my people were as common as the next person, no better or worse—blank slates on which to write whatever biographies we could.

For me, both Vermeer the painter and Vermeer the man fundamentally belong to the Europe and the era that the original Jennison brothers turned their backs on in favor of throwing their lots in with others daring to sail off into the unknown. In Tim's researching not just the artist, but the most intricate secrets of Vermeer's singular skills, my great-grandmother's cousin's descendent also has brought our family full circle. The children of the children of those who tore themselves away from Mother Europe to seek their fortunes elsewhere have, in turn, made their own fortunes and, so armed, returned to the Old World to reflect on not only our own roots, but where our branches, where future generations of "Americans" might take our culture next. By solving riddles about the past, Tim as well as cultural pioneers like him, open up the realm of what's possible not just in an amorphous future but now, today.

Tim Jenison with his mechanically assisted copy of Vermeer's The Music Lesson, *at his studio in San Antonio*

———

priest with altar boys at Belmond's St. Francis Xavier Church; teachers with pupils at Goodell school:
Religion and education have played key roles in the life of the Upper Midwest since its founding days.

PART IV b

Root-Sinking Settlers

Section 7:
Peter & Maren "Mary" (Nielsen Jørgensen) Juhl family

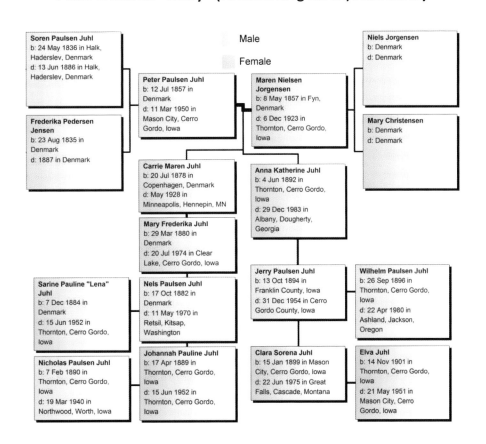

Soren Paulsen Juhl
b: 24 May 1836 in Halk, Haderslev, Denmark
d: 13 Jun 1886 in Halk, Haderslev, Denmark

Frederika Pedersen Jensen
b: 23 Aug 1835 in Denmark
d: 1887 in Denmark

Peter Paulsen Juhl
b: 12 Jul 1857 in Denmark
d: 11 Mar 1950 in Mason City, Cerro Gordo, Iowa

Male

Female

Maren Nielsen Jorgensen
b: 8 May 1857 in Fyn, Denmark
d: 6 Dec 1923 in Thornton, Cerro Gordo, Iowa

Niels Jorgensen
b: Denmark
d: Denmark

Mary Christensen
b: Denmark
d: Denmark

Carrie Maren Juhl
b: 20 Jul 1878 in Copenhagen, Denmark
d: May 1928 in Minneapolis, Hennepin, MN

Mary Frederika Juhl
b: 29 Mar 1880 in Denmark
d: 20 Jul 1974 in Clear Lake, Cerro Gordo, Iowa

Anna Katherine Juhl
b: 4 Jun 1892 in Thornton, Cerro Gordo, Iowa
d: 29 Dec 1983 in Albany, Dougherty, Georgia

Sarine Pauline "Lena" Juhl
b: 7 Dec 1884 in Denmark
d: 15 Jun 1952 in Thornton, Cerro Gordo, Iowa

Nels Paulsen Juhl
b: 17 Oct 1882 in Denmark
d: 11 May 1970 in Retsil, Kitsap, Washington

Jerry Paulsen Juhl
b: 13 Oct 1894 in Franklin County, Iowa
d: 31 Dec 1954 in Cerro Gordo County, Iowa

Wilhelm Paulsen Juhl
b: 26 Sep 1896 in Thornton, Cerro Gordo, Iowa
d: 22 Apr 1980 in Ashland, Jackson, Oregon

Nicholas Paulsen Juhl
b: 7 Feb 1890 in Thornton, Cerro Gordo, Iowa
d: 19 Mar 1940 in Northwood, Worth, Iowa

Johannah Pauline Juhl
b: 17 Apr 1889 in Thornton, Cerro Gordo, Iowa
d: 15 Jun 1952 in Thornton, Cerro Gordo, Iowa

Clara Sorena Juhl
b: 15 Jan 1899 in Mason City, Cerro Gordo, Iowa
d: 22 Jun 1975 in Great Falls, Cascade, Montana

Elva Juhl
b: 14 Nov 1901 in Thornton, Cerro Gordo, Iowa
d: 21 May 1951 in Mason City, Cerro Gordo, Iowa

Peter Paulsen Juhl's parents

Soren Paulsen Juhl
b: 24 May 1836 in Halk, Haderslev, Denmark
m: 27 Mar 1857 in Halk, Haderslev, Denmark
d: 13 Jun 1886 in Halk, Haderslev, Denmark

Peter Paulsen Juhl
b: 12 Jul 1857 in Denmark
d: 11 Mar 1950 in Mason City, Cerro Gordo, Iowa

Frederika Pedersen Jensen
b: 23 Aug 1835 in Denmark
d: 1887 in Denmark

tagged with inscription "Landphere with bike"

Peter Paulsen and Maren (Nielsen Jørgensen) Juhl

born:	12 July 1857	8 May 1857
where:	København/Danmark	Fyn/Danmark ["Funen/Denmark" in English]
married:	23 November 1877	**where:** København ["Copenhagen/Denmark"]
died:	11 March 1950	6 December 1923
where:	Clear Lake, Iowa/USA	Thornton, Iowa/USA

Is it just me, or when one looks long enough into the eyes of at least the five youngest of the nine Juhl children posing in the below photo (as well as those of their likely overwhelmed mother), do they seem to reflect a hybrid of sadness bred with dread? Or, fear-fed wariness? My paternal great-grandfather—Gramma Luick's father—Nick Juhl, stands in the middle of the large flock, the shaved-headed boy crouched between his subdued Danish-immigrant parents.

Sarine (standing), Carrie, Nels, Mary; Peter (seated), Nick (crouched between parents), Maren "Mary" (Nielsen Jørgensen) and Johannah (standing); Jerry (front row), Anna and Wilhelm; in Iowa, circa 1897

Yes, most Victorian family as well as individual portraits seem somber to us today. For one thing, the camera's aperture had to be open so long in order to allow in adequate light to cast clear positive-negative contrasts. For another, social mores ruling the times called for restrained sobriety over unleashed gaiety. And, many people—even those with the resources to afford studio-made portraits, what then were an expensive extravagance—could not easily erase from their faces the weight of lives marked by on-going toil and serial trials.

Still, I find this shot of the Peter and Maren Nielsen Juhl family particularly heartrending and haunting. And, I'm perplexed by why, having left a small kingdom recently torn by war and social unrest, then landing in a vast republic that at the time of their arrival warranted prosperity-driven optimism, the Juhls seem anxious and unhappy, at least in that frozen moment. They were, after all, among those lucky Danes who'd traded poverty and social displacement for relative wealth and political stability.

———

chapter 23: a fertile cradle

Leaving their tiny coastal country in search of the means to survive and of expanded opportunities, the Danes left Denmark in the 800s and went to England—which they conquered, then ruled for about two and a half centuries. A millennium later, Danes left Denmark for similar reasons but went to the likes of Iowa—which conquered them. One of the Danes that America's Heartland transformed into one of its own was Peter Paulsen Juhl. That hardy man, however, was not alone.

"Dannevirke," an extract from Olaus Magnus' Carta Marina, 1572; Copenhagen's Stock Exchange, 1860s

Among my known ancestors, the Juhls came from the land with the most fluxuating geographic fortunes. At one time *"Danmark"* extended to today's Estonia in the east, to the polar regions of northern Norway, west to the North Atlantic's Faroe Islands, all the way to Iceland and then on to Greenland, and south—as mentioned—to the bottom of England. Denmark, a minute land lacking large deposits of mineral wealth, historically always prowled for resources or at least trading partners who had them. Thus, as of 1536 it established commercial enclaves as far afield as along India's eastern shore, in the Caribbean and on Africa's Gold Coast, in today's Ghana—an exceptional feat in sail-powered sea-going days, sans motors, electricity or telecommunication.

Danish power reached its zenith in 1397 under Danish Queen Margaret I with the formation of the Kalmar Union, which united Denmark with most of present-day Norway and much of Sweden. Then, its clout within Europe eroded over centuries marked by inept kings, imprudent alliances with the likes of unreliable Russia, and, as of 1800, wars with Sweden, England (which in 1801 destroyed Denmark's fleet, then the second-largest in Europe) and Germany. It was the conflagration with ascending Prussia in 1864 that ended with Denmark's forced ceding of the border provinces of Schleswig, and thus cost Copenhagen a third of what remained of Denmark's home territory in Europe. The loss of land only exacerbated existing problems for an agrarian society undergoing disruptive industrialization and a growing flow of peasants to cities.

Vanggaard, the historical home of the Juhl family near Langetved in Jutland, Denmark, seen in the 1880s

Events of national, moreover global scope might often seem remote and abstract, but for those whose lives they touch directly, the effects are immediate and physical. The extended Juhl family, for one, experienced Denmark's defeat at the hands of the Prussians instantly and tangibly. A century later, in 1964, my cousin Paul Christopher Juhl—a farmboy from Webster County, Iowa—paid his first of several visits to the old Juhl homestead, where the family had lived for more than 435 years. He found the memory of Prussian occupation among older locals then still alive, deep and distressing. He wrote:

> Langetved, Denmark, is just a small spot along the road, midway across Jutland, between Kolding on the east and Ribe on the west. The Juhl homestead was part of an ancient living site with the main house having been built in 1534. The Juhl farm itself was about 190 acres [76.89 hectares] of level, productive land under-laid by sea shells, or marl, which was used to fertilize the land. Eels would often come into the small streams and could be eaten by the people in the village. The Juhl house originally had a straw roof but was replaced by tile centuries ago. It was just a short walk from the Skrave Kirke, the church that served the communities in that area. Family legend says that during the Black Plague in Denmark, the church was not attended for a hundred years. When services resumed, it was necessary to cut away trees to get to the entrance. The Langetved village, in the days of the 1864 war with Germany, lay just south of the stream that became the new border between the two countries, the Kongeå.

Thus, after the War of 1864 the Juhls lived on the "wrong" side of an artificial border between what remained of Denmark and what soon became part of the Second German Reich. Government officials began a campaign to encourage the people to think of themselves as Germans. The Juhl family and others in the area attempted to send their children to schools in the "new" Denmark since the border was so near. The schools were of great importance in keeping their heritage and every chance they could, the children crossed over.

Those who stuck it out, who did not flee to Copenhagen or abroad to seek a new life, had to live with a tense, costly cultural ambiguity. Paul's great uncle, Mads' son Hans Juhl, later wrote that

Germany ruled us with a very heavy hand: Replaced our Danish teachers with German teachers, destroyed our Danish school books and replaced them with German books. A German officer [rode] into this home every morning trying to find something in the way of Danish – for instance a boy or girl singing a Danish song or a small Danish flag in a window – promptly left a note saying, 'don't let me see this tomorrow morning.' This is why my father came to America – not wishing his sons to become German soldiers and shoot more bullets back into the home we loved so much. Mads Christopher Juhl, having lived for twenty years under almost unendurable pressure from

Ladegaarden, with a secured footbridge over the river, 1898

Germany, had to make a decision... live under this pressure or give up the homestead, give up his obligations to his parents whom he never expected to see again, and lastly strike out to find a new home in a country which he knew very little about... and penniless. He chose America. In order to fulfill his obligations to his parents, the homestead was sold under pressure to a German citizen. He gave a first mortgage for almost the full amount of the purchase price. This was considered a safe sale as German's economy at this time was unquestionable. After World War I, as we know, Germany's economy was shattered. Money was everywhere by the sack full. At this time the purchaser of our old homestead wisely decided this would be a good time to pay off this mortgage. So, bringing his attorney and two big sacks of money, he proceeded to pay off the mortgage. This money received would only buy two loaves of bread. Let me state by this sad experience that our economy is only as good as we keep it.

Eventually, after a plebiscite in 1920, the Danish-speaking majority of then-German northern Schleswig voted to cede from the young, post-WWI Weimar Republic and return to Denmark. In the late 1800s, though, the Juhls could not have foreseen with any certainty the eventual return of their farm to

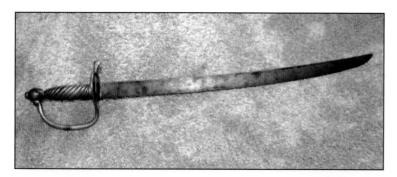

the sword Mads Christopher Juhl brought to Iowa as an emigrant, 1887

Danish territory. Assuming Prussian occupation as final and enduring, many drifted at least to the Danish cities, looking for a way to survive, if not to faraway *Amerika*, as a means to thrive. Those who out of desperation or a burning sense of adventure chose the latter option, considered very carefully what to include among the few things they could take with them. Paul's side of the family, which emigrated to Iowa

the same year as Peter Juhl and his brother-in-law, chose—among other items—to take with them a left-behind weapon. The story

that has been passed down concerning the Prussian sword is that German soldiers used the out buildings on the farm as a resting place during the war. The sword was being used to cut bread. When the word came that the soldiers needed to leave in a great hurry the sword was somehow left behind. When Mads Juhl immigrated to the United States in 1887, he brought the sword with him, perhaps being unsure of security needs for his family once he arrived. He brought it to Webster County, Iowa, about 15 miles southeast of Fort Dodge.

The Juhls came from common stock, with little say as powers greater then themselves—both Danish or foreign—determined their fates often with as little as a stroke of a feather-light quill pen. Most moderns possess some understanding of medieval feudalism. How many, though, can fully grasp that as late as 1788—a year after the U.S. Constitution was written and signed—Danish peasants "belonged" to estates controlled by an aristocracy resistant to emancipating what essentially were slaves.

A century later—the year that Maren (Nielsen Jørgensen) Juhl, with the first four of eventually eleven children, rejoined her husband of a

Denmark's Svanemøllen ("Swan Mill") before it burned down in 1892

dozen years, Peter, who'd preceded them to Iowa by one year—Danish peasants had lived freely for only a couple of generations. As of the official end of feudalism in 1788 they could have chosen to stay on the land or leave it, or even buy limited amounts of property, but the majority of freed serfs clung to a known minimal existence in the underdeveloped countryside rather than risk the unknown in the growing, increasingly mechanized cities. Before the Prussians arrived, it was persisting hunger in the mid-1800s that drove tens of thousands to the cities in search of food and work. Young Maren Nielsen was one of them. After leaving her native island of Fyn (known outside Denmark as "Funen"), she found both in København, ("Copenhagen," or "merchants' harbor" in English).

Christiansborg Slotskirke (1860), Toldboden, Amaliegade & Fra Lille Kongensgade—last three, 1870-90

At the time she arrived in the Danish capital, small-town-girl Maren found a city undergoing a period of intense cultural creativity that'd be known as the Danish Golden Age. Copenhagen's rising fortunes seemed all the more ironic, given that at the beginning of that century the city had survived a siege by thirty-thousand British troops—what some historians later deemed "the first terror attack against a major European city in modern times."

Only as of mid-century did the city tear down its defensive ramparts, making way for new districts to the north and west to house its many newcomers. In the expansive days of industrialization, painters and architects changed the face of Danish urban life, while engineers and mechanics—including Maren's brother—worked to improve public sanitation, expand canals and the harbor, introduce electrification and install electric-powered trams. Between 1840 and 1900 the metropolis' population more than tripled, from 120,000 to 400,000.

Besides the means to survive, in the nation's capital Maren found a husband, Peter—a "rock" in Greek and, like her, born in 1857. They married on 23 November 1877 and by Christmas 1884 had four children—three of them daughters. Among a multitude, Peter had come to the capital from the countryside. With few tangible resources, the couple could only afford a dark, damp apartment in a decrepit building. With little open, green space nearby, the children played in the cold, cramped courtyard, in all weather. The growing family ate poorly and irregularly. They wore a

streetcar workers outside Copenhagen's Central Hotel & Café Paraplyen

sparse wardrobe, sat or slept on used, worn furniture, and saved what little they could.

Gammelstrand market in Copenhagen's city center

Then, Peter found work at a factory, laboring long hours under dirty conditions, alongside other refugees from the prospectless countryside. The owner paid poorly, but there was little choice. When Maren ventured to the market, Peter's paltry wages could buy little more than basics. She often walked in slow, hungry circles, pricing food in one stall, then comparing it with the next. Sometimes, she visited a stall repeatedly before committing her few coins to a given monger. The money Peter brought home barely landed in his wife's thin hands before it swiftly vanished.

To not work meant to not eat. So, Peter did his job—but watched as boys barely older than his own children slaved away next to grown men. The unenclosed machinery often devoured a finger, even a limb. Both men and boys—in some factories a third of the workforce—had to work six days a week, ten-to-sixteen hour days, based on demand. While the owner grew rich and fat, the hollow stomachs of those who created his wealth growled in vain. A system had arisen, then refused to bend. It made the Juhls' urban existence seem harsh, meager and hopeless.

scenes of Copenhagen's slums around Amagergade, Baggaard and Borgergade-Aderlsgade, circa 1890

Alfred Benzon's factory at Vesterbrogade 62 in Copenhagen, 1883: Note "x" placed over owner's head.

By 1887, the young couple foresaw no future in Denmark. As Peter's father, Søren, had died a year earlier, they needn't stay to care for him. So, Peter and Maren's brother left for *"Amerika"*—the land of their dreams. It could not have been easy for them to decide to leave their homeland, for even with its then-shrinking size and stubborn hunger, Denmark was exceptionally homogenous ethnically and religiously, especially compared to its nearest neighbors, the Germans. And, Danish cultural identity remained strong: Denmark has the world's oldest state flag; each of the other Scandinavian nation's flags contains the Danish cross. At over a millennium old, Denmark's is one of the oldest surviving monarchies on the planet.

map of Odense province, circa 1900; Peter's mother, Frederika (Pedersen Jensen) Juhl , circa 1885

Despite bonds to the land of their birth that would bind them to Denmark till their deaths, Peter, Maren and several siblings remained fast in their decision to leave it. Unlike earlier compatriots who needed months to travel overseas by sail, the two brothers-in-law benefitted from a fully mechanized emigration process that mirrored the industrial age which by then Denmark also had entered. If their migratory experience was anything like Ane B. Hansen, Olga's hapless mother who left Denmark in 1888 and reached Dannebrog, Nebraska, within three weeks, the two men went from Copenhagen to Clear Lake within about a little more than a fortnight. Perhaps an apt metaphor to represent the scale of that technological wonder of their day would be for us to look at the moon, then a few hours later be there. My Danish ancestors' quick passage to Iowa was a modern miracle. It didn't come out of nowhere, however: It was a later stage of a cultural evolution that unfolded over a couple thousand years.

––––––

chapter 24: marketing the world

The rise of Western Europe as a global player would not have happened without its access to navigable oceans and seas on three sides. Eastern Europe, in contrast, shared genetic and cultural stock with the West, yet its development was far more introverted and slower than that of the Occident. Eastern Europe's Baltic access was seasonally limited by harsh winters, while its southern waterways ended in land-enclosed seas, not oceans; more accessible land routes at its disposal took longer to cover shorter distances and were fraught with dangers unknown at sea.

Already the ancient Romans declared the Mediterranean the "Middle of the Earth" and used that sea to stretch their peninsula-born empire from what we know as Scotland to Egypt, and from today's Morocco to Turkey. Even in the so-called Dark Ages long-distance trade and travel by sea sank to low levels relative to that of the Romans, yet did continue. The Renaissance that supplanted the Medieval period first arose alongside blossoming Italian sea trade with ports as far away as South Asia and West Africa. Later, Spanish and Portuguese exploration of what had been large swaths of a globe previously unknown to Westerners forever changed the course of world history. Once Europeans landed in the Americas, ascendant naval powers like Britain, the Netherlands and Denmark rushed to claim a share of unimaginable natural resources. Above all, Western connectivity via water facilitated the movement of peoples, ideas and material wealth.

Europe in 1190, with an inset showing Germanic tribal regions

As history remains ever symbiotic and never static, the rise of religious tumult in Europe at the end of the Middle Ages is more clearly seen and more fully understood in the context of the then-new Age of Exploration, an unmatched era of discoveries of both new lands and new ideas. In the exciting chaos of new possibilities never before realized, the calcified Catholic Church struggled—and ultimately failed—to maintain its monopoly over secular as well as sacred matters. As the Church's prohibition of Christians profiting from the loaning of money and accruing interest from it dissolved, more and more non-aristocrats amassed large fortunes. During the Reformation and afterwards city hall towers across Europe began to shoot towards the heavens in direct competition with church spires—an unmistakable assertion of increasing municipal over waning clerical might. At first private, then publically-traded companies began to dwarf the holdings and power of a declining Roman church.

"Luik" (in Flemish; Latin "Leodium," French "Liege," German "Lütich"), engraved by Matthäus Merian in 1650

As more and more, mostly Northern European provinces joined the gaining protest movement and papal authority declined accordingly, the balance of power shifted. Kings and lesser royalty who previously had been "elected" by councils of estate-holding lords or other property-owning elite no longer felt beholden to ever-distant Rome or even local king-makers. Such "appointed" kings, then, watching an expanding Europe, declared themselves to be "absolute" monarchs, no longer yielding to lesser powers such as "mere" electors. One of those kings, that of Denmark, set up such a monarchy that lasted almost two-hundred years. In contrast to their "elected" predecessors, absolute monarchs possessed, well, absolute power—which also meant they had at their disposal the material wealth to fund projects such as sending sailing ships to, say, the eastern shoreline of spice-rich India... or Africa's verdant Gold Coast... or rum-rice-indigo-cotton-producing islands of the Caribbean... or the whale- and fish-abundant shelves off of Greenland.

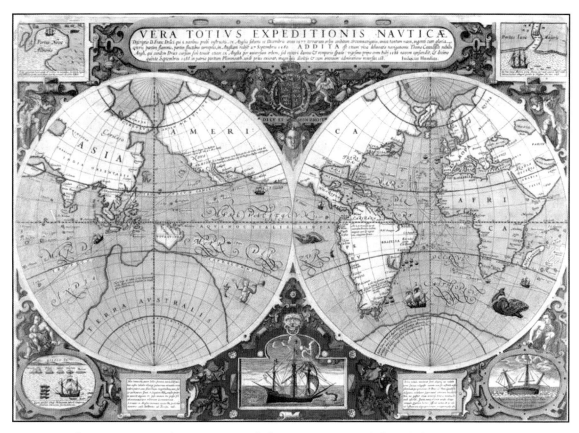

1595 map "Vera Totius Expeditionis Nauticae" showing Francis Drake's and Thomas Cavendish's voyages

Sending half-empty sailing ships on months-long voyages around the world in search of sellable cargo to eventually carry back to finicky European markets was one thing; later being able to export cheaply-produced goods to distant shores, then quickly turn those ships around with raw natural materials for processing in European mills and factories was another. And, once motorized ships and mass-produced freighters became cost-effective and commonplace, the shipping of goods to and from Europe expanded to include shipping *people*… like peasants from rural Denmark, who once had moved to the increasingly-crowded cities but could barely feed themselves—people like the Juhls, Nielsens, Hansens and countless others. A profitable solution to reducing the number of pesky paupers plaguing the expanding cities? Ship the urban poor out of Europe—to the inner cities or outer reaches of North or South America, Southern Africa or Britain's South-Pacific colonies—and charge *them* for the "service!"

It's no coincidence that in the evolution of capitalism, virtually all of the first trans-continental "companies" grew out of "royal charters" granted by European monarchs looking to increase still further their already-uncountable wealth. That was the case with Britain's East (1600) and the Dutch West (1621) India Companies, the Dano-Norwegian General Trade Company (1749) and Hudson's Bay Company—founded in 1670, the oldest continuously-operating corporation in North America, today the owner of companies such as Saks Fifth Avenue or Lord and Taylor. As monarchs' wealth later waned in the face of—or at least was increasingly approached by—that of non-aristocratic "bourgeois" tycoons, British, German and other leading shipping magnates had less and less need for royal funding of their ventures: They financed their own! While still fawning for the crown's favor and protection (vis-à-vis subsidies, privileges, protection afforded by national navies or armies), mammoth shipping companies expanded at breath-taking speeds. Once they saturated existing markets for transporting goods or, later, human beings, however, they looked for new, hopefully profitable undertakings—and thereby initiated some of the first "vertical-marketing" schemes of modern big-business. And, simple, striving folks like Peter and Maren Juhl's flock were among their millions of short-term, fast-turnover customers.

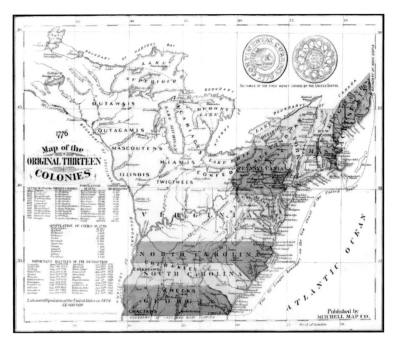

1876 map of the United States a century earlier, including territories

In the early years of emigration from Great Britain to its North American colonies, would-be settlers paid their own passage or, as often happened, "borrowed" the money in advance by agreeing to indenture themselves post-passage to usually unknown strangers for a period of time—typically, seven years—as laborers. African slaves, of course, were brought involuntarily as a way to enrich slave runners and, ultimately, slave owners—if, that is, the chained, underfed captives survived the overcrowded, unsanitary conditions they endured for weeks, even months on-board. Brought one way or the other, as of the mid-1600s the British crown had little trouble finding enough would-be laborers to keep the flow of bodies bound for the wilds of North America growing.

Before an ambitious elite formed the United States and broke away from "Mother England" towards the end of the 18th century, settlers to the American colonies came largely from Britain but also, in fewer numbers, from places as disparate as—for example—the Rheinland, Ulster, Sweden and Bohemia. Some did come in search of freedom of religion, but that exaggerated, relatively seldom occurrence aside, many more came to avoid military conscription, primogeniture or bad debts, for adventure or simply to make a lot of money in a short time.

After independence, while the clear majority of early 19th-century European immigrants came to the young republic from less-moneyed classes, the most destitute of the Old World's poor simply lacked the funds for ship's passage so stayed put. Until the days of the large-scale steamers following the American Civil War, often-misleading or scrupleless recruiters would comb Northern and Central—especially German-speaking—Europe for down-and-out land-owning peasants

original Ellis Island complex, built in 1892 but then burned in 1897

or small-townspeople who had modest savings to tap or some property to sell, with which to pay the fare to flee general, on-going poverty, or, during specific years, political turmoil or famine resulting from crop failures. The tempting pull to leave inherited material or social misery behind only grew as local presses eagerly published glowing letters of "native sons [and daughters]" who had fared well in and thus loudly touted "the land of opportunity."

With the advent of large steamers, however—coincidentally around the time of German unification under Otto von Bismarck, a half decade after Civil War had ceased in the U.S. and western expansion not only resumed but accelerated—the prosperity of the newly forged "German Empire" meant that the dire need that had pushed millions of Teutonic peoples to the Americas before 1871 no longer existed on the scale it had. Thus, British but, moreover, Continental shipping companies looked further into Europe for potential steerage-class customers. The wave of industrialization that had begun in Britain as early as the mid-1700s, then fanned out over France, the Germanic or Lowland states and later Scandinavia, and ultimately spread into Eastern Europe, Italy and Iberia, meant millions of new "sales."

A largely clever lot, the heads of the shipping industry kept a close eye on political and economic developments across Europe, so often knew when and how to cash-in on, say, Jewish pogroms in Eastern Europe, growing poverty in Southern Italy or unrest in the Balkans. As except for during mostly short periods of financial "panic"—the antiquated term for today's more clinical "recession"—the hunger for workers in 19th-century America remained mostly great, at times so insatiable that some shipping as well as even industrial groups sent early "head hunters" into areas of high unemployment to sign up entire work gangs (mostly, but not only consisting of men) to have would-be migrant labor sign work contracts already in the "old country" before ever stepping foot, fare-free, into the new.

poster touting the "speed steamer Deutschland, the world's fastest"

The promise of paid passage and thereafter jobs created pockets of Serbs in Omaha, Italians in Des Moines and Saint Paul, Poles in Chicago or even Greeks in Mason City. Steady improvements in Europe's roads as well as rail network made the mass movement of millions of even ordinary people with limited means from inland to coastal points of departure easier, faster and cheaper. Whereas earlier recruiting efforts had taken place nearer to the ports, by the late 19th and into the early 20th century, giant shipping firms siphoned off the "human excess" of even the farthest reaches of Europe and sent it sailing to the New World—and made incredible returns on their capital investments in the process.

To maximize profit-taking, first Le Havre, Liverpool and Rotterdam, then even more so Bremen[haven] and Hamburg became finely-organized hubs for emigrants bound for the Americas. The most resourceful companies expanded the range of services to go far beyond a mere ship's passage to the New World. Different moguls provided various packages, but their aggregate services ranged from printing authoritative guides tailored to would-be emigrants in target languages; strategically-placed newspapers articles and traveling lectures by "experts" about auspicious conditions "at the other end;" "emigrant kits" including items pushed as "essential" in the adopted country; chartered train cars from in-land Europe to coastal ports; medical services; clothing or other dry-good supplies for the crossing; hostels and cafeterias for those awaiting departure—and more. Some expenses were paid by the shipping companies to contractors on behalf of the emigrants, but the majority of the costs of such services and supporting goods were born by those risking all they had in order to gain all they dreamt of.

———

chapter 25: corners of sky

The vertical-marketing "packages" offered by steamship companies at the end of the 19th century did not end upon emigrants' arrival in New York, Halifax, São Paulo or Buenos Aires. The specially-designed immigrant-processing facility at Ellis Island, for one, included ferries and rail links to the New Jersey mainland that allowed new arrivals headed for points west to circumvent Gotham entirely, without having stepped a foot in expensive, seductive, "dangerous" New York City. While America's east coast contained several busy harbors—Boston, Baltimore, Norfolk, New Orleans—newcomers from Europe headed for destinations in the Northeast, Midwest or even the West mostly passed through New York. The Juhls did—and, like hundreds of thousands of other migrants at the time, jumped off the ship in New York only to jump onto trains headed for America's Heartland. While shipping companies didn't all do so, some further invested in commercial schemes to "answer every need of the newly-arrived American," from dorm-like "immigrant hotels" to travel agencies, whole trains, chartered wagons or at least the sale of train tickets, the publication of print media aimed to facilitate more easily establishing one's self in the adopted country—even English-language and "proper American etiquette" classes!

Ultimately, though, the most profit to be made off the backs of the aspiring "New Americans" laid in the ground—in land sales. Some agencies offered specific nationalities or other target groups further passage en masse to "colonies" in the West, "conducive to [their] special needs"—including for German-speaking Mennonites or Hutterites from Russia who, after a century of enjoying special status thanks to German-born Czarina Catherine the Great, no longer felt welcome in a later Czar's empire so sought steppe-like surroundings where they could transplant generations-old farming communities—in the latter case, religious-based communal ones. Publicity posters promised an overnight New Canaan to all.

1881 railroad booklet printed in German touting Nebraska's alleged rich farmland

Jews, another group fleeing recurring persecution in Czarist Russia, went to far-removed places on the prairie like North Dakota, looking for a safer corner of the sky they might call their own. Ironically, they first came to New York or regional centers like Saint Paul, Minnesota, only to be sent on per train tickets subsidized by German-American Jews, for reasons not fully altruistic. According to Dianne Ziskin Siegel, a granddaughter of some of those would-be Jewish settlers,

> German Jews had settled earlier in the United States. As a group better educated and more affluent, they had mixed feelings about the huge emigration of Russian Jews who were poorly educated, did not speak English and needed a great deal of help just to get started. There was a general sentiment among the German-Jewish population that there were too many Jewish refugees settling in large cities: First, life was often hard in the cities and, second, it was felt that this concentration of Jews in large cities might increase anti-Semitism. [Saint Paul's Mount Zion Temple's Rabbi Judah] Wechsler promoted the agricultural settlement idea. It would allow for some Jewish occupational redistribution and relieve the pressure on the Minnesota Jewish community, which was judged unable to absorb a large number of newcomers. Rabbi Wechsler obtained a grant in North Dakota on the Missouri River in 1882. Priority was given to Russian immigrants already living in St. Paul. Rabbi Wechsler gave $600-$800 to each family from the National Jewish Community, as the local one could not provide much. He formed the Hebrew Aid and Emigrant Society of St. Paul and was its president.

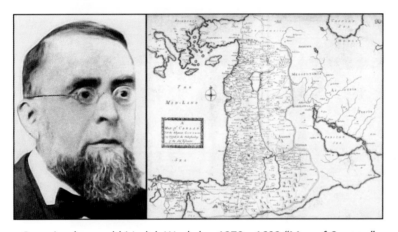

Bavarian-born rabbi Judah Wechsler, 1870s; 1692 "Map of Canaan"

The events on the Dakota plains unfolded parallel to Theodor Herzl's own distillation of what would become Zionism, which only as of 1909 gave rise to *kibbutzim*, Jewish communes meant to secure the future of Judaism in the world. Improbably, establishing Jewish, in part communal settlements—in this case on the steppes of North America—first took place in the Upper Midwest of the United States. And, they sank roots some three decades before the first *kibbutzim* were built, as well as almost seventy years before the founding of the state of Israel.

Of the fledgling pilot projects in Dakota Territory, among the most colorful and renowned was

> the new community called Painted Woods, located six hours from Bismarck by horse. [...] There were two different kinds of settlements [for Jews in North Dakota.] The first was establishing an agricultural settlement by bringing a group of Jewish people together, start a colony and support one another. Painted Woods exemplified this kind of settlement. The second type was by individuals who received some money from the Baron de Hirsch [Jewish-settlement philanthropic] Fund and came on their own in order to homestead. [...] There were undoubtedly many reasons why these families did not succeed as farmers. They had no knowledge of farming and had never done so in Russia; they apparently quarreled amongst themselves and with their neighbors, by whom they were often misused, reproached and despised; they had poor English language skills; their dress and appearance set them apart from their neighbors; many did not want to do physical work, and it was thought by some that making them the object of charity did not lead to independence. Also, they had married early, had many children, and they were disappointed by life in America and [thus] homesick.

In this 1913 group photo, Dianne Ziskin Siegel's grandmother, Ida Wilensky, wears the dark hat in the back row; her brother-in-law, Joe, is the capped young man in the back; some Wilensky children are mixed among their paternal/ maternal cousins, the Calof children. Abe Calof, left, and Herman Wilensky are shown sitting in a buggy, circa 1900.

Companies that offered later-coming immigrants such as my immigrating Danish ancestors land or services included European and American stock- as well as stakeholders. "Multi-national corporations," thus, are not a phenomenon of a "new" global economy. British companies, for example, built most of Argentina's and also much of the rest of South America's railways as 19th-century capital investments or direct, for-fee services. Despite widespread modern historical myopia that doesn't know it, American companies profited mightily from financing, production or sales in Europe and elsewhere around the world long before 1918 or 1945. And, European corporations did the same in the New World, already with the funding of the first sailing ships that set off in a westwardly direction for India—an investment that unwittingly yet fundamentally forever altered life in what became the "Old World." Both European and American companies—as another example—advertised the endless abundance of available rich soil in the heart of North America almost before the ink dried on the contracts Thomas Jefferson's agents signed with France's cash-strapped dictator, Napoleon, buying the Louisiana Purchase in 1803.

Just as land policies were central to expanding or at least maintaining power in Europe, the young U.S. government also turned to land as a political tool. Presidential candidate James Polk, for one, reportedly used the alliterative slogan "Fifty-four Forty or Fight" to fuel his 1844 bid for the White House—but after victory retreated to negotiate a compromise boundary for America's Oregon Territory with Britain along the 49th parallel, exactly as proposed by previous U.S. administrations. Almost two decades later, much of the motivation behind Abraham Lincoln's Homestead Act of 1862 consisted of political strategies. On one hand, it acknowledged calls from within the fledgling Republican Party to grant newly opened Federal territories to "yeoman farmers" rather than wealthy land speculators or, in their eyes worse, slave-owning Southerners. On the other, it offered a valve with which to release some of the mounting social pressures arising from the unpopular conscription of Northern men into the Union Army as well as from tense, crowded conditions in New York's Lower East Side that already had led to riots related to issues of both racial (African-American) and ethnic (Irish) background.

first homestead certificate, awarded Daniel Freeman, Beatrice, Nebraska, 1868; John & Marget (Axvig) Bakken with children, Tilda and Eddie, in front of "soddie" in North Dakota—per original caption: "John Bakken was the son of Norwegian immigrants who homesteaded and built a sod house in Milton in 1896 [used] for the design of the Homestead Act Commemorative Stamp of 1962. As living persons cannot be represented on US stamps, the children were blocked out by a haystack. Ironically, however, John Bakken was still alive at the age of 92 when the stamp was issued. This photograph was also used by Norway on a postage stamp in 1975, to commemorate the sesquicentennial of Norwegian emigration to America. The children were left in the picture for this stamp, rendering a more accurate image of the original photograph."

Following the Civil War, having settled the question if America's future would be more a slave-labor agrarian or a paid-labor industrial economy, westward expansion played a central role in national goals to create an ever-growing domestic market. Then, with the final defeat of Native-American resistance at the massacre of Wounded Knee in 1890, the U.S. government promoted unthreatened access to the Upper Midwest and Great Plains as assurance to would-be settlers from the American East and from Europe, as well as those already living there, that the enormous region was safe. The swarming arriving hordes—including dejected Danes—increasingly came straight from the ship, via rail. Their arrival in the middle of the vast North American continent, however, was foreseen—by both purported "friend" and perceived "foe" alike, even if with radically different points of view.

The ranks of those later reported to have "won" the West (please, from whom, exactly?) included railroad barons who claimed to be "self-made" men yet were beholden to business buddies, some of whom had bought cozy political offices in Washington, DC, from where they orchestrated empires. Allegedly to encourage America's march westward, fulfilling the "white-man's burden" of Manifest Destiny, the men invested with building the nation's rail network enjoyed numerous perks. Among the most lucrative, especially in regions like the Upper Great Plains, railway companies were handed alternate square-mile sections of land most of the length of their proposed lines. Congress meant the allowed sale of such land to help co-finance the cost of tying the country together via rail—a legitimate public project, yielding common gain. At the same time, however, the vertical-marketing-minded corporations—with both American as well as European stock holders—used some of the land to "plant" cookie-cutter communities across the prairies, like so many pearls in a chain laced across the plains. To this day, crossing the Dakotas—for example—one can watch a parade of fading towns pass by that resemble each other, featuring prop-like motifs: wooden but also later-built concrete grain silos, prairie-Gothic church spires, a broad-shouldered county courthouse constructed along classical lines, a stock-design post office, a smattering of wind-battered trees along motionless streets...

Earlier settlers, who populated previous waves of pioneers pushing westward, typically named new communities after ones they'd left or passed farther East or back in Europe, after one of the nation's founders, famous battles, geographical features, virtuous or noble images, or after a Native-American chief or tribe. Late-19th-century speculators, however, were wont to name the pop-up towns they grafted onto "empty" grasslands after—for example—their wives or board-of-director members' belle daughters, a faithful dog, a profitable race horse, a beloved poet or...

The monikers hung on patina-less places, however, mattered less than the intended towns' lack of existing social fabric. Filling them with folks already "assigned" a section of land before the immigrants ever left Scandinavia or Schenectady, railroad companies intended the new, generic "starter" towns they laid out like chessboards along promising rail sites to attract tens of thousands of ambitious individuals and families, looking for new lives with which to replace old.

aerial photo of Thornton, Iowa, circa 1940: Main Street is on the left.

―――――

chapter 26: waves of extraction

When the young surveyor Henry Luick reached the open prairies of North Central Iowa in the 1840s, he saw an unspoiled grassland that relatively few non-natives had ever seen. And, that millennia-old wilderness teemed with a number and diversity of flora and fauna that as a boy back in Europe he never could have imagined. Wooly, lumbering bisons and elk with towering antlers roamed the undulating plains around what would become "Belmond." After Henry returned a few years later with his younger brother, David, to stay, the two fed the first party of settlers on juicy buffalo steak and gamey leg of elk. With millions of buffalo grazing out behind the Luicks' cabin at that time, who would have ever thought that in little more than three decades the great mammals would be nearly extinct. "*No-o-o*, how could *that* ever be?"

When European Americans arrived on the Great Plains in larger numbers, those vast grasslands seemed deceptively barren to white-folk eyes. Problem was, they were, in fact, far from empty. For one, some fifty million bison roamed the Great Plains as late as 1875. After "dutiful" Americans—including cowboys, charter-train tourists shooting rapid-fire through open windows from padded seats, adventurer wannabes like future-US-president Teddy Roosevelt and too many others—flocked to the Plains to pick off a few dozen or several thousand head each, by 1890 only an estimated 750 pure-blood buffalo remained. Particularly during the most active years of railway construction, circa 1866 to 1886, pale-skinned newcomers fell so many bison, so fast, they just left the intact carcasses to rot—foul testimonies to the disbelieving Native Americans' fears that the arriving whites meant their demise. A few entrepreneurs thought of gathering millions of skulls to grind into fertilizer, while others fed a short-lived craze for buffalo hides to wear as lap robes during jolly sleigh rides. And, for a brief time, pickled buffalo-bull tongue graced the menu of most every gourmet restaurant across the young republic.

The mad rush to wipe out the North American Bison was a butchery as senseless as it was bloody.

pile of bison skulls waiting to be ground into fertilizer, mid-1870s

The enormous bisons' almost complete slaughter took its frenzied course with few opponents but millions and generations of victims. True, virtually erasing one of the world's largest land mammals from the planet forever did make way first for the cows and hens of hopeful peasants like Ane B. Hansen and her crazed second-husband, Stenholdt—and, later, endless paved parking lots or strips lined with Mac's and big-box stores. Even Grampa George's and Olga's beloved, edifying Stuhr Museum sits on the massive beasts' former grazing grounds and dusty wallows.

Buffalos, however, were not the settlers' only victims. Ashen bison skeletons strewn across the prairies, already then, marked the last days of freedom for a proud people who'd lived in seamless balance with their grass-covered world for thousands of years. As the "Iron Horse" and "talking wires" whites brought with them cut into, then tied open the wounds of the flesh of what the plains' original dwellers saw as Mother Earth, they despaired.

Although inhabiting a world where "travel" was limited to a scope and speed of what human or horse legs could muster, Native Americans understood astonishingly well what the ever-more-rapid arrival of "American," of Europe-stemming settlers meant for their people. And, they spoke from their hearts about what they saw. Sometimes offered beads, too often infected blankets, "firewater" or hollow "treaties" for land that they within their cultural framework couldn't conceive of "belonging" to them or anyone else, most resigned themselves to what they accepted as an unavoidable fate.

study for Albert Bierstadt's The Last of the Buffalo, *1888*

Indeed, seen in the larger flow of time, in almost no time the millions of natives who'd peopled an entire continent before Europeans came to conquer it, disappeared—from disease, from hunger, from bullets. As well-funded railways pushed their way across the prairies and the buffalo out, the natives of the Great Plains realized—as the Nez Perce's Chief Joseph later put it,

> there were a great many white people in our country, and many more would come; [Washington Territory governor Isaac Stevens said] he wanted the land marked out so that the Indians and the white man could be separated. [...] We gave up some of our country to the white men, thinking that then we could have peace. We were mistaken. The white man would not let us alone.

170

Ultimately, the continent's first humans felt expressly deceived by the strangers among them. One of the Upper Midwest's most legendary local chiefs, Black Hawk, said in his autobiography

> How smooth must be the language of the whites, when they can make right look like wrong, and wrong look like right.

Hinmahtooyahlatkekt ("Thunder Rolling Down the Mountain") or "Joseph;" with family, circa 1880

With Native Americans conveniently out of the way of white settlement, isolated homesteads attracted new towns, which in turn attracted more settlers, who then quickly fed the growing towns—some of which bore the names of the homes the land's new occupants had left, in search of new lives built upon the bones—or least broken lives—of those who'd gone before. Alone in Hall County, the adopted home of my Great-Grampa George Luick's future Danish-immigrant mother-in-law, Ane B. Hansen, the name its settlers bestowed virtually every community harked back to lives that once were. With the Swedes (re-)establishing "Gothenburg" in nearby Dawson County, the Danes decided to deem one of their Central-Nebraska enclaves "Nysted" after the coastal home some of them had known back on the Danish island of Lolland. They named a second one "Dannebrog," the cross-emblazoned "Danish cloth" or flag said to have fallen from the sky to lead the Danes to victory at the Battle of Lyndanisse ("Volmerslaget") in 1219 in today's Estonia.

More than any other immigrating ethnic group, the Danes

1881 railroad booklet printed in German showing Nebraska's railways

and their Scandinavian cousins comparatively easily midwifed in the New World what their compatriots who stayed home struggled hard to birth—cooperatives. Parallel to the adult-education *Folkehøjskole* movement that arose in Denmark in response to losing the 1864 war with Prussia (and inspired the founding of Danish "folk schools" in seven Midwestern states and in California), the cooperative movement there strove for social renewal and advancement through collective effort. Both projects reflected a revival of Danish identity and nationalism, and spurred reformist campaigns for popular "enlightenment." Earlier experiments in cooperative production or even ownership dated as far back as 1498 in Scotland, but those in Scandinavia countries almost four centuries later enjoyed more formal legal recognition and protection than late-Medieval models.

Transplanting Old World institutions—even new versions of earlier attempts to engineer a more peaceable humanity—onto New World soil couldn't succeed, however, without adapting them to the American reality. Various 19th-century cooperative projects across Europe and into the Progressive Era of the early 20th century in the U.S. tested mutual-assistance ideals as stores, workshops and mills, kindergartens or schools, banks, insurance providers, printing presses and more. In the early development of the yeoman-based agrarian Midwest, however, above all collective bargaining in selling commodities fanned the swift spread of farmers' grain cooperatives across the American Heartland. Even as they carried the burden of organizing, funding and then building such cooperatives as formal, legal entities, Midwest farmers continued to cooperate informally, starting vital harvesting and threshing or other "rings" that often survived for generations. By themselves, "American" or European settlers scarcely stood a chance of thriving under the often flip-flopping arctic-tropical climatic extremes or market-price whims they faced. And, they knew it. Whether or not they always liked each other, they banded together, as one.

The first generations of non-native peoples living on the North American prairie banded together not only based on geography, on physical proximity to one another, in order to get things physically done, but, moreover, on ethnicity, on emotional closeness to each other, in order to not become spiritually undone. Dutch-American residents of Holland, Michigan—for example—maintained contact with their peers in Pella or even in further-afield Orange City, Iowa, in order to read newspapers printed or

Midwest threshing crew breaking to pose for a photo, circa 1910s

periodically attend sacred services preached in Dutch, to study in denominationally-"pure" colleges, or profit from business connections. Danish Americans of Hall County, Nebraska, for another, did the same—with other folks with Danish roots in Iowa enclaves bearing Anglo-sounding names like Ames, Elk Horn, Kimballton… and Thornton, the future home of not only Olga Hansen Christensen Luick, but of Olga's future daughter-in-law's paternal grandparents, Peter and Maren "Mary" Juhl.

———

Some Danish-American historians hold that from 1820 to 1850 "about 60 Danes settled in the United States every year"—and cite three of the more notable of those mostly single Danish men who came between the colonial period and the American Civil War:

> one of George Washington's most trusted officers during the American Revolution, [a second] who died at the Alamo in March 1836 in the struggle for Texan independence, and [the third] a blacksmith from Copenhagen who led a group of adventurers from Missouri to California in 1839. The trail [he] established [...] was followed by the "forty-niners" during the California Gold Rush [and he] is considered one of the most important early settlers of California.

American steamer docked at Larsens Plads, 8 Toldbodgade in Copenhagen, circa 1890

After the Civil War, instead of young bachelors trickling to America searching solo for their fortunes, the majority of Danes came as families—extended ones, arriving piecemeal. When Peter Juhl and his wife's brother—who took the "American" name "Jerry" Nielsen when he arrived in the New World—stepped off the train at Thornton's dusty clapboard station in 1887, the men found Peter's sister, Anna, and her husband, Ole Nielson, waiting for them.

Peter Juhl and his brother-in-law "Jerry" Nielsen were met at the Thornton train station in 1887 by Peter's sister, Anna (right), who was married to Ole Nielsen and had immigrated to Iowa before her brother. It is a coincidence but no surprise that both Peter and his wife, Maren "Mary" Juhl, had sisters named "Anna" or that both Peter and his sister married people named "Nielsen" given the commonality of both forenames and surnames. By the late 1880s, hundreds of Danes had crossed the Atlantic to settle a swath reaching from Thornton southwards some 15 miles (25 km) to Latimer, Iowa—a true immigrant enclave on the prairie.

Happy to speak his mother tongue with his sister's family and the hundreds of other recent Danish immigrants who'd established a Nordic enclave that stretched south across the Franklin County line to the tiny town of Latimer, Peter immediately set to work as a farmhand. By chance having come to the last part of Cerro Gordon County to be settled, he witnessed the remaining native prairie succumb to the settler's plow. Everywhere he turned, abundant crops shot up from the freshly-turned sod, creating a bounty like none he'd ever known. Unlike in urban Denmark, in rural Iowa this former peasant could become the master of his own fate. As soon as he'd saved enough money, this future "American" would send for his wife and four children.

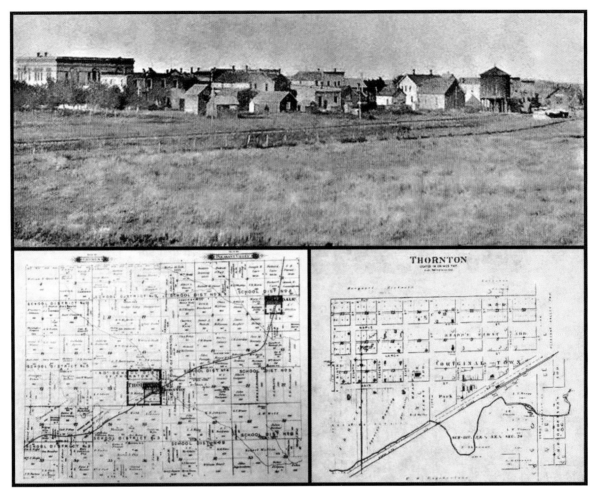

photo of Thornton's Main Street, seen from the south side, circa 1890; period maps of township & town

Diligent Peter Juhl enjoyed two auspicious advantages from the moment he arrived in what in Europe he had heard hailed as "The land of unlimited possibilities." For one, unlike tens of millions of other immigrants who'd arrived in the United States or other New-World countries such as Argentina or Australia, South Africa or San Salvador, he had established family members waiting for and ready to help him. And, those family members were tightly-connected: his sister Anna Nielsen's farm, for example, lay directly adjacent to that of his brother, Søren Juhl's.

Second, Peter happened to set himself up in farming during a period of prolonged boom in a country with annual growth rates that would have made modern China envious. With expanding cities out East and the endless West filling in with settlement, American agriculture had a growing stock of hungry customers. With that of the U.S. having reached fifty million by 1880, the country's farm population had reached almost twenty-three million; forty-nine percent of all employed persons were farmers—one-quarter of whom were tenants. With steady, committed assistance always available and more than enough work as a farm hand for hire to save money, Peter soon had the funds to send for his wife and four children, as well as to buy a farm.

175

Peter and Maren "Mary" (Nielsen Jørgensen) Juhl, circa 1910

After joining her hard-working husband on a Tuesday, 17 April 1888, "Mary"—as she henceforth called herself—set up housekeeping on a farm that Peter and she bought west of Sheffield, spread out against a slight rise on the otherwise flat prairie between Thornton and Latimer. As they found the funds, the Juhls—whose surname comes from the Danish word for mid-winter, "*Jul*"—added to the existing small farmhouse that had come with the young farmstead they had bought, for already in spring 1889 the first of another seven little Juhls arrived. The couple clearly prospered, for they kept expanding the house. They added at least two wings, and afforded themselves such amenities as floor-to-ceiling porch screens to keep out flies as the family enjoyed fresh air in amble, light space to work or unwind after a long day. Indoors, stained glass lent the large bay window a refining finishing touch and shades adorned each window. Nearby, a sleek windmill saved the family hand-pumping its water, while rows of conifers broke prairie winds in winter and leafy trees encircling the house provided much-needed summer shade.

By appearances at least, it seemed that by the first decade of a new and optimistic century, after only little more than a dozen years of living in their adopted country, the Juhls had realized their American Dream. Reaching it with impressive speed, however, did not assure that everything about their hard-won "American" lives would be to their liking. As the Old-World parents of decidedly New-World offspring were to discover, the Juhl children differed mightily from their subservient-raised parents and dared do as they please—as made embarrassingly public on 16 June 1910 when the *Oxford Mirror* in far-away Oxford Junction, Iowa, tattled on the elopement a fortnight earlier of Peter and Mary's third of seven Iowa-born children:

Elva, Willy, Clara, Peter & Mary on Juhl farm near Thornton, circa 1905

Iowa State News

Events of Recent Occurrence Throughout the Commonwealth

Returning home for the parental forgiveness, Mr. and Mrs. Fred Lunstrum [sic] and Mr. and Mrs. Colburn, a quartet of Clear Lake young people who went to Chicago where they were married, got the cold mitt from the home folks. Serious results were prevented by officers who hovered near when the young people came to town after their brief honeymoon. Mrs. Lunstrum, who was known as Miss Anna Juhl, was a well-known young clerk, and her husband is a tailor and has been running a business there for some time. The marriage was forbidden by the parents. Mrs. Colburn was Miss Flossie Pramer, who has been engaged as a singer at a local theater, and is the daughter of Mr. and Mrs. Walter Pramer, well-known residents. Mr. Colburn is a carpenter.

BHS photo identified only as "Cora Mosman"

Maren "Mary" and Peter Juhl, circa 1920

Over time, as the first generation of "new Americans" turned into adults, married and moved out to pursue lives of their own making, the long, white-frame farmhouse the Juhls had erected grew evermore empty. One of Peter and Mary's children—their second of four sons, Nick—found a bride from nearby Rockwell, and a job as station clerk in Burchinal, the quiet railroad stop halfway between Thornton and Cerro Gordo County's seat, Mason City. When, in mid-April 1913, "at the quiet hour of two o'clock in the morning, the spirit of the life of [Nick's young wife] Lottie Esther Moorehead Juhl fled to its maker and eternal home," why didn't the baby's paternal grandparents take their son's two-day-old, half-orphaned child to live with them?

True, their youngest of eleven children, Elva, was almost twelve by that time, so the 55-year-old immigrants could see the end of almost three and a half decades of parenting. Perhaps they had no desire to add almost twenty years to it. Or, maybe their deceased daughter-in-law's parents, the Mooreheads, proved readier to take the girl. Or, maybe Mary's health wouldn't allow it. In any case, within a decade she and her husband had sold the farm they'd toiled so hard to establish and moved to Clear Lake, where they owned a fruit farm and orchard on the east end of Main Street, the site today of the town's junior and senior high schools. There, according to an obituary printed in the growing resort's *Mirror-Reporter* in early December 1923,

> Mrs. Peter Juhl, who had been ill for about two years and had been confined to her bed for at least one year, passed away at her home at South Fourth Street last Thursday. She had suffered greatly during the greater part of her illness. Everything that medical skill could do was done, but nothing could stay the progress of her ailment.
>
> Mrs. Juhl was a very active worker in the Zion Lutheran church, she was a woman in whose life was exemplified the real Christ spirit.
>
> Mary Neilson [sic] Juhl was born in Denmark, May 8, 1857, and was married to Peter Juhl Nov. 23, 1877 in Denmark. They came to Iowa April 17, 1888.
>
> She leaves to mourn her passing: her husband and [children, as well as] 21 grand-children, two great grand-children, and brother Jerry Neilson [sic] of Thornton, Iowa, sister Mrs. Anna Hansen of Thornton, and two brothers and a sister in Denmark.
>
> **CARD OF THANKS**
> We desire to thank our many friends and neighbors for all the kindness shown us during our recent bereavement, and for the floral offering.
>
> Peter Juhl and Family

the Juhls' simple, weathered gravestone in Clear Lake Cemetery, across a fence from what once was their fruit farm

The Peter Juhl family lost a key member with Mary's passing, but it gained another within two years when aging Peter took a second, "American" wife, Laura Sommers Sutton. According to "Grampa Juhl's" granddaughter Charlotte, the two kept the fruit and vegetable business thriving, with an orchard boasting not just the standard apple but peach, pear, cherry and other trees, as well as many sorts of berry bushes and diverse beds of vegetables. Such productive later years would not last long, however, for as the *Globe-Gazette* reported on 31 August 1931,

> Mrs. Peter Juhl, 69, died at her home on Grant Street at 8 o'clock Sunday morning after an illness which had bothered her all summer. She returned a week ago from the hospital where she had received treatment. Funeral services will be held at 3 o'clock Wednesday afternoon at the Ward Funeral home, East Main Street with burial at Algona, where a short service will be held in the chapel.
>
> Laura E. Sommers was born at Gallopolis, Ohio, March 25, 1862. She moved with her parents to Ripon, Wis., and later to Owen's Grove, Cerro Gordo county [sic]. Here she was married to Joseph Lewis Sutton, Sept. 1, 1878. The young couple pioneered in Clark county, S. Dak., returning to Cerro Gordo county in 1890. They resided in Mason City for a short time and moved to Algona in the fall of 1891. In 1910 her husband died. Ten years later she moved to Clear Lake and was married to Peter Juhl of Clear Lake in 1925.

Widowed a second time at age 74, Peter went on living, but rather than finding a new companion for what were supposed to be his "golden years" he focused on his growing list of direct descendants—many of whom were on hand to observe his reaching nine decades of a rich life. As the *Globe-Gazette* announced on Friday, 11 July 1947,

JUST BEFORE SUNSET   CLEAR LAKE, IOWA

Peter Juhl, who will be 90 years old Saturday, was honored Sunday at a family picnic at State Park lodge with 71 relatives gathering for the celebration which also observed the 61st birthday of Mrs. Mata Nelson, Thornton, daughter-in-law of Mr. Juhl, whose birthday was Sunday. Each was presented a gift of money. Mr. Juhl, who is in excellent health for his years, has lived in Clear Lake and Thornton since a young man. He was born in Denmark July 12, 1857, was educated there and was married to Mary Nelson [sic]. He, accompanied by his brother-in-law, came to America in 1889 [sic], going to Thornton, where he stayed with his sister. The next year his wife and 4 children came to America and joined him there. They started farming west of Thornton and stayed in that vicinity for many years.

Some years after his wife's death he was married to Mrs. Sutton of Clear Lake, who succumbed in 1931. Since her death he has made his home in Clear Lake and for the past few months has been living with his daughter, Mrs. Mervin Jensen, East Lake Place. He has 9 [other] children [...]

Attending the affair were the following: Matt Juhl, Clear Water, Minn., Mr. and Mrs. Vale Law and family, Emmons, Minn. Mr. and Mrs. Jay Miller and family, Hanlontown; Mr. and Mrs. Donald Gullickson and family, Mr. and Mrs. Reuben Hanson and daughter, Mrs. Bertha Juhl and Phyllis, Northwood and Mr. and Mrs. Jerry Juhl and family, Manly; Mr. and Einer Madsen and family, Alden; Mr. and Mrs. Ray Nielsen and family, Sheffield; Mr. and Mrs. Delbert Juhl and family, Rockwell: Mr. and Mrs. Harry Welker, Mr. and Mrs. Roy Badker and daughter, Theone, Clear Lake; Mr. and Mrs. Arnold Troe and son, Swaledale and **Mr. and Mrs. Peter Juhl and daughters, Mr. and Mrs. Donald Luick and family**, Mr. and Mrs. Soren Nielsen, Mr. and Mrs. Leonard Nielsen and sons, Mr. and Mrs. Martin Nielsen and family, all of Thornton.

If Peter Paulsen's grandson "Peter Juhl [with] daughters" was present at the big bash, was the mood not a bit crimped, were Lynann and her baby—Donald's illegitimate baby, Lois—also present? The article lists my paternal grandparents "and family" as having been in attendance, too: Wasn't the intended festive atmosphere compromised by the discomfort of the open secret that unavoidably accompanied fate-tainted Mr. and Mrs. Donald Luick to the momentous event? I can only imagine that as my grandmother, Charlotte, later told my cousin Barbara that due to the whole affair "a part of [her] just curled up and died." She likely suffered immensely. Our grandparents' last, legitimate daughter, Sheranne, however, tells a different story:

> My family got along fine with the Juhl family! Mom's half-sisters were closer to her as if they were sisters. They all knew what happened with Dad and the hired girl! It was no secret---the whole town knew! I always remember the family reunions at State Park every August. A lot of good food and we kids went swimming. My cousins were all there and one or another of them would come home with us and their parents would come the next Sunday for dinner and to pick up my cousin. Those were real families! I dearly loved my aunts and uncles. I still keep in touch with my cousins---even though I lost track of one. At moms funeral a cousin from Northwood took a long lunch break and came down to see me! She was standing by the church door when we got back from the cemetery. Jeandelle and Bud walked past her and didn't even recognize her, which didn't surprise me as they had nothing to do with their cousins for some reason or another---don't know why! Bud's went to one family reunion at the shelter house when Deb was a baby! I remember my folks always wishing that the kids would go to the reunions! Jeandelle carried on for many years saying that she didn't even know her cousins---I finally had enough and told her all she needed to do was pick up the phone and call them and invite them over! They all lived around Hanlontown, Northwood, Hampton, and on the edge of [Minnesota]! She was miffed when she found out that I still kept in touch with them. We had that discussion a few weeks before Mom died! So much for my rambling on---I just wanted mainly to let you know that my family had no problem with the Juhls---they were a true family. Mom forgave Dad and healed long ago!

Regardless to the degree—or not—that the Juhl clan recovered from the disconcerting shock and awkward social stigma of one grandchild's husband having a baby out of wedlock with a minor, who then by coincidence later married another grandchild's son, patriarch Peter would not survive to be a binding presence in the family much longer. As the *Globe-Gazette* informed its North Central Iowa readership a short time later, on Thursday, 16 March 1950,

> Funeral services for Peter P. Juhl, 92, who died suddenly at a Mason City hospital Saturday evening, were held at the Wilcox funeral chapel Tuesday afternoon with the Rev. Axel Shefveland, pastor of the Zion Lutheran church, conducting the rites. Burial was in Clear Lake cemetery. Pallbearers were 6 grandsons: Raymond and Leonard Nielsen, James and Andrew Jenson, and [Lois Luick Juhl's adopted grandfather] Peter and Gerhardt Juhl. Mrs. A. E. Folkmann, accompanied by Mrs. Irving R. Morgan, sang "Rock of Ages" and "My Jesus, as Thou Wilt." Members of the Lakeside Ladies' aid served dinner at the Harry Welker home at noon and a lunch following the services. Relatives were present from Grand Lake, Ill., Minneapolis and Maple Lake, Minn., and Manly, Mason City, Northwood, Sheffield, Thornton, Klemme and Rowan.

———

chapter 28: seeking Danish homelands

When, as a boy, Gramma Luick used to reel off the various nationalities comprising the Luick-Juhl lineage, singing "We're Scotch-Irish, English, Welsh, German, Dutch and Dane!" I always had the feeling that any Danish blood was but a drop on an already-full palette of deep, oozing red. Besides Great-Grampa Luick's seldom-seen second wife, "weird" Olga, and Gramma's own, supposedly disowning father, it seemed to me then that not a hint of Scandinavian-ness soiled our otherwise "pure" British-Germanic pedigree. Then, the Bi-centennial came—and teen-age Mike began digging deeper behind the dominant, age-old Luick-Thrams family narratives.

My grandmother Charlotte often cited as proof for the source of her life's long list of woes the charge that "neither my father nor his Danish parents wanted me." Taking Gramma at her word, I, too, wondered why that might have been, as even to juvenile me it seemed rather brutal to...

So, I set off to find out!

Thornton's Picnic Day, circa 1910: Oxen were roasted, a band marched down Main Street, crowds came.

As Gramma once mentioned in passing that Thornton's red-haired former postmaster, Carl Hansen, was her father's cousin—Maren Juhl's sister Anna's son—he seemed like a logical place to start digging. In an attempt to uncover a reason why the Juhl clan might have wanted nothing to do with the two-day-old baby who eventually became my cute, diminutive granny, I marched to his small, white-asbestos-shingled house on Thornton's north side, at the bottom of the hill on which white-fenced Pleasant View Cemetery quietly sits, savoring its commanding view of those living in the village below, dying to get in.

typical Upper-Midwest frame house from first half of the 20th century—"home" for millions of Americans

After I pounded forcefully on the door, sure that the humming air conditioner half-hanging out the shaded window would drown out my knocking, a frail bird of an old woman with florescent-orange hair eventually pried the swollen door open and inquired weakly "*Ye-e-es*?"

"Good day" I began loudly, already unable to hide that I pointedly wanted something, "might Carl Hansen be at home?"

After a moment of visible indecision she turned and, as she closed the door firmly, let the faint words trail over her finely-dressed shoulder "I'll *a-a-ask*."

Standing there on the top of steaming, poured-concrete steps, I cast my eyes around and noted that the sole living creature I could see—a sad-looking dog with slumping head and shoulders—barely had the energy to pant under such a scorching summer sun as it slowly scuttled from one shady spot to the next. Just as I heard a car motor lazily turn over and strain to push its pile of red-hot-metal-on-wheels away from a curb, then roll listlessly down a tarred street simmering from the merciless heat, the inner house door opened with a *"swoosh!"*

"Can I help you, young man?" a tall, once-handsome male figure inquired suspiciously, veiled behind the obscuring mesh of the screen door.

While I was still explaining who I was, my relationship to him and my mission, the square-shouldered stranger stepped halfway out the door with one foot, threw a nervous glance down the street, then pressed both of my upper arms to my torso with his large hands and said "Do come in" as he already was squeezing me past him, into the cold-as-ice cottage.

Once inside the living room, Bird Lady reappeared, standing before me, but this time supporting a hollow smile. "Oh" she chirped, "Carl has *lots* of family!" Stepping back and sweeping a frail hand in the direction of several French-Imperial-style padded chairs with fussy, "antiqued" curved legs, she motioned for the teen in their frigid midst to take a seat. "It's just" her voice again trailed off, with her forced smile following it, "that we don't have any family of our own."

three examples of French-Imperial-Style furnishings, decoration and architectural embellishments

As the storms were tightly screwed in battened-down position on all the windows, and every shade in the house was drawn to its sill and tightly tucked behind thick, gold-lamé drapes, their chilly, stuffy den should have been dark. As it was chock-full with glitter and shine exploding forth everywhere, from everything—from the embossed cushions on the pastel-covered French-Imperial-style chairs with the fussy, curved legs to the gilded, curly-cued frames holding back heavy canvases smothered in suspended globs of stale-smelling oil paint—at first I found the place more blinding than the debilitating summer sun outside, busy frying everything to a crisp.

As Bird Lady prepared some bitter instant iced tea with fake lemon juice, Carl fetched some deeply-buried albums. As he started taking me on a rushed tour through their black-but-faded, construction-paper pages, Bird Lady returned and began posing one distracting, insignificant question after the next. Sitting there, uncomfortably perched on the edge of an absurd French-Imperial-style chair with fussy, curved legs, I politely tried—certainly in vain—to pretend to take seriously Bird Lady's inane chirpings even while trying to keep pace with page-flipping Carl. As if in covert cahoots and in tandem, the aged couple refused to let me either linger over a given photo or pursue one, coherent line of questioning to its satisfying conclusion. I tried desperately to brake their dash for the photo-album finish line, for in the blur of images that fluttered past my dizzy eyes I saw the photo of Peter, Maren and nine of their eleven children; I spied a white farmhouse with tall, screened-in porches… plus the couple as retirees… but 'twas all so *rushed*!

Afraid that I'd soon betray my growing impatience with the odd duo's bait-and-switch tactics, I stopped a moment, sat silently and surveyed the many beveled mirrors hanging round the place next to overdone sconces holding never-lit, gold-dipped candles. Then, watching out the corner of an eye (made dry from the blasting air conditioning) to monitor my hosts' reaction, I slowly dropped my head and stared a moment at the overdone French rugs and fussy parquet flooring.

Caving in, Carl quietly offered—noticeably reluctantly—to let me take a half-dozen images of the Juhl-Nielsen clan to be camera-copied, then returned by a solemnly-sworn date shortly hence. He had hesitated, that is, until I revealed that the amateur photographer who'd shoot the copies was none other than Gerald Allen, the well-respected Cerro Gordo County sheriff who twenty-one years after the infamous crash discovered Buddy Holly's signature glasses in a forgotten envelope in some old court files. "Jerry" was also Gramma Luick's twice-over cousin and the doting father of my high-school-age "cousin" Jennifer, with whom I was collaborating to write a booklet about our shared, pioneering ancestors. Hearing such placating credentials, Carl consented to sharing the family treasure which he and Bird Lady had been hoArding: I had won!

As I finally fulcrumed my sweating ass out of the sinking seat of that hideous French-Imperial-style chair with the fussy, curved legs and managed to stand erect again, facing the door I noticed a photo album on the floor next to Carl's ridiculous French-Imperial-style chair with fussy, curved legs. "What's that?" I asked, innocently.

"Oh, that" Carl dismissed, scarcely looking at the intentionally neglected volume at the bottom of the heap of albums he'd brought from another room, "it's nothing, really."

I peered at Bird Lady for a second—and when she then reflexively quickly looked away knew "it" *wasn't* "nothing."

"Mind if I have a look at that one, too?" I asked even as I bent over to pick it up before Carl could answer.

Metro-Goldwyn-Mayer studios, Culver City, California, 1922; Rudolph Valentino in A Sainted Devil, *1924*

When the stiff binding finally surrendered and let the glossy Art-Deco cover go enough to open, I found a young, debonair man dressed like Rudy Valentino on the frontispiece who could only have been Carl in the full bloom of virile, swarthy young manhood. A quick thumbing through just the next few pages revealed image after revealing image of Carl at the center of uninhibited streamer-laced parties, Carl in big topless cars full of cone-breasted girls, Carl on-set under bright lights while surrounded by knickers-wearing crew members, all focused on Carl's every move.

"*Ah-h-h*, Carl?" I stammered. "What are—?"

"Yes, that's me" he blurted out as if confessing an undeniable accusation. "In Hollywood. In the Twenties. Before talkies came in—an' I went out."

"*Wow-w-w*" I marveled as I reverently turned the taut pages. "Why didn't you tell me you were in Hollywood in its Golden Age?"

"You asked about Danish-immigrant farmers."

"Yeah, Carl" I interrupted him, "but this—"

"...is no big deal" he finished my imprudent sentence. "Look, it was a long, very long time ago."

Falling back absently into the bottomless seat of that stupid French-Imperial-style chair with the... whatever they were... wherever I was... WHERE *was* I? Was this Boondocks or Beverly Hills? Had I stepped inside an over-decorated Midwestern parlor or a displaced Parisian drawing room? WHAT *was* all this glitter and shine about? And, *WHO* WERE THESE *BIZARRE* PEOPLE?!

————

Place—and space; people—and how they fill, how they move through that space. With frigid, overdone, fussy lives, or in bare-boned, stripped-down pursuit of fully being in a fluid present? Whose space "is" it, anyway? Does a given place "belong" to marauding Vikings, meglo French dictators, shunned Jews or cute-but-deranged little Luick grannies? Who has a "right" to fill a space—soulful native chiefs, sad-eyed immigrant wives or their first-generation, Hollywood star offspring? Do we pull the shades down and close ourselves off in an entombing space, or knock down the ramparts and let our civilization spread to the hills? What pop-up "towns" do we fill our spaces with; whose cookie-cutter concepts do we steal or at least import from other places? What do we want, what do we "need" space to mean and to "do" for us?

These were a few of the images I meditated on some twenty years ago as I biked across the Danish island of Fyn, against hellish early-summer gusts from a nearby sea. I'd kissed "*adieu*" to my first German partner, Wolfgang Wagner, and set off from our shabby *Hinterhofwohnung* back in Kreuzberg, before that then-rough-an'-tumble part of former-West Berlin ever imagined it one day might be chic. Alone for the first time in months, I communed with the indulgent spirits of the open road and whispered to muses who flew alongside me, right behind my helmeted head.

Fyn offered fertile ground for imaginings, as the Danish writer and Dickens devotee, Hans Christian Andersen, had grown up in its seat, in half-timbered Odense—a detour through which I pedaled despite the exhaust-spewing trucks carrying Fyn's abundant farm wealth to market. I thought of Karen "Isak Dinesen" Blixen, the Danish writer who had spent her early years at Rungstedlund manor on an estate north of Copenhagen. As I pushed my two-wheeler through the grounds of Egeskov—said to be Europe's best-preserved Renaissance water castle, but a magnificent, many-gabled monument to brick construction in any event—I entertained visions of that aristocrat-cum-writer. "*How ironic*" I thought to myself, "*that she had to put into Africa a heart and soul of hers that at first had refused to come out in Denmark.*"

men and boys from America's fourth-largest tribe, the Ojibwa; 1800s

Perhaps, in trekking to the farthest hinterland in order to wade into her deepest inner land, the future Nobel-nominee was taking cues from her father, Wilhelm Dinesen, who spent thirteen months among the Ojibwa (or "Chippewa") of Wisconsin in the early 1870s. What had they found abroad that they could never find at home? Did Danes have to wander to places like East Africa and America's Midwest in order to see their olden Nordic homeland fully anew? Did they have to forsake their native country and set off on grand adventures in foreign ones in order to grow new eyes through which to see the world more clearly, in brighter fullness? Already for them, even in what we moderns consider a backward world, in shortest time the whole globe had become their "field." The question remains: during all those journeys, did they travel hopefully, or stay blinded by thoughts of arrival?

"Chippewa lodges, Beaver Bay" from B.F. Childs' late-19th-century series "Gems of Lake Superior Scenery"

However, it was not thoughts of aristocratic or artistic Danes which most busied my mind during that hard-won bike ride across my ancient ancestors' windswept island home. Instead, images of "my" Danes occupied me most—thoughts of my great-great-grandfather Peter Paulsen Juhl, surrounded at ninety by zillions of admiring descendants from dozens of far-flung towns and states. Some of his and Maren's myriad progeny first became mostly Midwestern farmers, but then their children's children became shopkeepers, soldiers and silent-screen stars; we greats and great-greats became teachers and preachers, doctors, dentists, pilots... or historian-writers.

Peter and Maren's forbearers likely included Viking raiders who by turns terrorized then pillaged North Europe's coasts, or, later, maybe were sea-faring traders who plied East Indian or West African shores. Certainly, they included hungering masses, yearning to be free of local tyranny, longing to choose fuller, happier futures... seeking their own corner of the sky to call their own.

———

185

postscript: from another world

In late October 2014 Christian and I left Dresden and drove to Denmark and Sweden for an eight-day break. Besides welcoming a week spent mostly in a secluded lakeside cabin in South Central Sweden's rural province of Småland, I wanted to pay a visit to the Juhl family's farm in Jutland, the peninsular anchor of the Danish archipelago, and to Växjö's emigration museum.

I had contacted Anton Boison, the Juhl homestead's current owner, per postal letter the previous week. (Yes, I should have approached him earlier, but proofing galleys for publishing volume one of this serialized book a month hence preempted all thoughts of short-term practicalities.) In just the little time he had before our planned arrival, Anton organized a heartrending family reunion of sorts.

Anton Boison telling Michael Luick-Thrams about local history over creamy pudding and strong coffee

When we arrived in nearby Rødding, at the home where retired widower Anton now lives with his fellow-senior-citizen girlfriend, an elaborate table of butter-slathered sweet breads, brandied cream pudding, strong Danish coffee (an unintended tribute to Olga's long-gone, thick-brew repute?) and even home-distilled blackberry snaps awaited us. So did former farmer Arne Juhl, an 85-year-old cousin I didn't know I had.

Bespectacled, neatly combed Arne came exceptionally well prepared. Eating rich pastries and sipping fine coffee took place amongst scattered maps of Langetved, the village surrounding "Vanggaard," the Juhls' historical homestead, as well as family-tree charts, photocopied church records, outlines of familial relations cascading back to the 1700s, etc. ad infinitum.

As much as I appreciated the painstaking preparation for our rushed visit, I felt keen to set off on the final five kilometers of Christian's and my pilgrimage to Langetved. Late-fall darkness threatened to steal a good view, not to mention worthwhile photos. (I felt pressured by a shrinking sense of time anyway: the clocks were set to "fall back" an hour that night, plus I didn't feel at all ready for the 21 November layout deadline hovering above my head.)

"*Oh-h-h*, yes, yes!" Anton tried to placate me, "we go now. *Oh-h-h*, of course: yes, yes!"

Once we'd climbed into this avid hunter's high-floored utility, however, an unannounced stop soon waylaid us yet again. Pausing at Arne's pleasant home on the edge of Rødding, he took us in briefly to meet his sweet Swedish wife, moreover to see two heirlooms that had once graced Vanggaard's spacious ground-floor rooms. He proudly showed us an aged grandfather clock with family-scribbled inscriptions on the inside, and a rosemaling wall cabinet—both handcrafted in the early 1800s, brightly painted and to this day kept in pristine condition.

the author winds Juhl-family clock from 1806; Arne Juhl and author viewing house sign from 1860

Back in Anton's car, on the last leg of our day-long drive from Dresden to a farm I'd seen but never visited, Anton spoke of "American Juhls" he'd met over the years. Yes, my cousin Paul Christopher from Webster County, Iowa, had come a handful of times. But, already in 1959 as a teen of sixteen, Anton had met Paul's then-87-year-old great-uncle, Hans Juhl, who had returned to Jutland to inspect old family haunts, such as the farmhouse where he'd been born. Although Denmark was no longer the country his impoverished family had left, Anton said the man's eyes welled up several times as he recalled "I remember *this* so well…" or "Oh, *here* we…"

In line with the sad stories Paul Christopher had gathered on his numerous visits to our Danish homeland, then relayed to kin in America's heartland, Anton and Arne recounted the lingering impact of Jutland's division at the hands of the occupying "Prussians" a century and a half ago. Anton's grandfather's brother and oldest son—for example—had fallen on the battlefields of France in World War I, fighting for the German Kaiser not out of conviction but obligation. "As had some five thousand other men and boys from the area" Anton explained. "Everyone knew someone who had died." Arne nodded, then gazed out over the once-contested countryside.

"And loss through emigration?" I wondered. "Had this region also lost bodies through attrition?"

"*Oh-h-h*, yes, yes!" Anton replied. "Thousands went to København or even *Amerika* in that time. *Oh-h-h*, yes! The people here then was very poor. *Oh-h-h*" he sighed, "it was a hard, hard time."

At last reaching Vanggaard, Anton's heavy vehicle barreled into the gravel-lined barnyard at such a speed that he blindly drove right over a yellow-plastic sandbox shovel his grandkids had left lying outside. After a quick search for Anton's missing adult son and his young family, a brief cell-phone parley confirmed that they'd set off looking for break-away cows in the back pasture.

scenes from Vanggaard, the Juhl family's historical home in Langetved, in Denmark's verdant Jutland

As we four visitors poked about the deserted place I thought of Charlotte again and again, ever stronger, and wondered silently to myself, *What'd Gramma have said, had she been able to see her grandfather's boyhood home? Might that have tempered her venom towards despised Nick? Would she have hated him less, if she'd understood more, what the whole clan had come from?*

Such unanswerable queries, however, would remain unanswered, as the tour quickly resumed.

the author strolling around Vanggaard's farmyard in October 2014—scene of 1880s family heirloom photo

After a whirlwind run around the U-shaped barnyard—lined on three sides by long, sturdy brick-on-stone barns, faced on the fourth by the ancient farmhouse—then a peek at the nearby pasture, bisected by a trickling brook, our entourage relocated to the parish church in adjoining Skrave.

*scenes from Skrave village church near Langetved, including early-19*th*-century, Juhl-family gravestones*

While quaint Vanggaard had fed my hunger for a nostalgic sense of family and place, the village church interested and, unexpectedly, touched me more. Yes, Arne pointed out numerous gravestones with J U H L carved across them, but more than a familial connection to the place I sensed the weight of my Danish ancestors' wider story, a saga inseparable from a small nation's ageless search for resources and opportunities. And, its people's willingness to chase them.

"How ironic," I grinned to myself, *"the Juhls left here only to land on a Danish island in a sea of Iowa prairie."* Meditating on Gramma's neighbors after she sold the farm and moved into town in 1973—the Ingebretsens, Jacobsens, Christensens, Hansens, Olesens and all the rest—it struck me that hopeful emigrants might swap landscapes, but cannot so easily sidestep certain fates.

As we meandered through the quiet churchyard Anton explained that in his family's case his son and his wife have rented out most of the fields and taken jobs "in town" as "farming just doesn't pay." Langetved's creamery closed in 1995: "In my youth the milk of a hundred dairy farmers kept it open, but now the village is home to only fifteen. A few farmers buy up more and more the smaller parcels of land, so what's left for the rest?" Pointing to a crawling metal mammoth on the other side of the churchyard's stone wall, he lamented "The machinery—it gets more complicated and more expensive every year. *Oh-h-h*, the costs—they are too high, the prices too low. We love this land" he swore, looking out over meadows and woods, "but what to do? We grew a dozen crops—barley most of all— but now it's corn, corn, corn. We're killing the land; it's so tired by now. The farmers—they feel lost and angry. They have so few and such bad choices."

I knew what Anton meant: I'm from Iowa.

Although they had risked an oceanic passage and braved hardships entailed in forsaking their homeland and wandering off in search of new lives in the New World, "my" Juhls had felt compelled to leave the land—not just in Denmark but, almost a century ago, in Iowa, too. *"Was all their effort worth it? They could have stayed in Europe just as easily and lost land here, too!"*

Just then, Arne said something. As I looked up—it might have been the pronounced light of the sinking autumnal sun or something unconscious but significant—my distant Danish cousin and our guide looked so familiar, like the Astrups back in Burchinal or the Jensens across our fence. *"Come to think of it, the folks in Langetved look a lot like those back home. Gosh,"* I marveled as my eyes focused on Medieval carvings on the eight-hundred-year-old church, *"the Juhls could've just stayed here all along. They could've saved themselves the bother an' costs to build a 'Danish Lutheran Church' in Thornton if they'd jus' stayed put an' kept attending this one…"*

only one of several Medieval facial or other decorative carved features built into Skrave's village church

Then, it struck me:

"But, wait a minute! Maybe it's less important what my people did in Amerika*, and more important what America did to my people."*

Looking into Arne's and Anton's questioning eyes just then, I thought *"These sweet souls look like us, but they sure don't act like us. Somptin' over there changed us"* (as I thought all this through, I could feel my heart beating under my breastbone) *"in here. We who left this place turned out different from the folks who stayed behind—and that difference makes all the difference."*

At that moment, I knew I'd found a truth deeper and more basic than I'd expected as I packed the car, then sped off back in Dresden that morning.

The trip had been worth it.

———

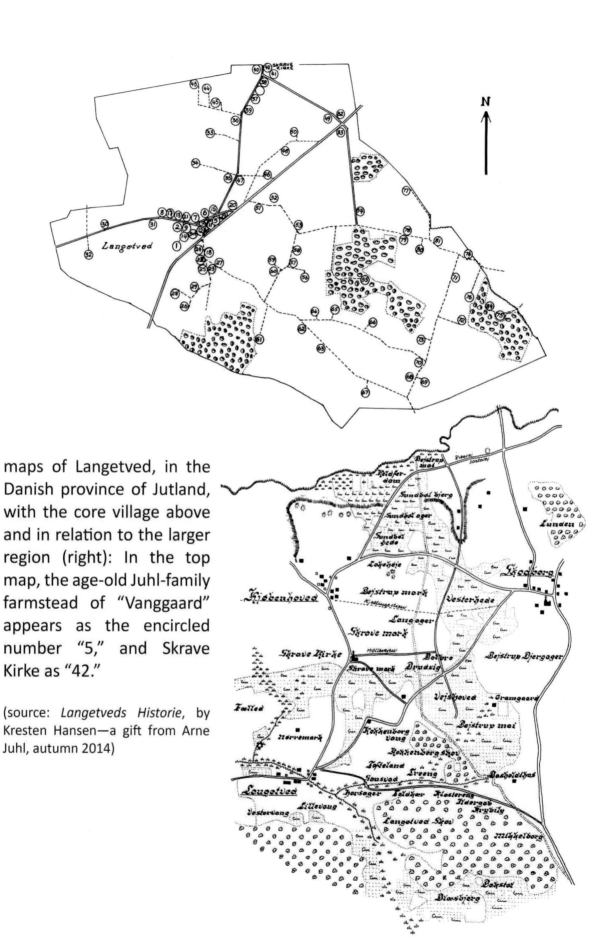

maps of Langetved, in the Danish province of Jutland, with the core village above and in relation to the larger region (right): In the top map, the age-old Juhl-family farmstead of "Vanggaard" appears as the encircled number "5," and Skrave Kirke as "42."

(source: *Langetveds Historie*, by Kresten Hansen—a gift from Arne Juhl, autumn 2014)

PART IV c

Root-Sinking Settlers

Section 8:
George & Lottie (Campbell) Moorehead family

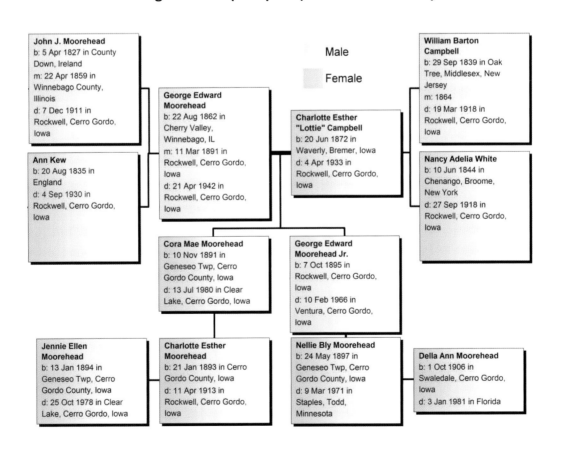

John J. Moorehead
b: 5 Apr 1827 in County Down, Ireland
m: 22 Apr 1859 in Winnebago County, Illinois
d: 7 Dec 1911 in Rockwell, Cerro Gordo, Iowa

Ann Kew
b: 20 Aug 1835 in England
d: 4 Sep 1930 in Rockwell, Cerro Gordo, Iowa

George Edward Moorehead
b: 22 Aug 1862 in Cherry Valley, Winnebago, IL
m: 11 Mar 1891 in Rockwell, Cerro Gordo, Iowa
d: 21 Apr 1942 in Rockwell, Cerro Gordo, Iowa

Male

Female

Charlotte Esther "Lottie" Campbell
b: 20 Jun 1872 in Waverly, Bremer, Iowa
d: 4 Apr 1933 in Rockwell, Cerro Gordo, Iowa

William Barton Campbell
b: 29 Sep 1839 in Oak Tree, Middlesex, New Jersey
m: 1864
d: 19 Mar 1918 in Rockwell, Cerro Gordo, Iowa

Nancy Adelia White
b: 10 Jun 1844 in Chenango, Broome, New York
d: 27 Sep 1918 in Rockwell, Cerro Gordo, Iowa

Cora Mae Moorehead
b: 10 Nov 1891 in Geneseo Twp, Cerro Gordo County, Iowa
d: 13 Jul 1980 in Clear Lake, Cerro Gordo, Iowa

George Edward Moorehead Jr.
b: 7 Oct 1895 in Rockwell, Cerro Gordo, Iowa
d: 10 Feb 1966 in Ventura, Cerro Gordo, Iowa

Jennie Ellen Moorehead
b: 13 Jan 1894 in Geneseo Twp, Cerro Gordo County, Iowa
d: 25 Oct 1978 in Clear Lake, Cerro Gordo, Iowa

Charlotte Esther Moorehead
b: 21 Jan 1893 in Cerro Gordo County, Iowa
d: 11 Apr 1913 in Rockwell, Cerro Gordo, Iowa

Nellie Bly Moorehead
b: 24 May 1897 in Geneseo Twp, Cerro Gordo County, Iowa
d: 9 Mar 1971 in Staples, Todd, Minnesota

Della Ann Moorehead
b: 1 Oct 1906 in Swaledale, Cerro Gordo, Iowa
d: 3 Jan 1981 in Florida

George Moorehead's and Charlotte "Lottie" Campbell's extended ancestors

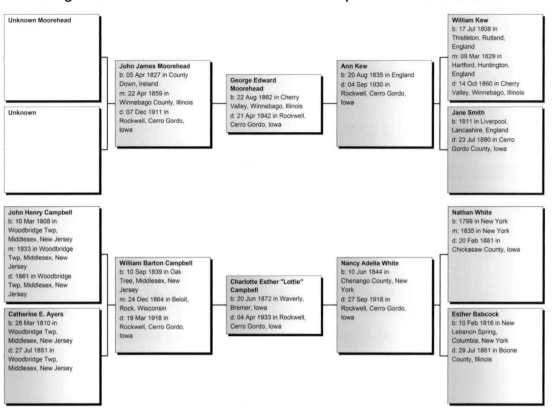

Unknown Moorehead

Unknown

John James Moorehead
b: 05 Apr 1827 in County Down, Ireland
m: 22 Apr 1859 in Winnebago County, Illinois
d: 07 Dec 1911 in Rockwell, Cerro Gordo, Iowa

George Edward Moorehead
b: 22 Aug 1862 in Cherry Valley, Winnebago, Illinois
d: 21 Apr 1942 in Rockwell, Cerro Gordo, Iowa

Ann Kew
b: 20 Aug 1835 in England
d: 04 Sep 1930 in Rockwell, Cerro Gordo, Iowa

William Kew
b: 17 Jul 1808 in Thistleton, Rutland, England
m: 09 Mar 1829 in Hartford, Huntington, England
d: 14 Oct 1860 in Cherry Valley, Winnebago, Illinois

Jane Smith
b: 1811 in Liverpool, Lancashire, England
d: 23 Jul 1890 in Cerro Gordo County, Iowa

John Henry Campbell
b: 10 Mar 1808 in Woodbridge Twp, Middlesex, New Jersey
m: 1833 in Woodbridge Twp, Middlesex, New Jersey
d: 1861 in Woodbridge Twp, Middlesex, New Jersey

Catherine E. Ayers
b: 28 Mar 1810 in Woodbridge Twp, Middlesex, New Jersey
d: 27 Jul 1851 in Woodbridge Twp, Middlesex, New Jersey

William Barton Campbell
b: 10 Sep 1839 in Oak Tree, Middlesex, New Jersey
m: 24 Dec 1864 in Beloit, Rock, Wisconsin
d: 19 Mar 1918 in Rockwell, Cerro Gordo, Iowa

Charlotte Esther "Lottie" Campbell
b: 20 Jun 1872 in Waverly, Bremer, Iowa
d: 04 Apr 1933 in Rockwell, Cerro Gordo, Iowa

Nancy Adelia White
b: 10 Jun 1844 in Chenango County, New York
d: 27 Sep 1918 in Rockwell, Cerro Gordo, Iowa

Nathan White
b: 1799 in New York
m: 1835 in New York
d: 20 Feb 1881 in Chickasaw County, Iowa

Esther Babcock
b: 10 Feb 1816 in New Lebanon Spring, Columbia, New York
d: 29 Jul 1861 in Boone County, Illinois

tagged with inscription "School Club"

George Edward and Charlotte Esther (Campbell) Moorehead

born:	22 August 1862	20 June 1872
where:	Cherry Valley, Illinois/USA	Frederika, Iowa/USA
married:	11 March 1891	where: Rockwell, Iowa/USA
died:	27 September 1943	4 April 1933
where:	Rockwell, Iowa/USA	Rockwell, Iowa/USA

George Edward and Charlotte "Lottie" Esther Campbell Moorehead, taken upon their marrying on 11 March 1891 in Rockwell, Iowa

"Death and disease, followed by disease and death—and despair" was all I ever heard in relation to this wedding photo of George Edward Moorehead and his decade-younger bride, Charlotte Esther Campbell, taken on the occasion of their marrying. All I saw, though, was the handsome, well-trimmed man and his doe-eyed, baby-faced bride, with her carefully-crinkled curls and tightly gathered, hourglass waist.

Cerro Gordo County's popular sheriff, Gerald Allen, came from Rockwell—at least, his people did, and in the North Central Iowa that I lived in, who you were *from* was as important as who you were *now*. His family later lived in Mason City, the ash-tree-lined county seat of about thirty thousand souls where, in the early Forties, he briefly dated my maternal aunt, Irene Thrams.

In the Seventies "Jerry's" daughter, Jennifer Allen, and I met and, over a short but productive period, collaborated. Discovering we were related through two interweaving lineages, we interviewed a dozen shared relatives and got from them a score of family photos that chronicled a rich but hard past we didn't know our people had.

chapter 16: a house divided

The world that guiltless George Edward Moorehead was born into was one of war. Even in his remote birthplace, the Illinois frontier village of Cherry Valley—which had incorporated only five years before, built around a mill and a railroad stop—there were at least three deep-seated, on-going conflicts unfolding at once. The loudest, deadliest of these was the American Civil War, an armed confrontation between two camps of states over how a new, diverse nation should develop—economically, socially and, therefore, politically. The quieter two, however, would also prove to be often violent and usually ruinous for all—albeit with far fewer corpses.

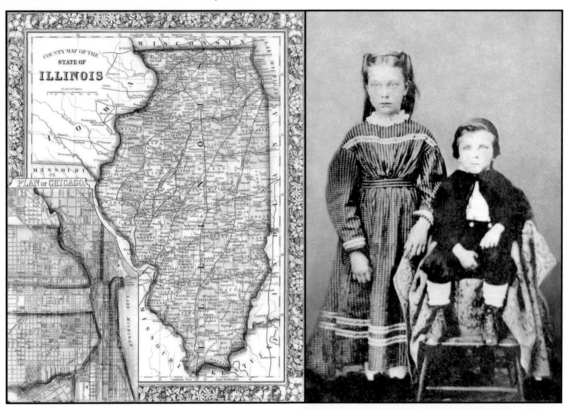

Illinois map, "Entered according to Act of Congress in the year 1861 by S. Augustus Mitchell Jr. in the Clerks Office of the U.S. District Court…;" Jennie and George Moorehead, circa 1865 in Illinois

Just two days before George's birth, *New York Tribune* publisher Horace Greeley—the ardently-abolitionist Republican who'd coined the term "Go West, young man, go West"—printed his *Prayer of Twenty Millions*, a polemical public plea for President Lincoln to liberate slaves in Union-held territory. The issues tearing apart the young nation, however, went far beyond that of slavery. Worldviews embodied by skin color afforded, first, a visible badge to hang campaign slogans on, with which to coax citizens into parting with prized votes or newspaper readers into parting with their precious pennies. It provided, then, after all discussion had stopped, the most motivating flag behind which to goad young men into thrusting bayonets into a cousin's or brother's chest. Indeed, what Southerners called "The War Between the States" went beyond facile fronts like pro- or anti-slavery. Sadly, in late summer 1862, as his English-immigrant mother Ann Kew Moorehead gave birth to baby George, the armed debate between the Blue and the Gray was a long way—and an even longer body count—from being settled.

The other two economic-cum-political struggles hanging over the Moorehead household into which little George arrived also had to do with intractable issues around personal identity and how people "move through the city"—as ancient Greeks millennia earlier had summed up human relations and power-sharing. The more palpable of the two involved ethnicity—that of George's Irish-born father, John James Moorehead from Balleywalter, a fishing village on the Ulster coast, in County Down. The oft-rabid anti-Irish sentiment that raged in 19th-century America in recurring waves wasn't new: It had surfaced already in colonial times, but broke out again with a vengeance with the potato famines

Confederate dead at Marye's Heights, Virginia, killed on 3 May 1863

that commenced in 1845 and sent over a million sons and daughters of Eire across the Irish Sea as well as the Atlantic Ocean in search of work and food. Did the anti-Catholics of Cherry Valley care that their village blacksmith, John James Moorehead, stemmed from a Protestant part of Ireland or that his people had Scottish—so, Presbyterian—roots? Probably not: stupidity rarely cares for facts or decisive details.

Ann (Kew) and John Moorehead at the occasion of son George's wedding in Rockwell, Iowa; March 1891

The last of the three essential conflicts hanging over tiny Cherry Valley—along with the rest of 19th-century America—at the time of George's birth, was also the most benign of them, even though it stemmed back at least to Medieval Europe. This divisive social cancer arises from the unequal yet essential relationship between the producers of food, and those who buy it from them *and*, in the next moment, turn around to sell tillers of the land the goods they need both to live as well as to pursue their livelihood, yet cannot create themselves. The hate-flamed fires of the Civil War burned themselves out.

The bigotry-based waves of anti-Irish discrimination—as finally demonstrated when a majority of U.S. voters elected its first Catholic, Irish-American president, John F. Kennedy, in 1960—eventually faded away. The unsettling, justice-imbalanced tension between food producers and food consumers, though, persists to this very day.

These three separate-but-related themes—how people of different backgrounds or with varied interests can live together peacefully, even while pursing varied goals or fulfilling seemingly opposing needs—accompanied George all his life. They influenced many of the paths he chose to take, including later political office. At their core, the overriding issues of his day involved how George and those around him—in his family, in the communities in which they lived, and in the nation, the dominant culture of which dictated the realm of possibilities perceived by the Mooreheads—shared both resources and the power to divide them, or not.

While overriding, often abstract social issues direct the arch of each of our lives, most mortals do not live primarily focused on the distant or eternal; most of us live our lives preoccupied with the immediate and temporal. And, many tend to deal with daily-world affairs more out of emotional rather than intellectual modes. We live, however, not alone: Forced to, we juggle the private and personal against the demands of the public and political. George Moorehead was no different. In his biography we find strands of our own struggles; in his story we find semblances of our own trials—as well as our own triumphs, as modest as they might be.

————

chapter 17: trailing restless souls

"Ol' Aunt Winnie Campbell"—as the Allens called the aged woman who was Jerry's deceased mother, Lorna's decade-older "old-maid" sister—shuffled around her small, musty retirement-center flat like an aged trapeze queen inching her way along a wilting wire. A veil of fried-fish grease mixed with jellied dust hung in the air, so that even the worn padded chairs from the Thirties that Winnie refused to replace stuck to the bottom of our butts. Still, we hardly noticed and cared even less, for Jennifer and I had driven down after our respective high schools had let out—hers in Mason City, mine at Clear Lake—to grill Ol' Aunt Winnie about "all she knows." What eager Jennifer and I didn't know, though, was what a *lot* 85-year-old willing Winnie knew!

Although I'd been in Rockwell maybe fifty times until then, I'd never met this hunched, white-haired woman who seemed to have met half of all of Dad's maternal relatives who I knew ever existed—right up to my Gramma Luick. (When Winnie mentioned "naughty Della Moorehead" among the myriad members she had known among my extended family, she added only a quiet "Oh, you'll find out" when I inquired who that could be.) It took no time, however, for me to realize that Winnie Campbell was to the Moorehead-Campbell-Kew clan what my maternal grandmother, Erma, was to the Thrams-Falcon-Ehrhardt multitudes—a captivating story-teller with an exceptional ability to remember and recount endless rounds of names, dates and places, in minute detail. Thus, I became an immediate fan of hers.

The problem was, even armed with fresh pens and lined paper, Jennifer and I—both honors students—soon got lost in the maze of blood-ties and vanished kin. At that point Winnie whispered "I know how ta take care o' that!" and waddled off behind a big curtain cloaking small treasures. After she'd returned to the sagging seat of her worn-arm armchair, she opened the lid of a vintage shoebox full of disintegrating, cardboard-backed photos.

"Oh" Winnie sighed within seconds of starting her hunt, "that helps—but it's *not* what I want."

"Whadjya find?" I fished.

Maude (standing), Ray, Grace, Charles "Gus", DeWitt, Will & Lottie, with William (seated), Mae & Nancy (White) Campbell, circa 1895; William Campbell outside Rockwell's post office, circa 1915. Not only the Whites were touched by war: According to family lore William's great grandfather, Neil Campbell (born 1734, died 16 October 1777) "was taken from his sickbed and removed from his home near Oak Hill [New Jersey] by the British. He escaped, but later died from the exposure." The family was Yankee, back to 1600s.

"Here" our distracted hostess explained, "is a picture of Uncle Bill at the Rockwell post office, and a portrait of the Campbells—that's your Lottie on the right side—but they're not what I was lookin' for."

"*Uh-h-h*, I'm thrilled to see 'em" I offered feebly as Jennifer's aging aunt pushed on, digging deeper into the photographic graveyard splayed across the soiled apron she'd pulled tautly over her packed lap. She plucked crumbling newspaper clippings and long-unseen pictures out of the box like so many unresisting threads from a jammed loom.

"So, Winnie, what ya know 'bout these folks?" I asked as I dragged the stiff, crowded family scene from her lap and held it in the air, suspended like a milky x-ray bearing confounding results.

Without looking up from a mission she clearly saw as dead serious, Winnie reeled off in one long, shallow breath "My grandfather William Barton Campbell came from Oak Tree back in New Jersey and his wife Nancy Adelia White five years younger from Norwich New York had sent five of seven brothers off to fight the Johnny Rebs because their dead mother couldn't—"

"Gosh" I marveled as the ancient raconteur briefly came up for a breath, then resumed.

"—she met William in Illinois during the war and married him in Beloit across the border in Wisconsin on Christmas Eve eighteen-hundred-and-sixty-three although he'd only had an eighth-grade education but a year later they moved to Frederika Iowa near Waverly before finally settling in Rockwell where by the time I was a wee girl he was an ice dealer."

"Oh!" I brightly chimed, feeling as idiotic as I likely sounded.

original caption: "The charge of the First Iowa Regiment, with General Lyon at its head, the Battle of Wilson's Creek, near Springfield, Missouri, August 10, 1861" from a sketch by "special artist" in Fremont's Division. Adelia's five soldier brothers were Elias, Charles, George, Lucius & Alonzo.

Perhaps as a distraction offered out of pity for my embarrassing stupidity, Jennifer cited "That girl in the foreground—the angelic-looking one in all white—that's Aunt Mae. Ever heard of her?"

Having never heard anything about any of the souls slowly floating out of the magic box, I answered my double-cousin only with a stony look.

"She looks sweet an' lovely here, but she later ran a saloon on Main Street, in Rockwell. Yeah" Jennifer smiled as she recycled conversations with Ol' Aunt Winnie from long before our shared project, "she kept a squirrel perched on her shoulder as she made the rounds and bantered with the boys in the bar. I guess" she tsk-tsked as she slowly shook her head, "she was quite a character—despite her parents, William and Nancy, having been devout Congregationalists. Yep—Aunt Mae was kinda rough."

Without looking up from that frayed shoebox during her flurry of hand movements inside it, Winnie mused quietly to no one in particular "I wonder if that's who taught Della ta drink."

"Say" I protested, "who's this 'Della' person you keep mentioning?"

Winnie said nothing but handed me a brittle, yellowed report—undated and anonymous—of a Campbell-White family reunion. I examined it cursorily, then peered at her, much confused.

"See that list of attendees at the bottom?" she drilled.

"Yes-s-s" Jennifer softly answered in my stead as I studied the artifact raptly, in stunned silence.

"Mike's Lottie, with her George Moorehead, was there—and, oh, those were the days of *real* family get-togethers! Those of today" she sighed, "well, they jus' ain't the same."

A tense quiet then fell upon us as Jennifer mutely read the article over my hunched shoulder.

Belmond characters captured by Martin Thoe; report on White family gathering in Bremer County, Iowa

As she absently continued to sort through the contents of the crowded box, without looking up from the task on her lap, she handed me a faded, crumbling article. "The Whites and Campbells were very close. Our people always attended their people's gatherings—like this one, over jus' northa Waverly."

Before she finished her sentence, I was studying the list of names provided at the article's long end.

"Here!" Winnie then exclaimed as, with a trembling hand, she proudly waved a long-lost sepia image in front of Jennifer's and my faces, muttering over her loose dentures "Here's George Moorehead and Aunt Lottie's wedding picture! I was *sure* I'd it tucked away somewhere here."

"*Wow-w-w*, Winnie—that's great!" I enthused, but my thoughts already were racing ahead, trying to map in my mind how all these people she kept weaving between fit together. When I eventually understood that she had uncovered an early image of the couple that raised my Gramma Luick, I smiled and nodded in silent satisfaction. Problem was, having just conquered that mental riddle, Winnie began to rattle off so many "Campbells," Kews" and "Dillinghams," scattered amidst "Sweets," "Whites" and "Mooreheads," I simply closed my notebook and stared at her, blankly.

Focused again on the contents of the still-overflowing shoebox, our busy hostess began fishing out yet more yellow, feather-light layers of packing paper or rubber bands that had dried out and burst well before the Vietnam if not Korean War. "Oh, here it is!" Winnie called out as if finding a long-lost lottery number. "Here's that photo of the Kews' cottage back in Thistleton!"

"In Illinois" I asked inattentively, as all that info flying at Jen and me had lulled me into a stupor.

"No" she looked at me, incredulous, as if I were dense beyond belief, "in England."

"Wait a minute" I countered, slowly coming to, "what year did the Kews leave England?"

For once Winnie fell silent, peered up at the light fixture, then disappeared into some parallel universe to calculate something. "Well" she sighed, finally coming back to us, in nineteen-hundred-seventy-nine in a place called "Rockwell" in Iowa, "it must have been 1855, because—"

"Hey" I interrupted her equation, jerking back to life but still finding it hard to believe Jennifer's and my extraordinary luck, "just imagine! We now know what the Kews' thatched cottage looked like back in mer-ry ol' Eng-o-land… way, way back—even before the American Civil War!"

"You know why the Kews left the border country between Rutland and Lincolnshire?" Winnie asked from her thread-worn throne.

"No—but *do* tell us, please" I begged.

"Poverty."

"*Poverty*?"

"I mean to tell you" little Winnie underscored her one-word sermon, "the Kews was *so* poor they couldn't even afford to give the children middle names."

"Seriously?" I stared at the diminutive woman dumbly. "How poor were they? I mean—"

"Well" Winnie recited without pausing, "William Kew worked as a butler in the local lord's castle and got to wear fine red-and-blue-velvet serving jackets with fancy brass buttons and smart britches but couldn't feed Jane and their six little ones back home in Thistleton and that's why the English have their 'Boxing Day' for the servants to take Christmas dinner leftovers home to their families but it was never enough so the Kews snuck off ta Liverpool and in spring eighteen-hundred-and-fifty-five set sail but there was pinkeye on board with only hardtack or dried meat and salty sea air that cracked their lips as the captain barked at them to go back to the dark decks below during the many storms and—"

"*How* in the world do you remember all this, Aunt Winnie?" I wanted to know.

painting of Guy Mannering, *which brought Kews to America*

"—when they got to New York on June 14th they took a train to Cherry Valley where they found a shanty to live in while William and the boys hired out by the month as farmhands to put bread on—"

"Yes, Aunt Winnie" Jennifer jumped in, "it's *so-o-o* nice of you to have had us, but…"

"—and the Kew daughters they worked as stock-girls in Cherry Valley shops and cleaned houses or took seamstress jobs to help pay for what the family needed but Ann at home couldn't grow, make or…"

By the time we finally succeeded in tearing ourselves away from inexhaustible Ol' Aunt Winnie, she was starting yet another round of stories, always told in looping sets, over stained, wear-rounded dentures that kept clacking in her mouth and that her probing tongue kept playing with, as if trying to dislodge a poppy seed or angel's hair. We two novice family historians felt overwhelmed by more material than even we bookish-types could quickly digest, so we made a date for the following week. As Jennifer and I parted my dutiful cohort promised that she would draft a chart to make visible what both she and I were having trouble making sense of in our swirling minds.

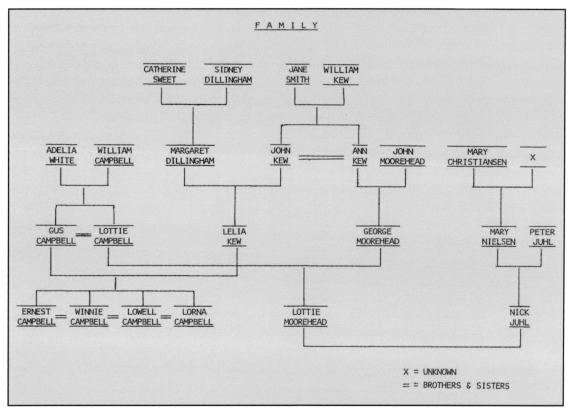

family-tree chart Jennifer Allen made in 1979 to clarify how she and the author are "double relations"

"Oh, that's jus' fine" Winnie waved behind us as we headed for the door. "I'll be here—I don't have anything planned." As the door to her flat creaked shut, I heard her softly say to herself "Well, at least I don't think I do."

———

chapter 18: the unending journey

The following week, having already filed through layer upon layer of nameless faces and hollow biographies, Winnie began to fill in gaps in the full, mostly long lives that led to… us. "The oldest of the three Moorehead boys, George"—childless Winnie somehow seemed to know, as if she'd herself witnessed all the delicious details she relayed to her eager audience—"loved to hunt and fish, tell jokes and tease the prettiest girls at church or ice-cream socials. He especially loved to fly across the open prairie in his sleek gig, his horse sweating in the summer sun. In winter, George glided over the frozen buffalo grass in his lightning-fast sleigh; the brass bells hanging under the panting horse's heaving belly jingled in the crisp, cold air…

It was a compelling story that Ol Aunt Winnie told us—and I've retold it here as she recounted it to then-teenage Jennifer and me, some thirty-five years ago. Problem is, fantastic family lore thrives on myths and soars with impassioned retelling, but at times withers in the face of facts that seem clunky or, worse, outright inconvenient when held against the lovely lilt of lulling lore.

For sure, death dictated the direction of George Moorehead's life already at an early age. It was the premature death from pneumonia at 52 of his maternal grandfather, William Kew, that once the Civil War had ended led young George's widowed grandmother and uncle—Ann's mother, Jane (Smith) Kew, and brother, George Kew—to consider a move west in search of new opportunities. Ann Kew Moorehead and her blacksmith husband decided to go with them—at least for a while.

Frank, George (both standing) & Burt Moorehead,
& George Kew (both sitting), in Iowa, circa 1890

Dubuque, Iowa, circa 1850s, from a lithograph printed by Herrmann Meyer in New York, in German

201

In 1869, after the winter snows had melted and worst of spring's bottomless mud abated, they set off by wagon from Cherry Valley, in Northwest Illinois, and crossed the wide Mississippi by ferry, which was cheaper than crossing the new toll bridge. After a rest in what was then, with eighteen-thousand people, one of the hundred largest urban areas in America, the emigrants guided their groaning wagons up and over the bluffs that kept the busy river port pushed up against the Mighty Miss. As the relative comforts of boomtown Dubuque faded behind them, these transplants from England, Erie and Illinois ventured out onto the frontier of the Great American West in search of available virgin prairie in Iowa.

Dubuque and the Mississippi as seen from a ridge west of the city, 1872

After a few days of traveling over poor roads or none at all, they arrived at Winneshiek County's seat, Decorah, a bustling, predominantly Norwegian settlement of about two thousand souls. That first night they found lodging in an inn and, as they eyed the town the next morning, they swarmed around the pin-up boards at the local land office, seeking a spot to call their own.

Stiles Hotel and stables, circa 1875 (left) and early Water Street businesses in Decorah, circa 1860

They must have found one, for the 1870 census cited John Moorehead—"born Ireland, [a] farm laborer"—as living in Madison Township with Ann, "born England, keeping house." They lived with Ann's mother, 62, and Ann's brother George, 24, who of the six Kew children had been afforded the most schooling—which wasn't much. On the frontier, brawn often trumped brain.

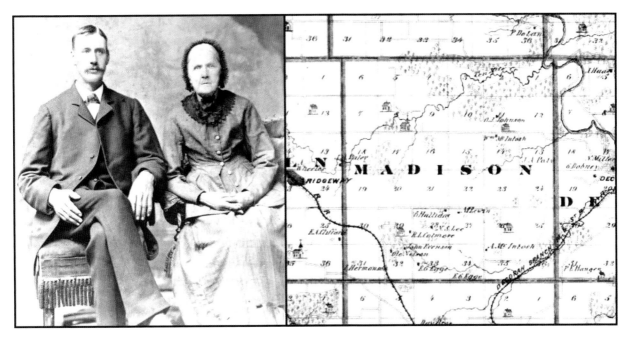

George & mother Jane (Smith) Kew, circa 1880; Madison Township in Iowa's Winneshiek County, 1870s

The five Moorehead children then on the ground ranged in age from eleven (Jennie) to baby Ann, two. Mother Ann had named her little son after her youngest brother, George Kew. The oldest brother, John, had left Cherry Valley two years earlier and moved west by oxcart to North Central Iowa. Apparently he found his travel companions, Sidney and Catherine (Sweet) Dillingham, agreeable, for soon after arriving in Cerro Gordo County and building a makeshift shelter near Linn Grove (later renamed "Rockwell"), 28-year-old John married the Dillinghams' sixteen-year-old daughter, Margaret.

Catherine (Sweet) Dillingham as painted on tin in the 1860s; John & Margaret (Dillingham) Kew's wedding picture, late December 1867

At the time the Moorehead-Kew party arrived in Winneshiek County, Decorah pulsated with a dynamism unusual for the already-then staid Midwest. Although less than twenty years old when four of my ancestors sojourned there a spell, the atypical town—built on the site of where an asteroid hit Earth and left a crater four miles (six km) wide, just as early life was emerging in the oceans—had already proven to be an early Iowa hotbed of individualism, a hunger for freedom, and rebellion.

203

Scandinavian settlers had begun pouring into "Little Switzerland"— so nicknamed for its dramatic, river-carved hilly landscapes—just after the U.S. Army removed the last Native Americans in 1848. (Ironically, the arriving settlers named Winneshiek County, Decorah and the nearby county seat of Waukon in Allamakee County for Winnebago leaders who had supported the Americans during the Upper Midwest's then-recent Black Hawk War—before, that is, the newcomers then forced their erstwhile Native-American allies onto reservations.)

Decorah, on the banks of Oneota Valley's Upper Iowa River, mid-1870s

The pious Norwegian Lutherans populating Northeast Iowa initially received their pastors from a seminary in Saint Louis, a journey of couple days by paddleboat up the resisting Mississippi River, or a couple weeks by land. In 1862 pastor Ulrik Vilhelm Koren successfully moved a fledgling Lutheran seminary from nearby La Crosse, Wisconsin to nascent Decorah. He didn't expect a rebellion from within only four years later, but one came—at the pen of a bookish farmboy from Dane County, Wisconsin.

Luther College's student body in front of Old Main—and below; circa 1880

On the heels of a just-concluded civil war, eighteen-year-old student Rasmus Anderson headed a cohort of boys to proclaim a "Bill of Rights" in opposition to what they saw as a "rigid" schedule, rules about visits into town—less than a mile away—and to dish-scouring, wood-cutting as well as shoe-shining chores. The proclamation ended with their assertion that "there was not enough freedom" but members of a pastoral conference saw matters differently. The administration deemed the handiwork of the all-male radical cadre (women wouldn't be admitted at Luther College for another seven decades and only then as a remedy to Depression-wracked finances) as "the worse of sins" and expelled its treasonous leader.

Rasmus B. Anderson (left) may not have met much success as a student at Luther College, but he clearly did later - as detailed in the footnotes at the end of volume III.

Luther's first campus pastor Nils Brandt, wife Diderikke (Otteson) & family taking tea on campus lawn, 1870s

The Mooreheads and Kews, however, had more immediate matters on their minds than radicals' freedom fights. Namely, they wanted to eat—and feed their family. That they could do in rural Decorah, but not without exhausting effort. Thousands of years of erosion had filled pockets of the Upper Iowa River tributaries' bottoms with deep, rich soil. Other spots in what's known as the "Oneota Valley," however, stayed thinly-covered, gravely alluvium atop crumbly bedrock. (The fossiliferous layer of limestone characteristic of the region is so distinctive that it earned its own geological designation, "Decorah Shale.") Thick underbrush between meandering streambeds complicated their work of scratching fields out of the newly won land.

In short: Establishing viable farmland would prove a hit-or-miss gamble for the Mooreheads and Kews. While cheaper than what remained available back in Cherry Valley, the land of Northeast Iowa entailed numerous challenges. And, beyond those, the family faced the typical travails confronting most pioneer families: unreliable weather and fickle markets, recurring waves of disease against which they had few effective antidotes, declining stocks of game to hunt, etc. But, their hardships were not unique.

19th-century scenes of the Upper Iowa River from Benjamin Gue's History of Iowa, *written over 17 years*

While nearby Protestant seminarians might be busy protesting, up the road 13 miles (21 km) some of the Moorehead-Kew clan's neighbors to the north would later be embroiled in deep conflicts of their own. Charles and Caroline (Quiner) Ingalls—the "Pa" and "Ma" of Laura Ingalls Wilder's later landmark *Little House* series—struggled to survive an unhappy sojourn in tiny Burr Oak, Iowa. The only segment of her family's convoluted career as Upper-Midwest pioneers that Laura later omitted from her family chronicle, the Ingalls' stay in the Hawkeye State seems one of the few stations in their long journey in which even ever-optimistic Laura could not find redeeming light.

Only beginning her career as a published writer of books late in life, at age 65, perhaps as aging Laura finally took pen in hand she blended out the half-year her family spent in Winneshiek County because it came in a series of sad, dark events. Just before they arrived in fall 1877, Laura's only brother, Charles Frederick—named for their father and their mother's step-father—died at ten months of age. While she did not write about it in her children's-book series, Laura did refer to little Frederick's death in her unpublished manuscript *Pioneer Girl*, thought to be the basis of the later juvenile version of her family's trials. In her memoir, she confided

> Little Brother was not well [and that] one terrible day, he straightened out his little body and was dead.

According to one Wilder-family scholar, Laura wasn't the only one affected by Frederick's death.

> Nearly forty years after Freddie's death, Ma mourned him, telling relatives how different everything would be "if Freddie had lived."

As the Ingalls family had suffered two consecutive years of devastating grasshopper plagues at Walnut Creek, in Southwest Minnesota, then lost their first and only son (or brother) while taking refuge with relatives near South Troy, Minnesota, Charles and Caroline eagerly accepted some friends' offer to co-manage the Masters Hotel in Burr Oak, Iowa. They were happy to do so—at first.

After only three months, they walked away from that tense post, feeling they'd been unfairly treated. Per one source, the family moved

> two buildings to the south and lived above Kimball's Grocery Store. Charles started a feed mill, grinding farmers' corn and wheat with his horses. Between the hotel and Kimball's store stood a saloon. After a fire in the saloon, Charles moved his family to a red-brick house at the edge of Burr Oak. It was in this rented house that the youngest of the Ingalls, Grace, was born in May of 1877. Shortly after Grace's birth, the family decided to leave Burr Oak and return to Walnut Grove again after becoming burdened with doctor bills, grocery bills, and rent.

The Ingalls, however, were not the only family to come to Winneshiek County, then leave it for what promised to be greener fields elsewhere—further west, always further west.

Caroline Lake (Quiner) & Charles Phillip Ingalls (1860); second daughter, Laura (Ingalls) Wilder (1894)

Unlike protesting students and conflict-plagued hoteliers, Ann Kew's three sisters—Fanny, Jane and Emma—had more harmonious intentions in mind, like marrying. Which, they did. Solidly anchored in Northeast Iowa and Southeast Minnesota, they now headed households of their own, in an archipelago of settlements closely encircling Burr Oak—Hesper, Bluffton and Canton. Married with children, they were no longer part of the equation when their aging widowed mother, Ann, their brother George, sister Ann Kew Moorehead and brother-in-law John Moorehead contemplated the family's next move. Whatever—or wherever—it would be, it ultimately would be determined by King Wheat, which was then the reigning grain.

————

chapter 19: uncovering hidden layers

After only three years in Winneshiek County, the restless Moorehead-Kew clan moved again—this time some 200 miles (300 km) to Clay County, lured by the promise of "free" land "earned" by homesteading what until the European-American aliens' arrival had been a sea of grass for ten thousand years. Unlike the wooded hill country of Northeast Iowa, hardly a tree punctuated the grass-lined, windswept plains of Northwest Iowa.

1873 map of railroads in Minnesota and Iowa; George with sisters, Catherine and Jennie, circa 1875

As noted a century after the Moorehead-Kews ventured out onto the open prairie in search of a future better then what they perceived their past to have been,

The Spencer area was the last portion of the county, and of the state, to be settled due to the general absence of forests. But when the time came in which the head of the family could secure 160 acres of government land as a home for fourteen dollars, the hardy pioneers began to venture out upon the

207

treeless plains and devise ways to live without timber. Then it was that sod houses and stables were invented. They were made by running a broad-shire breaking plow over the wet prairie where the tough fiber of the sod of generations had accumulated. They cut it into long strips and then turned them over. The strips of sod were then cut up with spades into lengths suitable to handle. Then they were laid up like brick into walls. A few poles brought from the nearest timber supported a roof of slough hay, skillfully placed on like thatching. Thus a comfortable shelter was made. The ground was smoothed off for a floor, and until boards could be procured for doors, the skins of elk, deer or wolves shut out the wind and snow.

On one hand, without trees, even structures like the wagon shop in early Spencer had to be built out of sod, which bestowed even a new settlement a heavy, primeval feeling. On the other, with no forests to clear, the arriving settlers envisioned endless wheat fields where unending prairie still covered the flat, fertile land as far as the eye could see. Future stands of glimmering wheat, they thought, would make them rich.

a sod house built in Northwest Iowa; Dave Skinner's wagon shop, one of Spencer's first businesses, 1869

Since grain-bearing grasses had first been domesticated some ten millennia ago in what is today Turkey, crops like wheat transformed human existence. No longer needing to constantly roam in search of plants or animals to eat, humans could accumulate food reserves in one place while, under benevolent conditions, new crops continued to swell the supply of available sustenance. With stationary lifestyles, over time bigger groups of people could more easily develop large-scale projects (defensive structures, waterways, cities) or pursue cultural endeavors (written language, visual arts, concerted music). It was *that* "agricultural revolution," the domestication of plants and animals as reliable food supplies, that enabled the rise of what we understand as "civilization:" advanced, complex social organization and culture as facilitated by settlement.

Still, realizing how to manipulate plants to produce surpluses, as well as how to effectively store surpluses for later use, is one thing. The actual planting, cultivating and harvesting of crops, however, is another. For thousands of years such work meant grueling physical exhaustion for the masses. The recent rise of first effective, labor-saving mechanization, then mass-produced machinery increased agricultural production multifold. As railroads expanded into grain-growing regions like the Ukraine, Argentina, Southern Africa and North America's Great Plains, and mills pioneered processing in places such as Minneapolis and Sioux Falls, wheat grew into a global commodity.

latest American (reaper, left) and French (thresher, right) grain-harvesting technology of the 1880s

The Moorehead-Kew family, struck by cash-crop fever, left the comforts of Eastern Iowa for the West. Striking it rich raising grain, though, was not as easy as they had imagined. First, there were prairie fires. Later, fungal grain rot. Some years there was too little rain. Others, too much. Of all the serial trials they faced, however, recurring plagues of Rocky Mountain Locusts proved the most devastating.

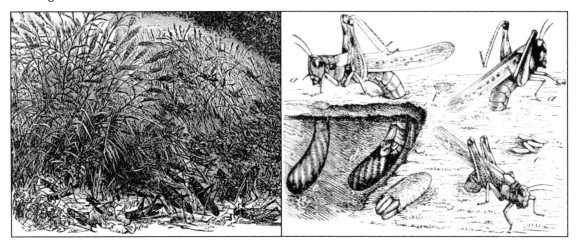

period depiction of locusts infesting grain field; 1877 illustration "Rocky Mountain Locust oviposition"

According to witnesses, on a June day in 1873 the midday sun suddenly disappeared without warning as waves of locusts—sounding like a rainstorm—descended upon those living on the prairie. In no time they shaved crops off at the ground, gnawed the wool on live sheep as well as devoured clothes off the backs of terrified children. The unstoppable invaders ate away on paper and tree bark, furniture, window and door frames—even wooden tool handles.

As one Clay County historian later recorded:

> The pests came down in countless millions like black snowflakes. They devoured most of the crops and later devoured all the growing grain. They had eaten the settlers' winter food and their spring seed. In fact, many of the settlers were left in such destitute circumstances they appealed to friends in other states for aid. Many aid societies were organized, and solicitors were sent to Illinois and Wisconsin to seek help for the area. The settlers drew up petitions to the legislature, asking for grain for the coming year. The legislature responded, sending out men to distribute seed grain. The grain was sown in the spring of 1874, and by the middle of May, the grasshoppers began to appear again. Though it looked as if everything would again be lost, the season was favorable. The grain came again, and about the first of June, the grasshoppers flew away. The farmers' crops were saved for that year.

Of aid sent by state government in faraway Des Moines, Ohio-born pioneer farmer George Monlux reported ruefully:

> Some relief came from the $75,000 appropriated by the Iowa legislature, but as is so often the case, the really destitute and needy were modest people, so did not receive their necessary, rightful amount of aid.

In September 1874, in Iowa's neighbor state to the southwest, the governor of heavily struck Kansas

> convened an extra session of the legislature hoping to find a way to help Kansans survive the calamity. The legislature determined that it did not have the power to take money directly from the state's treasury to help with the emergency. The plea for help went across America. Soon aid for the destitute Kansans began to arrive. Railroads provided free transportation of the barrels, boxes, and bales of supplies such as beans, pork, and rice. America's farmers even donated railcars full of barley and corn to assist Kansans with the next year's planting.

Harper's Weekly *illustration of farmfolk clearing field of locusts, 1875*

A lieutenant in Iowa's 8th Cavalry during the Civil War a decade earlier, Monlux also related how he in Lyon County, two counties northwest of the Moorehead-Kews, experienced the locusts' descent over a region full of struggling homesteaders and the resultant desolation. He said

the pests were so thick that tall slim forest trees, in two hours' time, were loaded so with them that their branches touched the earth; not a leaf would be left on the thrifty willow hedges. After stripping the gardens clean they left on an early morning breeze for the north. This was in June, and one month later, to a day, they returned from their northern journey. Small grain was nearly ripe and they literally swarmed in the grain fields, but left the prairies alone, so grass was good and hay plenty. [He] began to cut a thirty-acre field and before he had worked two hours, unhitched, for they had finished his harvesting for him! They were so thick that they crawled down the farmers' backs and up their pant legs and the bite was almost like the sting of a bee. When they left it was all at once and they were so numerous that the noonday sun was darkened and when they lighted in Cherokee County the track of the Illinois Central Railway was buried by grasshoppers. A freight train was stopped by reason of the wheels slipping on the greasy rails. They left their eggs on every bare spot of ground and plowing did not seem to hinder their maturing.

George Monlux, Compendium of History, Reminiscence & Biography of Lyon County, Iowa (1894); *"Iowa Prairie Farm" in* History of Iowa from the Earliest Times to the Beginning of the Twentieth Century *(1903)*

The Moorehead-Kews' distant neighbor to the north and west went on to describe the emotional toll the locusts inundation had exacted. The reportedly now-extinct creatures

even found their way into houses and if allowed to be amongst bedding and clothes, they would eat and finally ruin the fabrics. They girdled forest trees, ate harness, got into open wells and pumps, so no water could be drawn or used until removed. Farmers had to tie strings around the bottoms of their pant legs and wear handkerchiefs about the necks. Teamsters found it impossible to drive horse and ox teams against them. But very little could be done to save crops—strong men stood sullen and powerless and watched the devouring of fine crops, upon which they had depended for a living. Women shed bitter tears at the side of their cherished garden plots, from which they had expected a fall and winter living. They thought of their dear children and of the long, cold winter months. Too much credit cannot be given to those brave heroes and heroines who, year after year, held down their claims during these 'plague' years.

At the time of the 1874 infestation, Monlux recorded the vast extent of both the swarm's size and its impact:

cartoon showing Plains farmers "Grangers" battling locusts, mid-1870s

> At 5 p.m., Friday, a shower of grasshoppers descended upon this region, until the ground was literally covered with the devilish insects. The country was covered with them, from Little Rock to Sioux Falls, and north to LuVerne, Minnesota. They remained with us until Sunday at 10 a.m., when suddenly all arose and headed southward. The sky was black with them for many hours, and as they passed south of this place, the thickest of these swarms assumed the appearance of a black snake; a line of such clouds could be seen extending across the southern sky for several hours. More damage east and south is reported than here, which amounts to above one-third of the grain crop. It is believed they came from the Red River of the North and are making their exodus to the south, as they wait for north winds.

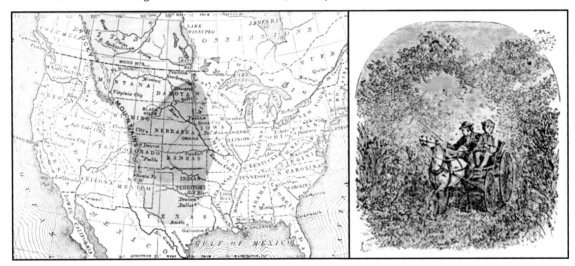

map of 1874 Rocky Mountain Locust infestation; "The Grasshopper Scourge" from the History of Iowa

Just as the Moorehead-Kews thought they had weathered a tribulation of biblical proportions, another round came to test them further. This time, they almost gave up and returned East.

> The second grasshopper invasion occurred the last part of July in 1876, just as the wheat and oats were ripening and the corn coming into tassel and silk. The grasshoppers ate the heads off the grain and settled on the corn until they broke it down with their weight, destroying all of the small grain. There was complete destruction. The settlers began to abandon their homes. Some of them turned their homes over to their creditors, while others sold them for little or nothing and left the country. There was great destitution the following winter, but kind friends again came to their aid. The next spring friends supplied seed, and the settlers paid for it when the crop was harvested. Some farmers on the border lands lost all of their crops once more from the grasshoppers, but for some reason, the pests flew away the early part of July. In other parts of the county the crops matured and were excellent…

> That was the last grasshopper invasion, and the county has never been troubled by one since.

———

211

In 19th-century America, especially on the frontier, conflicting interests often collided—too often resulting in bloodshed. Typically, on the local level, the owning and business classes' goals laid at odds with those of the renting and laboring classes. Only on rare occasions did all classes rally behind a unifying cause—one pressing exception being the popular clamor for better transportation. Since the movement of people and goods go both directions of any route, farmers sought reliable means to send produce to market, while would-be mercantile magnates knew that, long term, they could only compete with other shopkeepers if they could keep goods competitively priced. The fortunes of all in nascent settlements like Spencer, then, depended on an effective transportation infrastructure—at that time not paved roads, but rail-born ones.

> Scarcely had the people of Spencer settled on the new town site than they began to agitate the question of a railroad. They talked and sent representatives to present and impress their ideas upon those in authority. Their agents would return with no results. These settlers who stayed and struggled through the grasshopper invasions grew greatly discouraged. Many were to the point of leaving, and would have, if they had not been persuaded by the more hopeful and determined ones. The nearest railroad point was forty miles away, and over these long miles of road the merchandise must be transported by teams. The trip could not be made in less than three days and the cost of transportation was very expensive, and the merchant must therefore add this to the cost of his goods. This made the price of all classes of merchandise much more expensive than it would have otherwise been. The farmers had to pay this extra expense, and it was easy to see why they were anxious for the day when Spencer would have a railroad.

The coming of a railroad, however, wasn't the only sign of "civilization" arriving on the prairie. Unable to know that one day their local fair would become the largest, most-visited such annual event on the planet (billed for a reason as "The World's Greatest County Fair"), the early settlers found respite from the monotonous fare of trial and toil on open grasslands of Northwest Iowa.

As recorded a century later, Clay County's first fair, held in October 1871,

community event at Spencer's railroad station, circa 1885

> was a one day promotion by real estate agents. Their purpose was to display the products of the land in an effort to interest the public in the purchase of farms in this section. A farm, at that time, was little more than an undeveloped wild.

According to early Spencer pioneer Harry Chamberlain, that first fair displayed

> two or three pumpkins, a few ears of corn, some needlework, bed quilts, and a small amount of grain. He couldn't remember much more than these. He reminded us that there wasn't very much to work with in those days. It was a fair, anyway, and the Clay County people were proud of what they had accomplished.

The fair took place in and around a building on South Main Street. Harry Chamberlain held that

> an ordinary dray could have hauled all the exhibits. The livestock division was housed in a cattle shed near the main building. It aroused much favorable comment in respect to the two or three head of cattle and a team or two of horses that were shown.

The program for the day included a guest speaker who wasted no words in painting the glories of the county as an agricultural land destined to show great future progress. He predicted those in attendance would live to see the day when land in the county would sell for the unheard of figure of $25 per acre. The crowd indicated signs of disbelief.

There was planned activity for 200 people in attendance. Included were races and speed events to keep the celebration from becoming dull.

From reports, the fair was held again the following three years, and even though exerted effort was used to continue them, financial support was not available. One wonders how much land was sold by these estate promoters as a result of Clay County's first fair.

Finally—despite the welcome distraction of a first, albeit admittedly rather feeble county fair—devastating grasshopper plagues and delayed connections to vital markets pushed the fed-up, double-household Moorehead-Kew family to sell their homesteads in 1882. And, return east.

These English-Irish natives did not easily abandon their earlier dreams of wheat-wrought wealth on the prairie, but there was only so much disappointment and endless toil that a body could bear. Already the lack of cash meant that the two oldest girls, Jennie and Catherine—at the time of the 1880 Federal

Homer Barker showing abundant farm and garden produce, early 1900s

census respectively 21 and 17—lived with other families as live-in domestic servants. And, in any case:

original caption: "Spencer IA July 4th 1885"

Although the fledgling roadside stop of Spencer promised to be an up-and-coming outpost on the western plains, it was still little more than a wishful hamlet.

By now, though, at least both Jane and her adult son George Kew (a bachelor until 1893 when, at age 46, he married year-younger Sophia Bryant of Minneapolis), and John and his wife Ann Kew Moorehead, had "proved up" their claims after the required five-year minimum stay. The patch of prairie they'd endured so much to make theirs could now be cashed in on—then left behind. And, among everything else, in 1880 John had acquired American citizenship.

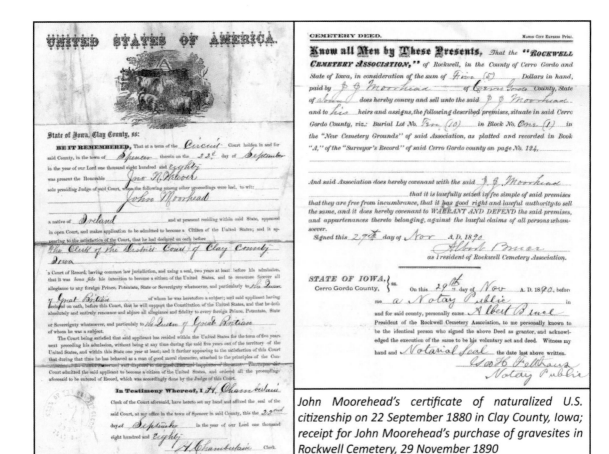

John Moorehead's certificate of naturalized U.S. citizenship on 22 September 1880 in Clay County, Iowa; receipt for John Moorehead's purchase of gravesites in Rockwell Cemetery, 29 November 1890

Immediate goals reached but long-term dreams seemingly impossible to realize in Clay County, the extended family retreated to Rockwell, where by then the elder of Ann's brothers, 50-year-old John Kew, had established a thriving farm among his young wife's people, the Dillingham-Sweets. The clan's matriarch, Jane (Smith) Kew, now 80, along with her 30-year-old bachelor son, George Kew, moved in with John and his family. As Ann's handsome son, George, was just shy of twenty when they arrived in the early '80s in prospering Rockwell (then home to about 300 industrious inhabitants), it had more to offer than struggling Spencer. He could not have known then, however, how the town would change his life forever—and in the process transform an adventuresome boy into a serious man.

The 1885 State of Iowa census, though, shows conflicting "facts" regarding what happened next. For one, it registered George Moorehead, "age 23, born Illinois," as married but living with his much-moved immigrant parents on their final farm, in Cerro Gordo County's six-by-six-square-mile Geneseo Township, which surrounds Rockwell.

Jennie (Barlow) and George Moorehead, 1884

214

For another, State of Iowa marriage records document that on Christmas day 1884 he took as his bride Jennie Elizabeth Barlow, the 21-year-old daughter of widower William Robert and the late Mary Alice (Willard) Barlow, who'd died the previous year. The family hailed from the Spoon River country of West Central Illinois.

As of the moment of that Christmas-day ceremony—likely intended to portend a happy and blessed life together—the available "facts" fade and the telling details behind what was clearly a personal disaster of soul-grinding proportions for George blur into a shroud of unbroken misery. It was upon uncovering this scenario of a living hell on Earth, which my paternal great-great grandfather somehow found the inner fortitude to survive, that I had to turn to Ol' Aunt Winnie.

George Kew, circa 1870s

———

Settling deeper into her dingy, upholstered chair, she looked straight ahead. As if her soul was hovering somewhere far away and long ago, she slowly began to recount that "When the Mooreheads arrived in Rockwell, dashing young George would hitch up his sleigh and attend parties in town during winter months, when work on the farm was slowest. It was there that he met a gay, lively girl with dancing eyes—Jennie Barlow, who squealed in delight to George's jokes and poured over his riddles, searching for clues to his clever puns and puzzles."

Jennie Barlow with friends, circa 1880; altered photo of a family friend waiting for a sleigh ride on the prairie

Without our understanding why, Winnie stopped her narration long enough to look Jennifer, then me straight in the eye for a silent second or two before resuming her telling of long-buried chapters in our family's never-ending chronicle. "Who could have guessed that within five years of George having married this china-doll-faced girl that he'd so quickly lose her *and* their two babes in a matter of months? Their baby boy, Leslie, only a few months old, died of pneumonia on a trip to Illinois to visit kinfolk. Tuberculosis took George and Jennie's little girl, Leila Ann, when she was only a little more than two-and-a-half. Then, it claimed her young mother, too—"

Leila Ann (top left), Jennie (Barlow) and baby Leslie Moorehead, last half of the 1880s; cardboard photo backing

Ol' Aunt Winnie's high-pitched, fragile voice trailed off, yet left a long wake that touched all of us in subtle, unsettling waves. The cramped living room was so quiet that when Jennifer and I swallowed hard, I swore our dry gulping could be heard all the way into the hallway.

Charlotte Campbell (top left) with friends, circa 1885

Finally, when she re-emerged from relaying her trance-like account, Winnie lowered her little head. She slowly adjusted her silver-trimmed, cat-eye glasses by their bowed bridge with a wobbly index finger and wrinkled thumb, then looked at us young people assembled an arm's length in front of her. Now solemn, she alleged "George did not act the same after the death of his young wife and two wee children. He quit joking and making riddles; he loathed life and despised laughter. His gig, sleigh and steed all lost their allure, for the biggest part of him had died with them."

Winnie broke her story once more, looked around the room to see if all was well, then shifted her quavering voice to a more up-beat tone and cadence. "Everything changed, though, when George met another maiden with dancing eyes and a girlish laugh, Charlotte Esther Campbell—my father's sister, daughter of William and Adelia White Campbell, who'd come to Iowa from out East. It was Aunt Lottie" Winnie held, "who revived the George Moorehead who loved to laugh and loved to live. For that, he married the pretty, petite girl in March o' '91."

Comforted by the thought that past-possessed

216

Ol' Aunt Winnie likely could make accurate assessments about her aunt's impact on tragedy-struck George Moorehead, I sat a moment and mediated on what it might have been like for him to have lost a baby boy, toddler daughter and young wife within seven months, between May and November 1889. I tried, but had no idea: Twas too much.

Margaret (standing), Jennie, Frank, Mary, Ann; John (sitting), Bert, Ann (Kew) & George Moorehead, 1880

"On top of that" Winnie added, "George had just lost four of his sisters, half of his family, to that same tuberculosis epidemic—and three before that. It was an awful time" Winnie shook her head, as if she had lived it although she only could have heard from her people about "when the whole town was shaken by unimaginable loss—all at once."

———

chapter 20: a community prevails

A community—a collection of families or individuals typically connected by shared origins, geography, values or interests—becomes bonded not only by coping with devastating loss, but by struggling in the face of common conditions, adversaries or goals. In an emerging farm town like Rockwell in its formative years, the most tangible, every-day hindrance to the collective welfare consisted of the supply of unjustly overpriced goods, squared with the sale of artificially underpriced commodities. In moving from Clay County to longer-established Cerro Gordo ("Fat Hill" in Spanish, named after a Mexican-American War battle) the Mooreheads suddenly found themselves to be one of the many families unwillingly held hostage to the banditry of Rockwell's unfair Main Street merchants.

ELEVATOR of GEO. FELTHOUS, ROCKWELL, CERRO GORDO CO.

My Moorehead-Kew ancestors also found, though, the inner resolve to reject economic tyranny and band together with several hundred other farm folk to create a self-run alternative—as featured in the here-excerpted, July 1903 edition of the monthly magazine, *World's Work*:

Farmer's Trust – Rockwell, Iowa

By H. A. Wood

In a weather-beaten, two-story farm building on the Iowa prairies is the headquarters of an industry in some ways more remarkable than any cooperative enterprise yet established, even that at [the pioneer, model cooperative in] Rochdale in England. It is a successful farmers' "trust".

The five hundred farmers who conduct the establishment were several years ago at the mercy of a single firm conducting the general store of the little town of Rockwell to which they went to do their trading. Their products were in good demand, but when they went to town for supplies and to market their grain and livestock, the shopman paid them what he wished and sold them supplies at any price he wished - there was no competition. The farmers stood it stoically for a time, but at last rebelled. They turned dealers themselves.

Last year, with an expense for salaries, rent, insurance, etc., of less than $4,000, they carried on a business of more than $620,000 on a capital of $25,000. During thirteen years, closing with March, 1903, this company of farmers has transacted more than $5,000,000 worth of business without the loss of a dollar. At no time has the capital stock been more than $25,000, and at no time has the indebtedness been more than $5,000.

The company is regularly incorporated under the laws of the State. The members come together only at the annual meeting. The articles of incorporation set forth the general nature of the business to be "buying and selling and dealing in all kinds of farm and dairy products, cattle, sheep, swine, poultry, dry-goods, boots and shoes, groceries, hardware, farm machinery, lumber, stone, brick, and all kinds of building material, grain and real estate; and dealing in all kinds of merchandise, and in buying and selling all such kinds of property on commission and otherwise".

The business is under the immediate charge of a general agent. The company has power to borrow money provided not more than $5,000 shall be borrowed at any one time while at no time may the firm be in debt more than $5,000. One of the provisions of the by-laws is that no shareholder "shall sign any bond, or sign, indorse or guarantee any note, bill, draft or contract, or in any way assume any liability, verbal or written, for the accommodation of any person, without the written consent of the director, in transacting any business for the society". No person may become a shareholder except a practical farmer, and no member may own more than ten shares of stock. Each share is worth $10. Provision is made for the expulsion of any shareholder who violates any of the provisions of the by-laws or constitution.

The staff of employees is very small. The business practically carries on itself. The company buys all the output of its members and sells to the farmers what they need. Others than members may buy, but such trade is not specially sought. Supplies are sold at a little above cost, though outsiders pay slightly more. The wares handled include farm implements and farm machinery, flour, fence wire, fuel, salt, lumber, oils, and the like. There has been so far very little retailing. The company does not come into competition with the small dealers. It owns its own elevator for the storage of grain and maintains its own lumberyard. Supplies of all sorts are bought in large quantities, in carload lots or more, and are then stored in warehouses.

Caption appearing in the original article, as placed here, from top to bottom, left to right:

- Gathering of farmers in Rockwell, Iowa
- Elevator of Farmers Coop in Rockwell, Iowa
- A favorite meeting place [and] Public School in Rockwell, Iowa
- President of the Farmers Coop [and a] Typical farm house in Rockwell, Iowa

The "gathering of farmers" may or may not have been one of the annual membership meetings, but includes members. In front of the "Opera House" are, among other things for sale by the coop, a horse-drawn hay rake, galvanized-metal wire fencing, and a one-row plow. It is likely that the cooperative offered social or even cultural programs to its members and the wider puplic.

In investigating the workings of this company in Rockwell, I found that these five hundred farmers are worth at least $5,000,000. Their farms are perhaps a hundred and sixty acres in size on an average, some of them considerably larger. The land has steadily increased in value in the last two decades, and particularly since the company was established, until such well-tilled, well-equipped farms as these men own are worth all the way from $50 to $80 per acre. As a body the members of the "trust" have nothing to do with politics.

The town of Rockwell has grown more than fourfold since the concern was established. More than half the population is made up of retired farmers, many of them members of the firm. They have administered the affairs of the town with discretion, economy and common sense. The town enjoys nearly all the modern public utilities - telephones, electric lights, a water system; it has fine public schools and a large private or parochial school, while there are the usual number of churches.

The home life of the farmers does not materially differ from that of other progressive Western farmers. As the beneficent results of the advanced agricultural education of the last twenty years have become more widespread, the farm life of the west has advanced, until today, in the home of the progressive farmer, music, the best of magazines and books - indeed, some primary show of a love for real art, are distinguishing features, separating the farmer, of the present, from the farmer of the past for all time to come.

As the success of the "trust" has been carried from farm to farm across the immediate country, similar organizations have been effected and favorable reports are being made. There appears to be no obstacle in the way of an indefinite expansion of the plan.

The "farmer of the past" to which the *World's Work* article refers as having been surpassed "for all time to come" was not some distant cave-dweller, but rather the croft-dweller of John Moorehead's days as a boy back in Ulster. The "typical farm house" featured in the periodical meant to serve as a dreamy contrast to Old-World thatched peasant hovels, the likes of which Ann and her mother, Jane (Smith) Kew, had left behind in then-not-so-merry rural England.

As the piece stated, given that "more than half the population [of Rockwell was] retired farmers" the town itself embodied the old-age pride of pioneers who'd turned crumbly sod into comfy, respectable nest eggs. As such, the townsfolk of that hard-working hamlet expected their swiftly-growing municipality to reflect in material ways the intangible motives that had led them to the prairie in the first place—for example through "all the modern public utilities - telephones, electric lights [and] a water system" that would have made even ancient Rome envious. Rockwell's array of "fine public schools and a large

19th-century photograph of the Kew home in Thistleton, England

parochial school [and] number of churches" offered further proof that the pioneers had "arrived," that leaving late-feudalist Europe and braving the unknowns and dangers of the New World had been worth all the risk, work and hardship.

———

chapter 21: the pioneers depart

It had taken conviction, bolstered by extraordinary hope, to be able to board those ships back in Belfast or Bremerhaven, Liverpool or Le Havre and turn one's back forever on all that one had ever known, then set sail into the great unknown. Once the brave souls who made their way to the New World arrived, it took courage to plant their feet on foreign ground, then set their hands to work building—often literally from the ground up—totally new lives, often with new names.

To be able to accomplish all that they did, those hearty individuals fed their families more than just jerky and cornbread. Many found spiritual sustenance in a powerful faith, a pronounced religiosity increasingly rare in the West—certainly in Europe but also in much of urban North America, Australia or various scattered outposts of the European realm. It wasn't always like that, though. As my pioneer ancestors began to leave this world, to surrender the fruits of their endless efforts, those left behind seemed keenly aware of the significance of what their now-gone loved ones had witnessed unfold, deep in the midpoint of North America. And, they wove those sensibilities into the eulogies they dedicated as lasting memorials to lost family members.

———

The pioneers' often unspoken assumption, that their god had rewarded them with such abundant earthly wealth for what they perceived to be individual and collective virtues, seemed tenable. While I have no documents suggesting that, by extension, the aging pioneers thought their god had "punished" the comparatively less-affluent neighbors, friends or kin they'd left behind in Europe or "out East," as a boy I absorbed the implicit belief modeled by my elders that we inhabiting the American Heartland had been granted a privileged place in a "Promised Land," our "New Canaan."

author visiting site of former Kew home in Thistleton, 1981; Eric & Vivian Kew, Swindon, England, 1982

Though now commonly seen with other, more wider-focused and critical eyes, as seen then by mostly poorly educated laborers themselves, the early settlers of the American frontier embodied a vanguard, the bringers of "civilization" to a once-wild land. They saw at the center of their civilizing efforts less the gun, more the plow—as in this frontispiece from *The Evolution of American Agriculture*, ironically published by a farm-workers union in the 1910s:

The deep, mostly unconscious assumptions to which I refer are not imagined—and they weren't only mine. Hobby-historian Elizabeth Lieuwen gave a presentation on the *Early History of Belmond* at a Wright County Historical Society meeting on a wintry Monday, 26 February 1951. She waxed:

"Civilization" as depicted in labor-movement publication, circa 1910

Let us picture the northeast corner of Wright County, known as the Belmond Area, in the spring of 1853 [when the first settlers, the Luick family arrived.] Nature held supreme sway. The grass was as green; the flowers as beautiful, as though admiring eyes had rested upon their loveliness. There was no eye but that of the maker's to notice the violet lift its face to the sun; or to note the change in nature's apparel as the seasons came and went. [What about the Native Americans' eyes? Did they, apparently, not count?]

The soil was deep and rich; the river abounded in fish; the groves had been strengthening for centuries, and the birds and water fowls were abundant. Every thing waiting the occupancy of man. "And God looked upon his work and saw that it was good."

Of course, an earthly plane ordained with such haloed, biblical attributes befitted only humans similarly so marked by the Divine. As Lieuwen asked,

Now that every thing was ready, where were the men and women who were naturally endowed with the fortitude and endurance, necessary to withstand the obstacles incident to pioneer life?

Lieuwen's own florid words offered epic images in response:

In the early autumn of 1853, two teams and covered wagons could be seen amidst the heat and dust of the northern Iowa prairie, slowly winding their way. In one wagon were Henry Luick, his wife and four children[.] In the other wagon was Dave, the younger brother, then seventeen years of age.

Although it's unclear on what source she based this assertion, Lieuwen's narrative held that for

many weary days they traveled on and on, until at last they came to the banks of a beautiful little lake, later called "Clear Lake." Then they came south, along the ridge east, until they came to the northwest side of Franklin Grove, where they decided to camp and rest on the banks of the Iowa River.

Having brought our heroic pioneers this far, the then-29-year-old granddaughter of early local settlers presented her audience with a prairieland Eden in which to forever plant them—and us:

Belmond-area couple, the "Pals," circa 1900

The weather that winter was good; the wild ducks and geese never left all winter. The children gathered butternuts and walnuts from the woods and went barefoot all winter. Wild game was plentiful, the river full of fish; large droves of elk were on the prairie. The family, standing in their log cabin door, counted several hundred elk in one drove going to the river at one time.

Some moderns might cringe upon reading or hearing such sappy sentiment today, but a half-dozen years after "America beat Hitler" the historical record of the previous half-century seemed to support such uncritical hyperbole. Then, a straight-faced speaker could dare swoon

Belmond residents, the "Lynches," circa 1900

These German families brought the true spirit of the pioneer with them, the knowledge of hard work and a desire for the possession of property and a home. They have been a God-fearing, industrious people and their efforts have been crowned with success. Pleasant Township in which this settlement was made, stands second to none in fertility of soil and high crop production.

224

Indeed, according to the selective, self-serving narratives we children of New Canaan were both weaned on and fed others, our people had stumbled upon an uninhabited paradise. In that vast, fertile garden, we as (mostly Protestant, Anglo-Saxon and almost exclusively white) yeomen, their distaff, offspring or attendant townspeople built a civilization where there had been none. It went without saying that such a happy state was divinely intended—and we, a chosen people.

———

When the pioneers' surviving descendants took pen in hand to immortalize the dead, however, they likely didn't meditate on motifs of "civilization." Rather, as they inventoried an entire life, they thought of what had been gained on personal levels, on what love the deceased had sown and what those tender seeds had yielded. And, they reviewed all that in context—as shown in an obituary the *Globe-Gazette* ran in March 1910 under the headline "John Kew Passes Away:"

John Kew was born in Thistleton, England, July 23, 1839, and died at Rockwell, Iowa, Feb. 28, 1910, of softening of the brain [encephalomalacia, typically caused by stroke or injury-induced hemorrhaging].

With his parents [William and Jane (Smith) Kew] he arrived in America, May 5th, 1855, and settled at Cherry Valley, Ill. In 1863 he made his first trip and purchased a portion of the land that now comprises the old homestead, and a couple of years later took up permanent residence here.

John Kew and Margaret L. Dillingham were united in marriage January 1, 1868, and to them four children were born, William, Lelia, wife of [Lottie Campbell Moorehead's brother and Jerry Allen's grandfather] A. C. Campbell, Edward, and Caroline, the latter dying when about two years of age. March 19, 1898, the wife and mother passed to the Great Beyond.

About two years later the subject of this sketch was united in marriage with Mrs. Eliza Johnson who today mourns the loss of a beloved companion and protector.

Four sisters, Mrs. Ann Moorehead of Rockwell, Mrs. Fanny Darrington of Hesper, Mrs. James Young of Canton, Minn., Mrs. Mary Casterton of Decorah, and one brother, George Kew of this place, yet remain of the original family to mourn the departed.

For nearly a half-century "Jack" Kew has been identified with the development of this community, and success in a material way has crowned his efforts. He has stood as an example and an exponent of agricultural thrift and business integrity. For years he has been identified with the church militant, and has stood for those things that make community life agreeable and to be desired.

In the passing of this pioneer citizen another of the fast receding landmarks of the '60s fades away. With earth's last, long farewell is coupled a well-founded belief that beyond the turbulent Jordan there comes the vision of the sweet fields of Eden and the Master's plaudit, "Well done" and "Enter thou in".

William, Edward & Leila; Margret (Dillingham, seated) & John Kew, 1889; Leila & "Will" as children, 1870s

When John Kew's brother-in-law, John Moorehead, died almost two years later, Rockwell lost yet another genuine pioneer among the townspeople's midst. Again, whoever announced the end of his life first reviewed its beginning; again, his attributed virtues were listed and heralded:

John Moorehead was born in County Down, Ireland, April 5, 1827. When he was about 24 years old, he came to America, remaining in Syracuse, N.Y. for two years. From thence he went to Cherry Valley, Illinois. He was united in marriage to Miss Ann Kew April 22, 1858. In 1868 [sic], Mr. and Mrs. Moorehead moved to Clay County, Iowa, where they took a homestead, making their home there for 14 years. In the spring of 1882 they came to Rockwell, Iowa, buying a home here from whence Mr. Moorehead passed to the eternal world December 7, 1911.

In his last hours he longed to see his favorite niece, Mrs. Levi Whitmore of Cherry Valley, Illinois. She arrived a few minutes before his death and he had the satisfaction of conversing with her before his spirit took its departure to the realm of immortal souls.

Mr. Moorehead united with the Free Will Baptist church sixty years ago. Soon after coming to Rockwell he and his wife united with the Methodist Episcopal church. He was a man of sterling qualities, a sincere Christian who carried his religion into every day life. He was of kind and cheerful disposition, being loved by all

who knew him.

To Mr. and Mrs. Moorehead nine children were born, six daughters and three sons. The daughters have all passed into the Beyond. The three sons remain, George, Frank and Bert, two of whom reside near Rockwell and one near Swaledale. There are living 14 grandchildren and five great-grandchildren. Mrs. Moorehead survives her husband. These, together with other relatives and many friends, mourn his loss.

The following verses handed the writer express the sentiments of the bereaved relatives:

Dearest father, you have left us,
   Your canoe rests on the sand
You have safely cross the river
   And have gained the happy land.
Oh, the peace and blessed comfort,
   Oh, the thought so grand and sweet
When we think that you are resting
   Safely now at Jesus' feet.
Rough and ragged was the pathway
   Which your weary feet have trod,
But the days seem so much brighter
   Since you made your peace with God.

No more sorrow, no more anguish
   No more pain nor weary sigh.
Pain nor sickness cannot reach you
   In your home beyond the sky.
Now your lifeless hands are folded
   On your calm and peaceful breast;
But how sad the mournful parting
   From the friends who loved you the best.
One less form about our fireside,
   One less voice, one vacant chair,
One more boat has crossed the river
   To that happy land so fair.

two of Ann (Kew) Moorehead's sisters (likely with offspring) who had married and so remained in Northeast Iowa/Southeast Minnesota when the rest of the Moorehead-Kew clan moved to Northwest Iowa in the 1870s to homestead

In an era when a man's many, purported accomplishments dominated the media, those of a woman often rated much less and more modest mention. While her husband's death warranted extensive billing, for example, when aged Ann (Kew) Moorehead died almost twenty years later, on 14 September 1930, her passing got only a brief, and then only factual, mention:

226

Ann (Kew) Moorehead (right) with sister & grandnieces, circa 1900; wheelchair-bound in Rockwell, 1920s

A longer, latter obituary did note the following about the life and soul of the deceased woman:

> Mrs. Moorehead became affiliated with the Methodist church soon after coming to Rockwell, and was a loyal member, taking an active interest in the welfare of the church until her health failed. Since then she has lived that Christianity by her kindly deeds, loyalty to her fellowmen, and her faith in the teachings of the word of God.
>
> For the past ten years she had suffered from a gradual decline which resulted in her death Thursday morning, September 4th [1930], at 9:30 o'clock, at the age of 95 years, 14 days.
>
> Weep not that her toils are over, Weep not that her race is run,
> God grant we may rest as calmly When our work, like hers, is done.
> 'Til then we yield with gladness, Our mother to Him to keep,
> And rejoice in the sweet assurance He giveth His loved one sleep.

That "Big Lottie's" mother's obituary—again undated and anonymous—should be so long and that praises of her should be so lofty, strikes this historian as telling:

AGED ROCKWELL RESIDENT DIES

Mrs. Ann Moorehead, 95, County Pioneer, Leaves Two Sons.

ROCKWELL, Sept. 4.—Mrs. Ann Moorehead, 95, pioneer resident here, died here this morning at the home of her grandson, Arthur Thomas, after a gradual decline.

Mrs. Moorehead was born in England and came to Rockwell about 50 years ago. She is survived by two sons, George Moorehead, Rockwel, and Frank Moorehead, three miles east of Mason City.

Funeral arrangements have not been announced.

Nancy Adelia White was born in Norwich, N.Y. June 10, 1844 and passed away at her late home in Rockwell, Iowa, Sept. 27, 1918.

She was married to W. B. Campbell at Beloit, Wis., Dec. 24, 1863, the companion of over half a century preceeding [sic] her to the Better Land but a few months ago.

In an early day the family located near Waverly, Iowa, and from there removed to this locality about thirty five years ago and during these long years the subject of this sketch has been known as a kind and devoted wife and mother. Mrs. Campbell is survived by eight children: Augustus Campbell, DeWitt Campbell, William Campbell, Charlotte Moorehead, Grace Sherwood, Maud Breeding, Ray Campbell and May Kelly, one daughter Della being deceased.

In addition to her children Mrs. Campbell has been blessed with thirty-three grand-children and eight great-grand-children, nearly all living in this community.

Mrs. Campbell was of a family of four sisters and seven brothers, six of whom survive her.

For many years Mrs. Campbell has been identified with the Congregational church of this place and died with a faith undimmed in the hope of immortal life in the spirit land.

To her children and to the community, Mrs. Campbell leaves as an abiding heritage the memory of an upright life, and the cherished belief that she has found eternal refuge beneath the sheltering branches of the Tree of Life whose leaves are for the healing of the nations.

Grace (Campbell) Sherwood (standing), Dewitt, Maude (Campbell) Breeding, William Jr., Mae (Campbell) Kelly, Ray; Gus (seated), Adelia (White) & William Campbell, with Lottie (Campbell) Moorehead, circa 1910

The passing of such men—as well as their distaff—marked a turning point for communities all across America. One generation, with its particular set of dreams, abilities and expectations, had determined the local world uncountable generations would inhabit after they were long gone. The communities they founded would live on—the majority of them, in any event—but would never fully depart from the course their earliest settlers cast more by example than dictate. For decades to come, those who followed would evoke and celebrate "the old pioneers." Only after two world wars had decimated the ranks of young men on the prairie, then cycles of boom and bust eventually emptied out whole towns, did the pioneers' flames finally die, leaving less light.

four females from one Belmond-area family, the Averys (left) and Belmond-area pioneers, the Aldredges, late-in-life

———

Its population having more than trebled since the Mooreheads arrived twenty-one years earlier, by the time the *World's Work* article appeared in summer 1903, Rockwell had grown from a patch of broken prairie into the home of "the progressive farmer [boasting] music, the best of magazines, books [and] some primary show of a love for real art" that in the "old country" many of the newcomers once had known, only the manor-born would have known and enjoyed. And, the fine communal structures they erected—from the "opera house" and grain elevator to the public school and several churches— each boasted some form of a vertical break (an auger-head shed, a decorative cupola, a bell tower or spire) from a previously-unbroken horizontal prairie, mutely stating "We have parted from what was before: Here, we have created a New Canaan."

Of course, all those recent monuments to a new order, to the "American century," needed a steward—and George Edward Moorehead happily volunteered.

George and Lottie (Campbell) Moorehead farm in section #20 of 1912 plat book map; George, circa 1920

Repeatedly elected to its town council and as mayor, the farm he and his once-petite wife had operated for a quarter century northwest of Swaledale actually lay geographically closer to Clear Lake and only a horse's trot from the future burg of Bob and Lorraine (Luick) Jones' brood. Still, he consciously chose to spend his later years in relatively progressive Rockwell rather than in a smug lakeside resort or a railroad siding with a few stray houses and a smattering of shops. Just as his future grandson-in-law Donald Luick would serve on Thornton's school board and my father on that of Burchinal's Farmers Co-op, Great-Great Grampa George Moorehead understood that if a community is to thrive, individuals must serve. If he was successful, he did as the *World's Work* reporter purported, and "administered the affairs of the town with discretion, economy and common sense". To have done otherwise would have been to betray the hopes, not to mention endless efforts of thousands of pioneers.

Burchinal Co-op in 1950s, 3 miles (5 km) due south of Ashlawn Farm:
The author's great-grandmother died in a cottage behind the erstwhile
train station (in this photo replaced by tall, squared grain silo), two days
after his paternal grandmother, Charlotte Juhl, was born in April 1913.
His father later was a member of the co-op and on its board of directors.

———

chapter 22: behind the scenes

Is there ever a private sphere which does not depart from public appearances? Such was the case, in any event, of the George and Lottie Moorehead family.

George & Lottie (Campbell) Moorehead, circa 1900

Some of their woes were visited upon them, while others arose out of their own lower angels. Of the latter, George's later, serial re-election as councilor or mayor of Rockwell suggests that his adopted townsfolk deemed him an able and reliable head for their aspiring metropolis. Before he moved to Rockwell in 1915 from the farm northwest of Swaledale that he and his wife owned for some two decades, and kept in the family for a couple generations, however, he wasn't always "right on it" when it came to overseeing basic maintenance on his own house in a timely manner—as shown in the photo of him and what remained of his still-at-home-family in about 1910. The severe water-triggered wood rot, clearly seen as creeping black mold where the back shed joined the two-storied section, could only have developed over time, fed by the lack of rain gutters to carry rainfall away from the house. Although the problem likely could have been easily fixed and was rather small, 'twas also telling—especially in light of other, far more serious "moral rot" among at least some of the Mooreheads (think deadly Della).

George, Della, Nellie, Lottie & George Jr. on the family's farm near Swaledale; Frank Gardner with George

Of the graver challenges facing the Mooreheads, could they have helped it, that one way or the other their beloved second-oldest daughter, "young Lottie," suffered a fall that would cost them her life—and their newborn granddaughter life-long her spiritual health? "Little Lottie"—my "Gramma Luick," the baby named after both her lost mother and the ailing grandmother who became one of her two legal custodians—later said she "pushed a broom by the time [she] was four" and took care of a house whose mistress was too bodily distressed to keep it herself. Charlotte Adelia—born a "Juhl" but raised a "Moorehead"—often claimed that at the time he married her grandmother, her grandfather

George "could close his two hands around her waist, with thumbs and forefingers touching, it was so small" yet "by the time she died, Gramma Moorehead had grown so fat from dropsy, they had to bury her in a piano crate."

George Moorehead, "Little Lottie" Juhl, Glen, Arlene & Nellie (Moorehead) Gardner fishing in North Minnesota; "Big Lottie" (Campbell) Moorehead, on the same fishing trip: late 1920s

To be sure, "Big Lottie's" physical health could not keep up with the passing years—which certainly had an impact on the Mooreheads' youngest of six, little Della, whose own children one day would pay for at least their mother's failing mental health if not also, indirectly, their grandmother's eroding corporeal vitality. In any event came the irreversible loss that George already had endured in 1889 with the passing of seven immediate family members in so many months—as the *Globe-Gazette* informed the people of Cerro Gordo County on 4 April 1933:

> Mrs. George Moorehead, about 63 years of age, died this morning at Rockwell at 6 o'clock. She had been in poor health for a long time. Funeral arrangements have not been announced. Mrs. Moorehead is survived by her husband and children: Mrs. Jennie Fuller, Mrs. Cora Miller and George, all of Clear Lake, Mrs. Della True of Thornton, Mrs. Jennie Gardner of Pine River, Minn., and Charlotte Moorehead at home. She was a member of the Methodist church. Mr. and Mrs. Moorehead were pioneer residents here.

Not even a decade later, George followed his second wife—after having taken, at the august age of 73, a third life-companion on Wednesday, 4 March 1936, Emily Eunice Patten, who out-lived him. Announcing in all-caps that the "FORMER MAYOR OF TOWN DIES," North Central Iowa's "paper of record" reported on Tuesday, 21 April 1942, that

> George Moorehead, 80 [sic], former mayor of Rockwell, died at a Rockwell hospital late Tuesday morning following a week's illness. A retired farmer, the Rockwell man was active in the civic life of the community. He was a former member of the school board. He was a member of the Methodist Church. Surviving are his widow, four daughters and a son. Funeral arrangements are incomplete. The Patterson funeral home is in charge.

A local obituary included grateful praise for the life tragedy-worn George had led "despite it all:"

For many years Mr. Moorehead had been affiliated with the Methodist church and at the time of his death was the highest ranking officer at the local Odd Fellows lodge.

Mr. Moorehead was prominent in local affairs, having served with distinction on the town council, as mayor, and for several years as a member of the board of directors of the Rockwell public school.

As agent and director for the Farmers Mutual Insurance association of Mason City, he ranked high, and through his work in that capacity won many friends throughout this section.

George Moorehead was a man of strict integrity, upright in his dealings with his fellow men, and one whom it was an honor to call friend.

George Moorehead's corpse during visitation, April 1942

Was it not merciful that duty-minded George Moorehead—who in some five-and-a-half decades had lost so many women and children close to him in his life—died, not knowing that his youngest daughter, less than half a year after his passing, would murder his youngest granddaughter, six-year-old Ardith True, and less than five months after that end the life of his youngest grandson, nine-year-old Merle True? As that double tragedy plagued George's family for decades thereafter, what would it have done to him, had he known about it while still alive?

scene from George Moorehead's interment service, April 1942

———

We all leave this Earth someday, fully and irrevocably. The "business" of our lives, however, which so occupied us for so long, leaves a lingering trail. My great-great grandfather's third wife, for one, thought that the fruit of George Moorehead's eight decades on the planet rightfully belonged to her, despite having been his spouse for six years—not even a tenth of his long life. Most, but interestingly not all, of the dead man's children believed otherwise, for before grass had fully grown over his grave, an item in the *Globe-Gazette* on 8 July 1942 warned—again in all caps—that "ATTEMPTS BEING MADE TO BREAK WILL OF LATE GEORGE MOOREHEAD."

> Three children and two grandchildren of the late George Moorehead, Rockwell, began a suit in district court here Tuesday to break the will which was signed on April 13, eight days before his death.
>
> The petition filed by George Moorehead, Jr., Della True and Nellie Gardner, children and Charlotte Luick and Delbert Juhl grandchildren, charges that Mr. Moorehead was of unsound mind at the time of the signing of the will because he was under the influence of narcotics given to relieve his illness and also under undue influence by his wife. The widow together with two daughters, Jennie Fuller and Cora Miller, and the executor of the Estate, Herbert A. Fuller (son-in-law) are the defendants.
>
> The petition asks that the will be set aside and Moorehead be declared by the court to have died intestate.

So, did three of George's six children and two co-suing grandchildren succeed in breaking a will they claimed that his third wife and half of his other children unduly influenced? Does it matter?

George with Emily, 1936; Frank Gardner, Emily & George, with Nellie (Moorehead) Gardner in Minnesota

Three and a half decades after we two geeky teens combed through the front parlors and back roads of autumnal North Central Iowa in late 1979, I sometimes meditate on the motives that fueled Jennifer's consenting to traipse about with a possessed "cousin" she didn't even know she had before I knocked on the Allens' ranch-style door one day. As we met about two decades later—too briefly, over a fast veggie taco in some hippie eatery in Eugene, Oregon—I have an idea. It's likely, though, that those of her half-orphaned, primly-coiffed sheriff father might be more revealing, more complex than those of his truly talented and accomplished daughter.

Gerald Allen's mother—Ol' Aunt Winnie's kid sister, Lorna—died in 1933, when "Jerry" was about five. At the time of Jennifer's and my feverish search for family roots, he often helped us in our exploration, but only now does it occur to me that it was always in the background—at times literally "underground" as he'd grab the photos our various raids yielded and run downstairs to the family's basement to copy them with a camera quietly borrowed from the courthouse crime lab. It was he, with few words and even fewer signs of sentiment, who helped preserve these precious images, these last traces of a now-vanished world. Having died in 2006, I can only wonder what images the lawman was trying to "capture" in helping us so tirelessly. Still, I'm thankful for the help he happily gave that now brings greater, visible knowledge about our family and,

Then-Cerro Gordo County sheriff Gerald Allen found a court file containing Buddy Holly's signature glasses, "Big Bopper's" watch, a cigarette lighter and dice in February 1980 — coincidentally during the time of Jennifer's and my family-history project. According to the Globe-Gazette, which shot this photo, the envelope was marked "Charles Hardin Holly – rec'd April 7, 1959" and the contents were returned to family. My father's youngest sister, Sheranne Luick, attended that concert at the Surf and later recalled "I WAS THERE! Cried my eyes out and threatened to never wash my arms where they autographed them!!! Course that threat didn't hold! I had an autograph book from all the singers there but I forgot it that night! Since then it was lost!"

perhaps, meaning or even a bit o' wisdom to thousands, far into the future.

"Don't look for any meaning in life" fellow Peace-Corp volunteer Cynthia Hoff told me as she and I were about to conclude our respective three- and two-year stints in Czechoslovakia in July 1993, "'cause there isn't any: You gotta make your own." In that spirit, each person will assign anything of value they might find in these stories meaning of their own making. For me, though, the long, convoluted story of my family in North America is a matter of life and death—literally.

Oh—and by the way: Gramma Luick and her co-plaintiffs *did* settle out-of-court with George Moorehead's widow and three co-defendants. The fractured family *all* lost even as none "won."

All that's left of 'em all on the physical plane are cold, pointy stones with scratchin's on top...

---

postscript: lack of one

On Ascension Day 1652 George Fox was in the North of England, headed to Pendle Hill, seeking an epiphany about his fold's future that he could offer his fellow "truth-publishing seekers." On Ascension Day 2014 I was in the heart of Rome, headed to Palatine Hill, seeking epiphanies from my family's past that I could offer my fellow "truth-in-family-history seekers," those who wish to understand more fully how who we are is a result of from where—and from whom—we hail. While Fox packed his epiphany in religious language, given their greater profundity and universal import, I had two more modest, personal epiphanies, which I tried to see in the plainest terms.

the first in a series of relics of Rome: modern depictions of the ancient city or of its ruins, and statuary

236

From the moment my German boyfriend, Christian, and I stepped off the airport shuttle in front of the massive, Mussolini-ordered Termini main train station, Rome surprised me. I'd stopped in the Italian capital a couple times—mostly enroute to other, more luring destinations—since my first sojourn there in summer 1980. For some unconscious reason that initial introduction to the Eternal City was more "in front of my eyes," as the Germans say, than the other, more transitory stops. I kept admiring, for example, how much cleaner and more polished the Rome of today is than that shabby, litter-strewn hole I encountered thirty-five years ago. Where were all those cars-on-roller-skates, I wondered—those cramped, comic little Fiats that then filled the streets and made crossing the buzzing squares a most likely lethal undertaking? And, the ubiquitous mangy, emaciated, puking cats? Again, simply gone!

Oh, how I (well, "almost") missed those draped-in-all-black Mamas, those brigades of little old Roman war widows who decades after The War still monitored the many churches to be sure that no man wearing shorts and not a single woman without a skirt or covered shoulders slipped into those sacred sites. They'd surely freak if they saw the skin-flashing, multi-tongued masses of today, shuffling their way through the city, shamelessly parading bare flesh for all to see. During our whole short stay in Rome, I suffered from a certain subtle-but-stubborn disorientation. Where were all those signs of embattled sin, of material as well as moral decay, of impending final doom that gave this, one of the Earth's longest-inhabited human settlements, the apocalyptic patina that once had both so fascinated and so put me off?

As Christian and I later merged with the flowing multitudes to tour first the Colosseum, then the Forum Romanum, it seemed to me as if all those massive stones were murmuring myriad tales of millions of souls. Standing there on the edge of the "arena"—Latin for the sand once strewn over those sites of theatrical, staged combat—in my mind I could see people, animals and props popping up in shifts via underground cages and ramps. Meditating on the fates of gladiators or the power-welding "editors" who managed their dramatic, prolonged murders, of sacrificed slaves or martyred Christians, I felt overwhelmed by the crushing force of pulsating humanity in all of its, in all of our endless manifestations and possible conditions. The solid walls of piled bricks seemed to bear silent witness to both the crippling terror and the intoxicating thrill of it all—the overall proportion of which my mind simply could not grasp.

I was mindful of standing in the erstwhile epicenter of so much movement—even then, sans motorized land or sea transport—of tens of millions of human beings, of unending waves of foodstuffs, grain, lumber or early manufactured goods. I saw traders' wares: pungent wine and slick olive oil, billowing silk and prickly fur, warm amber and cool diamonds, African lions and Balkan bears crisscrossing an empire stretching from Southern Egypt to Northern England, from the Black Sea to the shiny Strait of Gibraltar. I pictured an imperial city that at its apex boasted a population of a million yet in many ways functioned better than the skidding New York I witnessed in the '70s or the still-born

Berlin-Brandenburg Airport now languishing in the middle of once-mighty Prussia. I imagined the sensuality of the place then—the grandeur of gleaming white-marble walls juxtaposed by the earthiness of bulbous terra-cotta flasks, the lulling lilt of harpists' ballads punctuated by caged leopards' hisses as they awaited cruel slaughter. I could smell cedar-wood smoke waft by from up-wind thermal baths, even as scents of big-beast urine and dung burned my nose. I could feel the excitement and horror of it all creep up my skin.

imagined 19th-century scenes depicting Rome's colosseum, both from within and outside its walls

Standing there, oddly still amid the frenetic rush of unknown contemporaries all around me, I contemplated ancient Roman daily life—and marveled how "alive" it seemed as I watched both plebian commoners as well as finely-dressed senators take their seats among the 75,000 Roman ghosts gathered there that day. I observed men arguing over rising taxes or spilled wine goblets, while their distaff fussed with their ebony-haired ringlets, peering into bone-framed mirrors. I heard vendors hawk fowl drumsticks and greasy strips of pork, along with the charcoal needed to roast either on rentable grills. I overheard unintelligible talk between friends and foes...

Then, suddenly—in the midst all those faces and sounds, bodies and smells, sights and tastes from both an unseen but (for me, there, in that moment) "real" past and a visible but "surreal" present—I "saw" my ancestors... their faces... like those of stolid George Moorehead and his corseted, hopeful bride, Charlotte... of his peasant parents and her line-up of sturdy siblings... of babies and grannies, of offspring and upstarts, of sunburned farmers and chicly-dressed lasses...

 In the flash of a heady, thought-swirling moment, as a catalog of images fluttered afore my eyes, it struck me: "There for the lack of one, go I not"—and that thought literally left me cold. Despite the warm Roman sun bearing down, a frightful shudder truly did shake me by my spine.

A list of unnerving What If's began to rapidly run ticker-tape-style through my over-taxed head:

John James Moorehead was but a lad of thirteen when the Great Potato Famine of 1845 struck Ireland. He watched as a million of those around him on that crowded island literally wasted away; he joined a million others who fled in hopes of surviving the greatest disaster Ireland had ever known. One out of four people on the Emerald Isle either died or left in the subsequent diaspora. What if forebear John had fallen victim to hunger or disease rather than taken flight?

His future wife, Ann Kew, boarded the *Guy Mannering* in Liverpool with her parents and five siblings in June 1855 to set sail for America. What if that ship had gone down in an early-summer storm and slowly sunk to the murky, muted bottom of an indifferent Atlantic, or if she had succumbed, as many thousands of jam-packed passengers did, to on-board outbreaks of cholera or…?

What if, after both parties had arrived in Cherry Valley, John-the-village-blacksmith had fancied Ann's older sister, Fanny, more than her? Nothing against lovely Jennie Barlow, but what if John and Ann's later son, George's first wife had survived and he'd never married doe-eyed Lottie?

What if George and "Big Lottie's" future-killer daughter, Della, had practiced her later craft as a teen and poisoned her seven-year-younger "kid sister," her live-in niece, my Gramma Luick? Well… you'd have to be writing this book yourself, then—'cause I wouldn't be here.

What if "Little Lottie"—my prospectless, Depression-era paternal grandmother—had repelled Donald's advances in his car, after that dance, and not gotten pregnant with Lorraine? No spontaneous wedding at a colluding Little Brown Church in a quiet Vale… no Little Buddy…

What if…?

"There for the lack of one, go I not" I heard a merciless voice again whisper.

an imagined scene of Christians about to be fed to the lions as "sport" for spectators at Rome's colosseum

And then, I realized:

Each one of us hangs "here"—in some indefinite corner of an infinite cosmos—only by a literal genetic thread, an electrical impulse shot between protein-based bridges, a heartbeat passed from generation to generation, face to face, kiss by kiss, on a vulnerable-yet-persistent strand of Life encoded in the microscopic rungs of a "twisted ladder" we can never climb but always carry with us. Take a single "carrier" of that ladder out of your particular ancestral lineage, remove a single slave or gladiator, editor or emperor an' ya can forget all the rest! Do away with one soldier, shopkeeper, stagecoach driver… or Iowa farmer… and "time" stops, cuz *you* stop. Remove just <u>one</u> face from your family tree an' you can erase your own, cuz "you" wouldn't be "here." In the millions-of-years-long march of Life in search of life, "there for the lack of <u>one</u>, go *you* not."

VOLUME II

Conclusions

Volume I: *Roots of Darkness*

1) from the *persona*: my disrupted granny

Volume II: *Chasing Restless Roots*

2) about the *populi*: my disappearing people

Volume III: *Tap Roots Betrayed*

3) for the *polis*: my derailed country

conclusion about the *populi*: my disappearing people

Christian and I had been bopping about the Upper Midwest for a couple weeks. It fed my soul to see family and to meet with treasured old friends. I tanked up on authentic Mexican food, pumpkin pie, cranberry juice, maple syrup, root-beer malts, two-inch-thick beef steaks and other delectables not easily available in Dresden. Along the way, we'd combed through a revolving store of museums, archives and other sources of information, images or impulses for use in writing my Great American Saga.

By now, though, I felt spent.

Michael Luick-Thrams in Iowa City, pillaging state archives; in Mason City, with mother, Phyllis: summer 2014

After we'd driven in from the Twin Cities, though they'd never met, Mom and Christian became immediate buddies and—at times, to my consternation—allies. Seeing that I was sagging, my attentive mother suggested that she take my German boyfriend to see Mason City's Frank-Lloyd-Wright-designed hotel and other Prairie School gems, to poke about the old quarry that's now a county fossil park, and to pay respects at the sad remnants of what had been, once upon a time, for 105 years, "Ashlawn Farm."

"Oh" I feigned, "I don't want ya ta go ta any bother, Mom."

"'Bother'?" she protested. "Why, I'd be honored to show this fine young man around town!" and, with that, the two new Inseparables were out the door.

Alone for the first time in over a fortnight, I puffed out my chest, took an unusually deep breath, held it a meditative moment, digested the reality of having just been unexpectedly granted precious liberty, then let warm, moist air escape over my grinning lips.

At that moment, I simply fell onto Mom's plush carpeting and sprawled out over the living room floor. The mid-morning sun streamed in and soon was warming my cheery cheeks. For a few moments, my eyes took a slow survey of a space which had never been my home yet where the person I've known the longest on the entire planet now spends her every day. As I counted to myself *"an overstuffed sofa, an overfilled book case, an under-used electric organ"* my eyelids grew heavy and wanted to close. I obliged, and as the view around me faded into a dim haze, I observed my diaphragm... rising... falling... fresh air rushing in... my belly softening... rising... falling... stale air gushing out...

At some point, I opened my eyes just a crack, but then opened them wider when I found the bright, ranch-style room had fallen dark and, well, had grown. Instead of in Mom's cozy parlor, I found myself in a cavernous hall with ceilings so high I couldn't see them and corners so dark that "here" didn't end, but rather simply faded into an indistinct "there." The room was quiet, yet I could sense that any sounds would echo through this odd space. The summer sunshine had disappeared; a chill ran through me.

I sat up. "*Hey* I wondered, *where'd the plush carpeting go? And, the sofa, the book case, the—?*"

Suddenly, I heard soft footfalls reverberate and grow louder as a figure emerged out of the darkness.

"Who are you?" I blurted out, confused, as Mom and Christian had just left me on my own—or, so I thought.

"Who are *you*?" the young woman shot back.

Then, in a flash, I instinctively knew who it was, although this person hardly resembled the old woman I once had known, decades earlier, when I was but a boy. "Mattie?" I ventured. "Is that you?"

"Yes" she answered, perplexed. "But, who are *you*, I asked?"

"Don't you recognize me? It's me—the kid you knew as 'Mike Luick.'"

The young woman smiled, faintly but warmly. "Oh, I'm sorry" she replied, "but all the 'Mike Luicks' I know look nothing like you, Mister." At that point, as I realized that at 51 I must have looked like an old man to the youthful lass in front of me, who I, in turn, had known only as an ancient, distant relative. This Mattie lifted her young hand and began to count in the air with "There's ol' Michael Henry Luick, my father's elder brother. Then, there's young Mike Luick, who runs the—"

Martha "Mattie" Melissa Luick; mid-1910s

"But, Aunt Mattie, don't you remember *me*?"

"Should I—an' *why* are you calling me 'Aunt'?"

"I should certainly hope you recognize me! It's me, your brother George Michael's great-grandson."

At that, the doe-eyed figure protested "Don't try ta fool *me*! George's kids are only little tikes—so whaddaya mean with 'great-grandson?' Why, that's absurd!"

Then, I realized: I wasn't talking with the widowed great-aunt of *my* youth, but the unmarried maiden of *hers*. "Oh, I see" I mumbled as I wondered what to do next. On an impulse, it occurred to me to inquire coyly "Well, how many children does George have—and how old are they by now?"

Mattie studied my face for a moment, likely questioning if I was completely sane, then answered "Donald is—let me see" she looked upward as she counted with the fingers of one hand, "he must be four and a half years old, and Rena gave birth to little Voral last September, so she's not yet a year."

With that, I closed my eyes and flipped through my mental family-history Rolodex: *Gads, I've landed in summer 1916*, I thought to myself. At first, the idea shook me, but as I opened my eyes I went with it.

For a few heart beats, I said nothing. Neither did she. Then, when she saw that I wasn't playacting, Mattie simply bantered "You're not jokin', are ya?"

I dared not a peep, but only stared at a young woman who would have turned 19 in August of the eventful year in which I seemed to have landed. Still silent, I swallowed hard; my palms began to sweat.

"So" she abruptly punted, "what ya doin' here?" When I didn't immediately respond, she added "I mean, you must be here for a reason, otherwise—"

"Yeah" I replied, "I am—of course. I'm here... I'm here" I faltered, not knowing how to explain my inexplicable presence in a faraway world fully hers but not at all mine, "I'm here doing family research."

"That so? Perhaps, I can help" the fresh-faced young lady offered softly.

"Great" I accepted, then reflexively bid "Make yourself at home" before I realized there were no chairs in sight. "OK, then" I nodded as I stood up, prodded off my seat on the floor by a swelling sense of ineptness. Mattie knitted her brow for a second, then sat on the floor. I shrugged, then joined her.

"So, Mattie—well, tell me: What's up with you these days?"

Initially, the ghostly figure neither said nor did a thing. She only studied me, quietly, searching my anxious face for clues to what this encounter was all about. Then, she said "I'd like to ask you the same."

"*Ah-h-h*" I scratched the back of my head, "I'm in the middle of a month-long tour around the Midwest with my friend, Christian. We're here, visiting from Dresden."

"That sounds like a grand adventure! How's it goin'?" Mattie seemed to genuinely want to know.

"To be honest, it's a bit odd."

Belmond-area residents in diverse poses, as captured by local photographer Martin Thoe in the mid-1910s

Mattie didn't say anything, but I could tell she waited for me to substantiate my open statement.

"I mean, I've been gone awhile."

"You have? For how long—an' where've ya been?"

"I've been living abroad—including two years in New York, but for an Iowa farmboy that's being 'abroad,' too—for, let's see" I counted dryly, noticing that my attempt at levity had yielded not even the bat of an eye, "seventeen years. I lived in Yorkshire, Czechoslovakia and, longest of all, in Germany." Mattie wagged her head, clearly impressed. "Yeah, an' I also lived in the Twin Cities for a decade, so—"

"So how is it, Mike, being back in Iowa?"

As Mattie—or whoever this person was who seemed to be an earlier incarnation of my long-dead great-grandfather's sister—spoke, I asked myself how this tight-lipped young woman could possibly be the chatter-box old lady I knew first as a boy, and later again as a teen bearing a fresh driver's license. *The dead have no egos* I then recalled cousin Barbara once saying, so wondered if that were an explanation for this-Mattie's terseness. *If Barb's right* I reasoned, *a 'Mattie' apparition would have nothing to prove—nor fear, nor lose*. In any case, until now this supposed spirit was all ears, little mouth.

"I have the feeling that my people have disappeared." I reflected, then added "Or, are in the process of disappearing. I grew up here—and not that long ago—but most of the farms have vanished, down to the groves that used to shelter them from the prairie winds. And, the towns? They've dried up, too." I wagged my head, sadly. "More than the visible blight of a dying culture, though, it's the people I miss."

"Really? Whaddaya mean?" Mattie looked at me incredulously. "Have ya been down Belmond's busy Main Street? It's fulla people. And, as far as the farms being 'vanished' that's just too wild of an idea—"

"I know it seems like a horrible fiction to you" I interrupted, "and completely unimaginable, but—"

"Why should I believe any of this? What do *you* know about anything?"

"Good point" I granted. Then, an idea popped into my head. "Say, isn't your middle name 'Melissa'?" She nodded hollowly, but to the affirmative. Her eyes showed surprise that I'd know that about her.

"Wasn't Melissa Overacker Luick your grandmother?" Mattie nodded again. "And, didn't she later marry that Brethren, abolitionist pastor, John Arnold, and—"

"Where'd they go after they got married?" Mattie tested me.

"To California" I shot back, "where she died. Your dad, Louis, came back with your ma, Mary, in 18—"

"All right" Mattie capitulated, "all right—but what do you want to say with all this?"

"Good question" I mouthed quietly, almost under my breath, to myself. "What it is that I want…"

As my mumbling faded into ether, Mattie's head slowly turned and she peered into the darkness. Vexed, I turned, too, and, sure enough, spied silent, stone-faced Marion emerging from the shadows.

Mattie and I waited a moment or two for her kid sister to say something—anything—but exactly as I remembered her as an elderly woman, the girlish specter of 17-year-old Marion uttered not a word.

So, I turned back to Mattie. To both our surprise, however, at that instant Marion snapped to life and exclaimed, as if steered by remote, "Maybe you're not here to *say* something, but rather to *ask* it."

If I only knew what that'd be I quipped to myself, then said aloud "If only *you* knew." Though shocked by Marion's out-of-character boldness, I queried "What might it be that I'm supposed to ask?"

"Or, 'tell' *us*" Mattie chirped, visibly eager to hear what stories I had to share.

"You've been where we're not going, Mike. What's it like there?"

Mattie scolded her "*His* tellin's not *your* askin'!"

Ignoring her older sister, Marion repeated "What's it like there, Mike? Tell us—tell us, do!"

"All right, but where do I start? The world I dropped in from is a century from now." I waited for a reaction, but when none came I continued: "I dunno—how would you recap for me *your* world?"

"I see what ya mean" Mattie conceded, then thought a bit. "You seem to know us—right?"

"Indeed, I do."

Marion Marie Luick; mid-1910s

"So, then, instead of tellin' us about everythin' an' nothin', tell us what you think would interest the 'us' who ya know we are to become."

I found her assignment tricky, for various reasons. For one, how much time had we been allowed? For another, would I want someone to reveal to me, in detail, what *my* future would hold? Wouldn't that ruin the daily Surprise Effect of living each day, moment by moment, groping one's way forward?

"Mattie, you like food—right?" I improvised spontaneously.

"Oh, yes" she glowed. "Do I ever!"

245

scenes of food and drink in late-Victorian Belmond, Iowa; 1910s

"So, food in 2014—it's almost unrecognizable from what you folks eat. Yours comes mostly fresh from the garden or in bulk at the general store. Ours comes mostly trucked in from thousands of kilometers away, hauled from Mexico or flown in from New Zealand." Mattie's and Marion's eyes grew. "It comes wrapped in plastic or trapped in cardboard boxes. Juice comes frozen at the supermarket—"

"A 'supermarket'?" Marion echoed an unknown in my airing of modern America's culinary culture.

"—if you want. And, although the quality's often wooden an' pale, you can get strawberries at Christmas or kiwis at Easter. Entire strains of fruit and vegetables are grown to neatly fit packing crates."

"Waita sec: What are 'kiwis'?" Mattie wanted to know, catching up with my review in her mind.

"Some Belmond folks might have wooden iceboxes" I pushed on, "but we have big, metal boxes with rubber-rimmed doors—gigantic things to keep perishables cool or frozen. We have built-in kitchens—"

"Built-in where?" Mattie wondered, shaking her head as if not hearing something correctly.

"—that have more cupboards than many of your stores!" Both women fell dumbstruck, mesmerized by the image of such large kitchens. "The problem is, much of the food gets 'lost' in such endless storage and goes bad before we can use it." They wagged their heads in disbelieving unison. "But, Americans eat most of their food on the run, anyway, and seldom cook whole meals at home from scratch anymore."

Mattie crinkled her face, disapproval stretched from ear to ear. "How do they do *that*—an' *why*?"

"Oh, 'fast food' has reigned since the '50s and has grown to super sizes—as have two-thirds of the people." Noticing that my listeners weren't following me, I explained "Yeah, a third of our compatriots is 'just' overweight, but another third is outright obese." Seeing their jaws drop, I informed my two future great-aunts that "When I was a kid, our teachers and preachers warned of increasing global hunger, but instead we've got Michelin-man-shaped children from Chicago to Georgia, from China to Guatemala."

"But if what people is eatin' isn't good for 'em" Mattie asked, "why on Earth do they keep eatin' it?"

"As we say, 'Time's money.' And besides, gigantic companies make gigantic profits peddling poison." When I explained that the nation's food stocks are processed in factories and kept in warehouses, Mattie grilled "Can it have any taste at all? Why, I never heard of such a thing in all my days!" Destined to be a café owner a few decades later, she wrinkled her nose. "Where do they sell the stuff?"

"Oh, it's everywhere, in strips—"

Confused, Marion interjected with "What's a 'strip'?"

"—in airports," (noticing their incomprehension, I remembered that there were no "airports" in 1916 at all, anywhere) "malls," (again, a word that caused cocked heads) "college campuses and the like. You can drive your car alongside a building, press a button, speak into a box, idle up to a window and get food handed to you in a paper bag. You even can phone in an order and have pizza delivered."

Again, Marion: "A 'pizza'?"

At that, the sisters had heard enough about the staff of life—more than they could digest, as it were.

"An' family life?" normally quiet Marion piped up. "Tell us about families in 2014."

four generations of two Belmond families: the Ackersons (left) & Christies (Frank, Stanton, John, Marvin)

"Patch-work" I merely stated, each syllable in staccato.

"What's 'patchwork'?" Marion tilted her head and looked me in the eye as she awaited an answer.

"Well, since the Second World War—"

"*Which* war?" Marion interrupted.

"I'll come back to that—but since then, most American families have consisted of two, rarely more generations. And, we move a lot—something like a third of the nation, every five years. That's why many don't really know their cousins"—I could tell from their perplexed looks that the concept was as foreign to my paternal grandfather's aunts as it was to me, growing up as I did with dozens of cousins— "or even aunts and uncles. But don't forget" I swiftly noted, "when your grandfather, Henry Luick, left your grandmother, Melissa didn't miss a beat before she took her brood back to Michigan for a spell, before later returning to Iowa. Louis, your father, shifted between two households—both of which soon absorbed numerous 'Lathrops' and 'Arnolds' of various ages and roles. Indeed" I drove the point home, "those two generations were nothing if they weren't the product of a 'pioneer patchwork' family."

Visibly connecting the dots in her mind, Marion inquired "And, grandparents? What about them?"

"Never mind askin' him all that" an insistent voice broke in from the shadows behind me. Hearing a younger version of a voice I thought I recognized, I swirled on my butt to see not only a familiar-looking, 20-something brunette, but a set of worn, one-room-schoolhouse desks appearing just in front of her.

"My stars" Mattie called out, "if it isn't Cloe Jenison!"—who visibly enjoyed being an unwelcome surprise.

At that, Mattie, Marion and I took to our feet and met Cloe as she reached the desks, where all three of the "girls" quietly slid onto the cramped benches. I found myself drifting to the front of the "class."

"Don't think grandparents in his day have it much different than in ours. When the Jennisons came out here to Iowa from back in Crown Point" Cloe lectured the rest of us, "the family, they was tight as a bundle. After no time at all, though—when each of those Jennison boys got a family and a farm o' his own—why, at that point the families, they hardly knew each other anymore, let alone the grandfolks."

"You wouldn't be overstating it a bit now, would ya, Cloe?" Mattie challenged.

"Like I said, at first, as pioneers, our people—they needed each other to survive: Injuns, grasshopper plagues, diseases, blizzards an' cyclones. As the years went on and marriages and deaths took place, most of the families remained near each other and, in the early days, the families seemed to get along fairly well. If one family had sickness or death or family troubles or financial

Cloe LaVerne Jenison, mid-1910s

needs, they shared, but as the years went on some families moved away an' got more independent. As the children grew up, there was quarrelin'—an' bitter rows took place. Our grandfolks jus' stood by, sad, an' watched: What else could they do? They grew up in a diff'rent place an' knew a diff'rent time, when families held together."

"It sounds" Marion bid, "like the people lost each other: The more money they had of their own, the less they needed each other." She turned to me and asked "Does that sound right, Mike? Is that it?"

"That's certainly what my research reveals. When our people crossed America, the country was at a stage of development where most people had no choice but to depend on each other, to help each other literally move forward. If they hadn't worked as a team and stood together, they would have all gone down, each one alone. But, as the nation grew to be so powerful, so rich after two world wars—"

"Which 'world wars' you talkin' 'bout?" Marion insisted, but to no avail.

"—and the population grew to be mostly middle class, family ties faded, along with community ties. I saw that in my own postwar generation" I testified. "As we graduated, we grandchildren of the children of the pioneers largely drifted off to pursue our own riches: The best educated or those with the most moxie tended to leave, to chase careers in Des Moines, in the Twin Cities, Chicago, Denver—even Dallas. The ones who stayed in rural Iowa were mainly those who felt they had the least to gain elsewhere."

"But how can that be?" Mattie protested firmly. "There are *so* many families here now, with *so* many babies: How could we possibly die out a century from now? Surely, what you say simply *can't* be true!"

248

two Thoe-studio portraits of Belmond-area people; left photo with identifying inscription "Lynch"

"Well, what brought our people here in the first place?" Marion asked her older sister back. "Land!"

"And when did they come?" another, disembodied voice asked from somewhere in the dark void. Mattie, Marion, Cloe and I all looked around, but saw no one. Still, the voice spoke on: "It's 1916: Our people only arrived here sixty years ago. Before they came—" the female speaker continued, as the three women sitting at the school desks all peered at me, searchingly, "—what were there, maybe a hundred thousand Indians living in Iowa? In no time at all, a couple million came, looking for land or to make a buck, selling bobbles to the sodbusters." By this point, the faceless voice had grown louder as it drew nearer, and the women had taken to their feet, straining to see who it was speaking to us. "I tell

Ethel Mae Luick, 1920s

my pupils how good we have it. I tell them about the deep, rich earth and the healthy food it gives us. I remind them how set we are, that we have cozy houses and safe towns, strong schools, stable churches an' each other—but even at their young ages, they want more; they want something diff'rent..."

At that, as her words faded, a captivating young woman emerged from the darkness. As she did, the other three seemed to recognize her. Mattie and Marion smiled; Cloe did not—yet all three sat down. As she took a seat next to them, the sweet-faced blonde beamed, but Cloe muttered "Oh—Ethel: It's *you* again!"

Of course I marveled to myself, *that's who it is: It's Ethel Luick!* When I was a teenager, I knew her as a loveable ol' crone who used to bark commands at me while we drove around the countryside, but I loved it—and her!

"Why, look who's here" Ethel called out, "Cloe Jenison! I haven't seen you since, oh, not long enough." Ethel turned and said to me "It's time somebody around here called a spade a steam shovel!"

"Yes, we were just talkin' 'bout Iowa's history—"

"—an' its future" Marion finished my sentence. "Mike's here doing family research—an' since we're his fam'ly, he's researchin' *us*!"

"That so?" Cloe purred. "What's a 'Luick' got ta teach anybody 'bout hist'ry" she teased, "since they always turn it on its head anyways, ta fit what serves 'em best, when it serves 'em most."

Startled by Cloe's reflex aggressiveness, I barely managed to keep any composure at all. "Well, hard as it might be for all of you to see it—let alone believe it—in 1916, you and your families are anomalies."

"'A-what-alies'?" Marion inquired, shrugging even while she shook her head as if sipping old vinegar.

"You think the world you inhabit in or around Belmond is timeless, but it's not: You're riding a wave, a historical phenomenon, the stretching out of European culture, a foreign template laid over a vast continent previously occupied for ten thousand years by people very different from ourselves. The way we live, the system that's evolved over hundreds of years back in the Old World, has imposed itself upon the New, but this era of plowing asunder the prairie, of forcing it to yield food for livestock or for other uses, it's something new—and temporary. You, your families still farm it in tandem with the weather and the seasons, but it won't be long now, until wars around the world will lead your fathers and brothers to turn to ever-bigger machinery, then to hefty chemicals and gene-manipulated seeds—"

"'Jean Mann's pileated seats'?" Marion repeated, trying to make sense of what seemed nonsense.

"—to squeeze out of the ever-thinner, increasingly spent soil something to eat or to use as fuel." As all four young women began to shake their heads slowly or otherwise show incomprehension, I noted: "That dependence on machines, petroleum, chemicals, capital will decimate the entire region, leaving behind a fraction of the world you know here now: the people, your schools and churches, farms, shops, parks, cemeteries—everything. A century from now, it'll all be melting away into a blighted sleep."

identifying inscription on the negative for the photo on the far right as "Miss Saatoff"; photos circa 1910

As the "p" in "sleep" sprang off my tongue like a high-board diver into a waiting pool, I could feel waves of somberness settle upon my four listeners. It was if a nuclear bomb had exploded in the visible distance and they were all sitting dumbstruck, contemplating the weight of the words still echoing through their heads. *And I haven't even told them that humanity has the means to blow the world to bits* I thought to myself, *or about herpes, AIDs, Ebola or any other pestilences they've not even heard uttered.*

Even if they found the demise of themselves and everything, everyone they cared about unfathomable, I knew it would be historical fact—just like I knew that one day Mattie would fall deeply, helplessly, eternally in love with Ross Farmer, only to lose him, young and tragically. Looking to still-quiet Marion, I knew she'd play shadow to Mattie's majesty till the day death would finally separate the two—and that she adored her gay brother, whether or not she or he ever named what made Henry him.

It was mouthy Cloe, not at all surprisingly, who finally broke the silence with "An' I take it that we're jus' supposed ta sit an' let all that happen, without liftin' a finger? Is this some Luick trick to rob us all?"

"It's not 'our' scenario, ya know. My people, too, will be driven from the land, just like all the rest."

Looking at that damaged and damaging woman, early in her career as a lifelong naysayer and caster of doubts, I meditated on what had made her so bitter, so early. As the scene of her shotgun's barrel, poked into my chest, flashed across my mind, I got lost in thought as I tried to imagine how the fresh, nicely dressed, hair-in-a-bun schoolmarm in front of me could one day be a dried out, toothless ol' coot who wore musty, threadbare clothes and holed up in a shabby, dank, junk-filled dump.

Was the total disaster that became Cloe's life really the result of one unplanned pregnancy and being jilted at the altar? I wondered. *Can any hurt last that long and exact such an absolute price?* Just then, as a new wave of the dark pensiveness that has accompanied me all my life began to roll right over my inadequate mental barriers, I recalled a query from my Iowa-born historian friend living in Berlin, Alan:

> Michael, you always write from some moral standpoint, from some clear, black-and-white expectation of how the people populating your stories 'should' have acted or even lived, but rarely did. What is that unbending standard out of which you obviously operate, but never spell out?

Standing there, staring at caustic Cloe, I wished—for her, not for me, for I could always simply walk away from her toxic, mean-spirited, sorry-assed self—that she might, even if but for a few moments, be able to smile from her heart, to feel safe and happy in the world, even in these few ephemeral moments we'd have together in this dark, cavernous hall. Then, I heard Alan say *Hey, bud: I wish that for you, too!*

I've been fortunate, that even in the often penniless life of a public historian, where a cup of café-bought coffee can be a luxury, I've been rich in friends since my undergrad days at Iowa Straight. Alan's, too, has been a friendship that has challenged me to be more, to be better than I'd be were he not in my life... At *that* instant—still staring at future Hard Knocks graduate Cloe Jenison, meditating on which criteria I tap to judge if a given human life had been lived well, or not—a subdued man appeared.

At first, his sudden presence threw me off, but as soon as I realized that it was Mattie and Marion's older brother, Henry, I realized that Alan's recurring goading me to see bigger pictures just acquired an "Exhibit A." Here I'd just demoralized the whole group—Mattie, Marion, Ethel and Cloe—with my Doomsday-esque scenario for a world they helped plant on the Iowa prairies; even if what I confided to them was all true, as Alan again and again tried to make me see, my Truth was only one. Yes, the small-town world of late-Victorian Belmond was fated to evaporate one day like some Fata Morgana, but its passage also meant a loosening of stifling social codes that served too few and kept too many fettered.

It did not occur to me then, but when I later recounted to Alan these uncanny encounters, he wrote:

> It occurs to me that your [view of historical change is] a tad one-sided, and that instead of warning [a Mattie or a Marion] only about soulless shopping malls and fattening processed foods, you also could have informed her that in 2016 she would have full voting rights; she could control her own property and launch her own career without raising any eyebrows; she could

Henry Lorence Luick, circa 1910s

manage her menstruation without mess or discomfort, and could limit her pregnancies safely and legally with a latex condom or a pill; she wouldn't have to die of childbed fever; her children would never catch polio; she could stop a life-threatening infection with a simple shot of antibiotics; she could speed from one town to the other in her own air-conditioned car on a smooth super-highway; she could save up her pennies and jet down to Cancun for a cheap vacation; she would have hot and cold running water any

251

time she wanted; she would have access to all the world's knowledge at her fingertips [as] global communication would be instant and practically for free; and gay people could live as they saw fit and even marry each other rather than end up in prison cells or mental institutions. I imagine she'd be intrigued by the first of these prospects, and possibly shocked by the last, but that just goes to show how the world has changed. [...] So it's your call, but it might pay to admit at some point that there has been some progress since 1916. I mean, just ask any minority person - women, black people, Hispanics, gays, disabled people, you name it. You see, it goes back to Dickens' notion of 'the best of times, the worst of times.' Or, as Arthur Schopenhauer put it, 'Change alone is eternal, perpetual, immortal.'

Sincerely,

Alan

Instead of any of that, all I could think of in that moment, as Henry also emerged from the darkest crevices of my psyche, was *So, that's my gay great-uncle, huh?* I wondered *Will he recognize a kindred spirit? Did 'gaydar' exist in 1916, too?* As I looked the man over from head to toe, I hoped he could smell that he wasn't the only one in the room who was "diff'rent." But, given that Uncle Henry was 80 in June '69—in that steamy summer overflowing with rebellions and would-be revolutions, when homosexual fashion boys and drag queens stood up and pushed back for a change when the cops came into New York's Stonewall Inn for the zillioneth time to harass and extort them—"Hank" lived his entire life in a Midwestern world where our sort of love dared not speak its name, where his deepest desires to find closeness with other men went unuttered yet were a magnet for shame, from others or even his Self.

identities unknown, but the young woman, second from left, appears in several photos with Mattie Luick; 1910s

Oddly, decades and generations later, long after Henry's birth in 1889, even his nephew Gary resists naming "it" anything other than "Henry liked boys" and skirts the matter altogether as fast as possible. Yet, I grew up at the tail end of that small-town era rife with closed closets and "open secrets:" I really *have* been "there" and truly *did* do "that;" I know too well the crushing feelings born of grinding social disapproval. Until I went to Iowa Straight and braved my own coming-out in September 1982, I, too, maneuvered in a realm of blackness, of half-lies and fractured truths, of hollow "dates" with girls who appealed to me always for what was between their ears, never their legs. Henry, too, must have moved about in the shadows of benighted Belmond, in that pre-lib world of stony masculinity and sappy "feminine sensibilities." Of course, I could not be certain of the details behind Uncle Hank's homoerotic indulgences or dalliances, but I was sure of one thing, that he—and I—weren't "the only ones" like "us."

Eerily, exactly as I had that thought yet another young man sauntered up out of nowhere—but unlike the young women who'd appeared before him, he sat down not upon the school-desk bench, but rather took a seat and struck a commanding pose in a throne-like chair nearby. And, this time, none of my other visitors recognized the latest arrival—but, I did. "Carl?" I inquired: "Carl Hansen—is that *you*?"

Laying his cheek against a hand boasting a pinky ring, Carl read me in a flash. "Who else?" he jeered.

I had been as awkward a teen as ever there was, but even as an utterly unsavvy kid who didn't know who or what he was, when I met the retired Thornton postmaster that Carl would be some sixty years after this surreal encounter, on some level I entertained doubts about how "normal" he was. The "Bird Lady" with whom he shared that French-Empire-style icebox posing on the outside as a downhome Heartland cottage seemed like a personal page for his caprices, not a soulmate for his heart. I had no other reason, then, to ponder the man's most intimate depths further—not even local twiddle twaddle that left tongues wagging—and the couple's childlessness could have had numerous causes. Still, Carl's brief-but-secret career as a silent-screen film star in the heady Hollywood of the '20s let my mind run.

a Belmond-area young man resembling Carl Hansen; 1910s

"Carl" I punted, but then, realizing that in 1916 he could have had no inkling of the golden stint he'd have in the Golden State a decade hence, continued cautiously with "you're a talented fellow, I hear."

"You could say that" was all he managed to reply with an arrogance I'd not sensed when I met him for some stolen, icy minutes in the late Seventies. By then, his self-fascination likely had run its thin course; by then, he was at the end not only of his working life but, indeed, near the end of Life at all.

Having also been fuller of myself when I was Twenty-Something, I cut Carl slack yet found him trying.

"I sing in the Thornton glee club" he recounted as he rubbed his ring with his thumb, back and forth with the end of his long thumbnail, "and, of course, I was the star of the school play last fall—'Hamlet.'"

"I'm sure you were marvelous—but, look, we don't have much time left an' I wanna ask sompthin'."

"I'm all ears, sir—I'm all ears" he repeated as he shifted on his handsome-but-hard wooden seat.

"When you are up on stage acting, or even jus' out front, singing for a crowd, what do you want most to happen—what are you trying to *do*, to achieve?"

For a moment, cocky Carl searched for an answer. When he finally had one, he replied "I want them to see that I am here, and" his voice trailed off, "that I can…"

"You 'can' *what*, Carl?" I prompted.

"That I can help them forget for a moment that they are here, and that they can't."

Or, at least, you think you can do what they can't I editorialized under my breath. "Why would your audience want to forget that they are here or, as you put it, that they can't forget that they're here?"

"Because I want that most of the time, myself." Disclosing so much so quickly so casually, Carl recited his responses calmly yet grandly, as if he were the star witness at a trial of the century, where he knew that the whole world was watching, waiting for the wisest of soliloquies. "It's all so short, you see" he said, "so the people, they want to be you, even if for a few moments, and forget their Selves, their own petty daily worries as well as their great, existential *Angst*. They know what's coming one day—the final Final Curtain—so they turn to me, to anyone, to take the focus off their own, fleeting unimportance."

Albert Lee Luick, mid-1910s

"And that's also why" another male voice picked up Carl's monologue flawlessly, as if it had been his own, "we look to our families, to their histories, to who they've been, where they've been and where we guess they might be headed." Just as I wondered who this joker might be, who, like the others, quietly emerged from the dark, he elaborated: "The Luicks"—at which point I guessed that the buck who'd appeared must be no less than Albert Lee Luick, the young prince of the closest thing that the Belmond of 1916 had to royalty—"were an impressive parade of characters, for generations—that's for sure. Who wouldn't want to come from such a pedigree?" he, the first familial chronicler of my father's unusual people, boasted. He had a point, given they included a rebellious cavalry man, a frontier surveyor cum county judge, "Injun fighters," several generations of hightailing Romeos and other singular figures. "It sortta puffs out the ol' chest" self-assured Albert looked straight at me, "jus' knowin' what a colorful crowd you can hitch your weak ego to— doesn't it, Mike Luick?"

"Well" I stammered, "it's not quite, I mean, you make it sound so—but it's not as easy or clear as—"

"Why can't you jus' say it, Mike?" Albert pushed. "What's so hard in simply admitting 'I feared I was nothing, so I've been diggin' 'round my whole conscious life in my family's muck, to confirm that I was sompthin'—anything—over nothin' at all?' If you did you wouldn't be the only one—but one of zillions."

None of these photos bear an identifying inscription, but Belmond's Martin Thoe shot all of them around 1910.

At that, I began to feel increasingly uncomfortable, and uncertain about my lifelong interest in who I came from, my motives for uncovering those roots and what they meant to me. Unlike with the appearances of the four women—younger incarnations of relatives I had known as an earnest teenage genealogist—these three male figures who I knew of but not personally left me feeling insecure and sad.

a Belmond-area woman resembling Winnie May Campbell, mid-1910s

"You know, it's not easy for her, either" declared a high-pitched but resolute voice behind me.

As I swirled around me to see who it was who was stepping out of the collection of ghosts now paying me increasingly unsettling visits, I reflexively grilled "What's not 'easy' for whom?"

"Why, Little Lottie, of course! You've gotta think about her for once, too. It's real hard for that lass."

"*What* is so hard?" I demanded of the specter I quickly concluded must be of Winnie Campbell, talking about my Gramma Luick, Charlotte (Juhl) Luick.

"Life" Winnie shot back. "She's only three now, but she clearly shows that she knows that Big Lottie isn't her mother, that my ill and lumbering aunt would rather the lil' tike not be around—but she is."

"How do you know—what does 'clearly show' look like?"

"The girl seems to be always looking towards the door, waiting for a real, loving motherly type to walk onto the scene, but my dead cousin will never, ever come—an' Little Lottie jus' can't accept that."

Feeling slightly accosted by this quietly forceful figure in front of me, I took a slow, small step back. "My grandmother's mother fell down the stairs an' died the day after Gramma was born" I recounted gratuitously, given that great-cousin Winnie knew the tragic details, too well. "I'm sorry for that, but if Gramma had been able to deal with that—at least as an adult, if not as a half-orphaned kid, then—"

"Then *what*?" Winnie demanded as she took a step towards me, closing the gap I'd tried to put between us. "What would have happened—what would that have changed? Would it've helped *you*?"

Taking another subtle step back, I scrambled for an adequate response. "It sure wouldn't have hurt."

Following me flawlessly as I moved backwards across the room, as if we were tango partners and not clan members at odds over the meaning or relevance of events tsunamic but long past, Winnie shuffled towards me just as quickly as I increasingly urgently backed away from her. "Fact is, she didn't" she said.

At that, I'd backed up against the front of the school-desk bench and, losing my balance, fell backwards, leaving me sitting and Winnie standing immediately in front of and, threateningly, over me.

"Gosh" she asked rhetorically, "have there ever been things in your life that you've not dealt with?"

"Yes, of course" I stammered, aware that at this scene's beginning I'd been at the head of the "class" and now, somehow, was *in* it, "but, I didn't create a family, which then had to deal with *my* leftovers."

"Why'd Lottie's tragedy become *yours*? It wasn't your mother who died on your second day of life!"

By now having had enough of being on trial, I sat up and grew louder: "Because she was one of the most important people in my life, we spent a lot of time together and"—I teared—"I loved her deeply."

"I'm sure" Winnie sighed, "she loved you, too—the best she could, even if it wasn't a perfect love. She's a lively, loving child" the woman in front of me said softly but firmly, "an' she's doing her best."

Touched by Winnie's words, mine grew quieter, too, as I lamented "It's too bad, that her unslain inner demons seemed to mate so well with her later husband's, with Donald's—of which he had many."

"I was waitin' for ya ta pull lil' Donald inta all this" grumbled yet another young woman, as she stepped out from behind retreating Winnie. "He's now four-and-a-half and *such* a sensitive little boy!"

Anyone else gonna come to testify today? I wondered to no one but the taxed sap inside my head. "Are you" I ventured, "Mona, Donald's aunt—his mother's younger sister?"

"Indeed" she shined—but then her smile evaporated as she added "even if I can't make his home life much sweeter though I try." As Mona spoke, the others—Mattie, Marion, Cloe, Ethel, Henry, Carl, Albert and Winnie—gathered behind her in a loose half-circle. "Sis hasn't had it easy—having lost little Mildred soon after that babe was born, then having to deal with George's constant dreamin' an' changin' jobs or homes or both. George's too hard on the boy—and Rena too harsh in her scolding—so I attempt to add a bit o' sunshine wherever I can: a postcard here, a lil' present there, a visit when I can find the time."

Having never been able to ask the man myself what happened to him to make him effectively a near-mute, I gingerly asked Mona "So, does he speak to you, actually?"—at which she peered at me oddly.

Mona Jenison, mid-1910s

"Why, of course he does" she countered—but, then, upon reflection, added "It *is* true: His spark's become a bit dimmed as of late. Maybe that's outta fear that if he says something 'wrong' there'll be

hell to pay to either stressed George or, well, severe Lorena. As I said" Mona paused, "I do what I can."

As Mona finished explaining my grandfather's increasing withdrawal as a little boy as a response to the adults around him, I noticed that the assorted faces standing behind her had begun to disappear, one by one, almost imperceptibly.

"Oh, you guys!" I called out, "don't leave—not yet! Hey, come back here" I protested as my father's kin drifted off, one by one, until only Mattie remained. Once again, she and I were alone, together.

"Where'd they all go?" I asked. "Marion, Ethel—even crazy Cloe" I mourned; "What happened to—"

"Gone" Mattie interrupted, "—they're all gone, never to return."

"But, they'd just gotten here!"

"Life on Earth isn't forever, ya know."

"I know that—but losing you children of pioneers is a one-time, watermark event: A generation like yours will exist only once. That you're now forever gone, though—it's a tragedy; it's jus' too much."

Mattie Luick, head-on

256

"Is it?" she asked. Mattie's face betrayed not a hint of uncertainty, but rather an intent to provoke. I wondered what it was she wanted to achieve—and "who" or what sent her to visit me, a century later.

"Sure—but it's only one of the senses I meant when I told you I have the feeling that 'My people are disappearing.' I didn't mean just you specific people, with your individual personalities and biographies."

"So, what was the other sense you meant?" Mattie prodded.

I reflected quietly to myself for a moment, then explained "I mean also the passage of a *kind* of people, of certain characteristics that were so typical of you all, but now are as good as vanished." I looked up at Mattie and confided "Ya know, I miss you people *so* much! You were *such* a big part of us. You did things that I'm not sure we alive today could endure long enough to accomplish. You were—."

"Well, I suppose each generation has its own traits, an' leaves its own stamp on those around 'em."

"Lemme tell ya, you folks didn't jus' leave a 'stamp' on us; you basically threw the pot on the wheel!"

For the first time smiling more than just a faint grin, Mattie demurred "I don't know about that—"

"I can't speak for others, but you sure left deep imprints on me" I confided. "You're the ones Brokaw called the 'Greatest Generation' and I, for one, looked up to you. Sure" I shook my head slightly, "we *listened* to our folks—we would've gotten a swift lickin' if we hadn't—but we *looked up* to all of you."

Mattie's smile continued to widen as she bobbed her head slowly in grateful acknowledgment.

"And, the folks today?" she grilled. "Don't you look up to them?"

"Don't get me started" I warned. "Deb an' Dave an' all the cousins; my classmates an' the rest of our generation? Forget it!" I barked.

Mattie looked at me, expectantly, but I didn't continue.

"Why 'forget it'?" she finally pushed.

"Our folks grew up in material poverty—Mom and her sisters wore sugar sacks for underwear during the Depression! Then, there was The War, with scrap drives an' rationing an' all the rest. Our parents' young lives were marked by hardship, which was tough, but, hey—didn't it build character?" I shook my head in a silent *tsk-tsk* as I asked "And, we kids? They weaned us on the post-war fat they found so mesmerizing, then as teens we got high sniffin' our own navels. If you think the kids today don't know much about much at all, they're only symptoms of their parents', of *my* generation's self-absorption."

Suddenly spooked by the depth and rabidity of my own quick, damning anger, I fell silent.

A soft "Oh" was all that Mattie could slowly muster—until, that is, she looked up and over my shoulder. "Marion" she summoned to someone somewhere behind me, "what do you think?"

I turned and, sure enough, saw that in non-Life as in Life, Marion still played shadow to her Big Sis.

Marion said not a word, yet I "heard" her think *So, what's the question that he's here to ask?*

"You were all here once" I started saying to Mattie, "jus' as Mom and Christian and I are here now"—at which point I heard a car door slam and footfalls on concrete. "Someday, we won't be here, either."

"You're here now" Mattie reminded me with a breathless rush, "so live each day as best, as fully as you can—for if nothing else, you owe it to those of us who passed Life on to you, and to those who will come in the future and live on whatever Life you leave behind when you've lived out your share of it."

With that, Mattie, her shadow named "Marion," and the dark, cavernous hall where this most unusual of family reunions had just taken place, all vanished. Once again sprawled out on my mother's plush living-room carpet, I opened my eyes just as the door opened, with Mom followed closely by Christian, and not a few shopping bags bounding behind them into the room.

"Well, hello there, you two" I bid, as if wakening from a deep sleep. "Did ya see a bit o' Mason City?"

"Oh" they sang in such a synchronized chorus that I couldn't tell who said what, "we saw Rock Glen an' the Prairie-School architecture, Frank Lloyd Wright's hotel an' a deer below the Public Library an'…"

"That's grand" I said dismissively as I brushed aside the rest of their excited recounting. "I'm so glad."

"We thought of you" Phyllis beamed as she took a slip of paper out of her pursue. "Look what we found as I showed Christian around the library." As Mom handed me a poem, she noted "Dorothy from the genealogical society, in the history room there, gave us this." As I looked down and started to read, she asked "Didn't you used to attend their meetings when you were a teenager, jus' starting to…"

257

The soldier portrait likely comes from the World War I era. The only tagged photo, the doubled one, reads "Paul."

As my mother's voice grew ever dimmer in my ears, I read:

If you could see your ancestors
all standing in a row,
would you be proud of them or not,
or don't you really know?
Some strange discoveries are made
in climbing family trees.
And some of them, you don't know,
do not particularly please.
If you could see your ancestors
all standing in a row,
there might be some of them perhaps
you shouldn't care to know.
But here's another question
which requires a different view—
If you could meet your ancestors
would they be proud of you?

Phyllis (Thrams) Luick with Christian in Iowa, summer 2014; the left photo tagged with inscription "1908"— perhaps referencing a Belmond-area high school class

VOLUME II

Supplements

Published in 1903, fifty years after Henry and David Luick arrived in what would become "Belmond," their fellow adopted Iowan, hobby-historian Benjamin Gue reflected on the Hawkeye State's early years:

> As the pioneer period began to give way to the advancing tide of immigration coming into the Mississippi Valley with the progress of railroad extension, Iowa experienced many of the advantages of incoming capital and gladly welcomed the luxuries brought by material progress. But, among the new settlers there were regrets over the innovations which banished in some degree the universal hospitality of the early days of common poverty, when every cabin was a house of entertainment for the white-topped wagon loaded with "new comers" — men, women, and bright-eyed, bare-footed children seeking new homes.

> [Considering the years leading] to the dark days of the Civil War, which even then was beginning to seem slowly gathering in the not distant future, we may take a backward glance at the log-cabin era which will linger in the memory of the gray-haired few who were of that generation.

> The early settlements in Iowa were largely made by men and women with little of worldly possessions beyond youth, health, industrious habits and a determination to better their condition in a new country where most of the people were similarly situated.

> It was not from the well-to-do classes that the pioneers set forth on their westward journeys, to explore new and unknown countries. The middle-aged man with a family, who from some misfortune had found it a hard struggle in the East to accumulate any surplus over bare subsistence, could not endure the thought that his sons must be left with only an inheritance of industry; that his daughters must serve as servants in the families of strangers; that the long years of toil for a frugal living must go on among his descendants through the succeeding generations. He looked around among his neighbors and saw boys no brighter and girls no worthier than his own, enjoying the advantages of education, the best society and all that wealth could bring. His sons and daughters were as dear to him as those who were highly favored by fortune were to their parents. There were no class divisions in America to exclude his children from aspiring to higher positions; no exclusive social circles which they might not enter; the field was open to all. Misfortune or poverty alone kept the ambitious from participation in the luxuries of life. There were great unsettled regions in the far West where industry, perseverance and privations for this generation would give all of these advantages to the children of the poor.

It was hard to sever all social and kindred ties and seek among unsettled regions a place to make new homes; endure the stern privations, slavish toil and long, slow waiting for the coming in late years of life of the advantages that the children might some distant day enjoy. The whole West of fifty years ago was dotted over with log cabins, where, amid hardships, sickness, want and unending toil, the best years of the lives of brave self-sacrificing men and women were given to the building up of a new civilization from little more than nature had provided.

The younger generation of the closing years of the Nineteenth Century can know little of the slow progress of evolution which has transformed the bleak prairies of fifty years ago into beautiful farms of unsurpassed fertility, adorned with shady groves, fruitful orchards, large barns, modern homes and generous equipments of the best labor-saving implements. They cannot realize that our network of railroads, telegraphs and telephones has so recently displaced the stage coach, the emigrant wagon drawn by oxen, the weekly horseback mail carrier. That our cities and thriving villages with their modern homes, imposing business blocks and public buildings, with factories, banks, elegant churches and stately school-houses have, within the memory of the older citizens, crowded out the Indian's wigwam and the pioneer's log cabin and sod house.

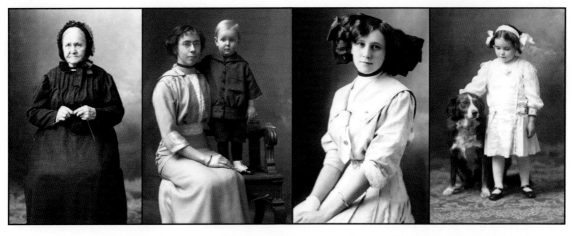

four Belmond-area females representing four various generations, with young son and family dog

Looking back upon a picture of pioneer life as it was in the years beginning with the early "30s," "40s" and "50s" [of the 1800s,] we find a land where the Indians, buffalo, deer and elk were reluctantly retiring before the invasion of the hunter, trapper and pioneer farmer. The well-worn paths of these early inhabitants of the wild groves and boundless prairies were found along the wooded banks of the rivers and creeks. Before the deadly rifle of the hunters and the snares of the stealthy trappers, the red men and wild animals rapidly but most reluctantly retreated. Next came the resounding echoes of the wood-chopper's axe as the lofty walnut, oak and hickory trees were converted into cabins and fences for new homes of the pioneer and his family.

Toil had no terrors for the early settlers; all were workers. There was a charm in choosing a home in the wild, unsettled country, as the family journeyed on day after day in the solitude of the vast rolling prairies, fording the streams, winding along the trackless ridges, exploring the fringe of woodland that bordered the creeks and rivers; passing beautiful groves that in the distance slowly loomed up like islands in the ocean, where earlier immigrants had camped and staked off their claims. The finding of a spring in an unoccupied grove and taking possession for a home; getting acquainted with the neighbors who had preceded them; exploring the thickets for wild plums, grapes, crab-apples, hazel and hickory nuts. Choosing the site for the cabin, cutting the logs which the neighbors helped to raise into a rude house, hunting the deer, elk, wild turkeys, prairie chickens, ducks and geese for subsistence until sod corn could be raised; going two or three days' journey to mill or market and camping out nights on the way; constructing tables, bedsteads, stools and shelves; breaking the prairie with five or six yoke of oxen and the huge breaking plow and planting the sod corn. The women of the household were among the constant toilers. In addition to the ordinary housework of later times, living remote from towns, stores or factories, they were artisans and manufacturers as well as housekeepers. They had to spin, weave, cut and make clothing for the family, and often were the teachers of their children.

There were compensations for the privations and hard toil. Hospitality was nowhere more general and genuine than among the early settlers. Entertainment of "new comers" was generally free and cordial. The one room of the cabin was never too full to furnish shelter and food for the traveler. Neighbors gathered together for miles around at corn huskings, which ended with a frolic for the youngsters in the evening. Shooting matches were made where the winners went home loaded with turkeys won; camp meetings were held by the light of blazing log piles where old and young assembled to listen to the rude eloquence of the uncultured preacher, lurid with fire and brimstone and endless wrath for sinners, which suited the sturdy pioneers. All joined in singing the grand old hymns with a fervor that raised enthusiasm to the highest pitch. The annual Fourth of July celebration appealed to the patriotism of every citizen, old and young. The oration of the young lawyer from a distant town was listened to with rapt attention and the national songs resounded through the grove. A picnic dinner spread beneath the sheltering trees, and a country ball in the evening, made up a day of general enjoyment for the entire population. Wolf hunts in the winter were occasions of excitement and political meetings in the country school-house at long intervals brought the widely separated settlers together and varied the monotony of their lives of toil.

Belmond-area men (one with unidentified small girl) in various poses; first from left captioned "Larson"

The malaria generated from decaying vegetation brought fevers and ague; when sickness came, often no doctor was within reach, neighborly help and kindness were never lacking, good-will and sympathy were the substitutes for skilled physicians. When death cast its shadow over the home, willing hands and warm hearts ministered to the stricken family and tenderly performed the last sad offices for the dead. A rude box enclosed the lifeless form borne by neighbors to the lonely grave. Often there was no minister, music or flowers. No carved marble or granite shaft told the name of the dead; the sturdy oak or lofty elm cast a grateful shadow over the grassy mound that alone marked the last resting place of the departed pioneer.

This period in northwestern Iowa lingered along well into the "60s," as that portion of the State was the last to be settled, owing to the general absence of forests. The prairies were vast in extent, generally inclined to be level and in many places defective in surface drainage, with frequent ponds and marshes, the home of the muskrat. It was not until the homestead law was enacted by Congress that people began to venture out upon the great bleak prairies of northwestern Iowa to make homes. Mostly destitute of timber for cabins and fencing, with few deep ravines for shelter from the fierce blizzards that swept over them in winter, they long remained unoccupied after other portions of the State were fairly well settled.

But, when the time came in which the head of the family could secure a hundred and sixty acres of government land, as a home, for fourteen dollars, the hardy pioneers began to venture out upon the treeless plains and devise ways to live without timber. Then it was that sod houses and stables were invented. They were made by running a broad-shire breaking-plow over the wet prairie where the tough fiber of the sod of generations had accumulated, cutting it into long strips and turning them over. These strips of sod were then cut up with the spades into lengths suitable to handle and laid up like brick into walls for houses and stables. A few poles brought from the nearest timber supported a roof of slough hay, skillfully placed on like thatching, and a comfortable shelter was made for man and beast. The ground was smoothed off for a floor and until boards could be procured for doors, the skins of deer and wolves shut out the wind and snow.

Then it was that the swarms of muskrats which inhabited every pond were utilized to supply the family with groceries. Muskrat pelts were always salable for cash at the nearest town, where buyers had agents to gather up all kinds of furs and hides of wild animals. During the first year of life on the prairie, before crops could be raised for market, thousands of homestead families were dependent upon trapping muskrats for the cash they must have to buy bacon and coffee. The homestead was exempt from taxes; deer and prairie chickens furnished meat for portions of the year; with industrious mending and the skins of wild animals the clothing was made to do long service; but some money was indispensable for fuel and such scant groceries as were indulged in.

Most of the homestead settlers were many miles from timber or coal. Their teams were usually oxen, which could live on prairie grass and wild hay, and break up the sod for cultivation. It was always a perilous journey in the winter to the nearest town or timber, or coal bank, for fuel or other supplies. It must be made generally by one man alone, over a trackless prairie covered with deep snow. No human foresight could guard against danger from the fearful blizzards of flinty snow driven with an ever-increasing wind and an ever-falling temperature that were so common in early days. With the sun obscured, nothing was left to guide the bewildered driver toward his destination, as the changing wind often misled him and many were the victims who perished in the early years of settling the great prairies.

Another danger that was encountered by the first settlers on the prairies came from the annual fires. Early in the fall frosts killed the wild grass and in a few weeks it became dry and would readily burn. Many of the recent settlers were not aware of the danger and neglected to take the proper precaution for safety of their buildings, stacks and even the families. Emigrants crossing the great prairies and camping at night where water could be found, late in the autumn, were often the victims of carelessness or ignorance of danger. There can be no more fearful sight or situation than the approach of a prairie fire before a strong wind in the night. The horizon is lighted up in the distance with a vivid glow, and dense columns of black smoke ascend in darkening clouds as the long line of fire circles far to the right and left. At first the sight is grand beyond description as the rays of the glowing red rise higher and higher and the smoke rolls upward in increasing density. But soon an ominous roar is heard in the distance as the hurricane of fire is driven with an ever-increasing wind, exceeding the speed of a race horse, and the stifling atmosphere glows with the smothering heat of a sirocco from a parched desert. Escape for man or beast is impossible unless a back fire has been started in time to meet the advancing tornado of resistless heat that can only be staid by a counter-fire. Houses, barns, stacks, fences, bridges and all animal life are quickly destroyed as the hot blasts strike them and in a moment the ground is left a blackened, blistering waste of desolation. The ruin of the camp or farm is as complete as the wreck of a burning town, or the track of a tornado. Scores of people and hundreds of homes were annual victims of these fires in the early years of scattered farms on the great prairies, before experience brought to emigrants and settlers the wisdom to protect their lives and property by timely back-fires as soon as the frost had killed the grass.

It was during these years of hard winters when the homestead settlers ventured far out on the wild prairies at great distances from timber and before railroads had penetrated the great plains, that they began to use corn and slough hay for fuel. There was no market for corn within one or two days' travel and when the market was reached, eight or ten cents a bushel was all that a farmer could get for his load. A large load would sometimes bring him from four to five dollars.

This was the pay for raising forty bushels of corn on an acre of his farm, husking it and transporting the load a journey of two or three days with his team. The proceeds of his load would pay for about a ton of coal which he must draw back to his home and which would furnish about as much heat as the load of corn sold. It did not take the settler long to see that he might far better burn the corn at home and save a perilous journey in mid-winter over the bleak prairies, often at the risk of his life. He learned to twist the long coarse slough hay into ropes with which to start his corn fire and utilized a home grown vegetable production to furnish heat in place of the expensive foreign mineral production of the same earth upon which he lived. Persons of the luxurious homes of distant countries and states read of the burning of corn, in the morning paper by a comfortable grate fire, and were horrified at the reckless destruction of food by the western prairie farmers.

As the railroads were slowly extended westward in Iowa settlements were made along the projected lines far out on the wild prairies in anticipation of their coming. Towns were laid out along the lines of survey and a new impetus was given to all branches of business. […] Stage lines conveyed passengers, mail and express packages in various directions from the terminus of the railroad. Freight lines were established to transport goods, lumber and coal to the chief towns of the interior and western portions of the State and bring back farm produce for the eastern markets. […]

The earlier settlers were building frame houses and barns. Pretentious business blocks, substantial churches, better school-houses and tasteful private dwellings were beginning to take the place in village and city of the log structures which everywhere prevailed in earlier years. Factories were relieving the overworked women in making cloth for the family clothing. Farmers were buying reapers to displace the grain cradles and mowers were taking the place of the scythe. Pine lumber was coming down the Mississippi River in huge rafts, supplying boards to relieve the slavish toil of rail-making for fencing, and lumber for farm buildings in place of logs. Improved cattle and swine were driving out the scrubs, while spring wagons and carriages were slowly coming into use in place of the saddle horse and lumber wagon. The young men in many localities wore factory made clothing in place of the home made butternut or linsey-woolsey, and the women dressed themselves in calico and muslin, which was a desirable and comfortable substitute for the home-woven fabrics of pioneer times. This relief from spinning and weaving gave the women and girls a little rest from the never ending drudgery of the household and leisure in evenings to read. Many ambitious girls now found time to study and prepare for teaching the country schools. High schools and colleges were affording facilities for better education and the bright farm girls began to crowd out the ancient men teachers who had long ruled with the birch rod. Boys from the farm were beginning to turn their eyes to the learned professions where social advantages were within their reach and visions of public offices in the future spurred them to acquire knowledge of the world in broader fields than those of the father's acres.

The slow but sure accumulation of property on the fertile prairie farms had brought a degree of prosperity to all classes and there was gradual relief from continuous toil and rigid economy that was unavoidable in the pioneer years. The new system of banks had for the first time furnished a safe currency for the transaction of business and eastern capital was now seeking investment in the State, facilitating the building of railroads and thus furnishing better markets. The liberal grants of public lands for railroad building attracted the attention of outside capitalists and far-seeing men realized that these fertile millions of acres must become valuable as they were made accessible to markets by the extension of railroads.

The hard times beginning with 1857 were passing away, and a steady and heavy immigration was annually coming into the State in search of cheap homes. Thousands of eastern men of wealth were sending money where the legal rate of interest was ten per cent, and the security as fertile lands as any in the world. The reports of the discovery of rich gold deposits in the eastern range of the Rocky Mountains, near Pike's Peak in 1859, attracted thousands of Iowa people to that region, and it is likely that these departures in search of gold nearly equaled the immigration from eastern States into Iowa. But the tide soon turned back and most of the gold seekers returned to the prairies of Iowa again, better content to rely upon the steady gains derived with certainty from the fertile soil of well-tilled farms.

—from Benjamin Gue's *History of Iowa from the Earliest Times to the Beginning of the Twentieth Century*, 1903

———

To be continued in: *Oceans of Darkness, Oceans of Light—a Pentalogy:*
Volume III: *Tap Roots Betrayed: How Our Dreams Got Derailed in America*, ending with conclusion for the *polis*: my derailed country

Prairie Spring
(1913)

by Willa Cather

Evening and the flat land,
Rich and sombre and always silent;
The miles of fresh-plowed soil,
Heavy and black, full of strength and harshness;
The growing wheat, the growing weeds,
The toiling horses, the tired men;
The long empty roads,
Sullen fires of sunset, fading.
The eternal, unresponsive sky.
Against all this, Youth,
Flaming like wild roses,
Singing like the larks over the plowed fields,
Flashing like a star out of the twilight;
Youth with its insupportable sweetness,
Its fierce necessity,
Its sharp desire,
Singing and singing,
Out of the lips of silence,
Out of the earthy dusk.

Willa Cather, photographed by Carl Van Vechten, 1936

Sherwood Anderson, by Carl Van Vechten, 1933

from Sherwood Anderson's *Winesburg, Ohio* (1919):

There is something memorable in the experience to be had by going into a fair ground that stands at the edge of a Middle Western town on a night after the annual fair has been held. The sensation is one never to be forgotten. On all sides are ghosts, not of the dead, but of living people. Here, during the day just passed, have come the people pouring in from the town and the country around. Farmers with their wives and children and all the people from the hundreds of little frame houses have gathered within these board walls. Young girls have laughed and men with beards have talked of the affairs of their lives. The place has been filled to overflowing with life. It has itched and squirmed with life and now it is night and the life has all gone away. The silence is almost terrifying. One conceals oneself standing silently beside the trunk of a tree and what there is of a reflective tendency in his nature is intensified. One shudders at the thought of the meaninglessness of life while at the same instant, and if the people of the town are his people, one lives life so intensely that tears come into the eyes...